It's Rangers for Me?

New Perspectives on a Scottish Institution

Ronnie Esplin and Graham Walker (eds.)

Fort Publishing Ltd

First published in 2007 by Fort Publishing Ltd, Old Belmont House,
12 Robsland Avenue, Ayr, KA7 2RW

Printed by Bell and Bain Ltd, Glasgow

Front-cover photograph courtesy of SNSpix: Ibrox stadium,
22 February 2007. Rangers versus Hapoel Tel Aviv, UEFA Cup, round of 32

Graphic design by Mark Blackadder

Typeset by Senga Fairgrieve

ISBN: 978-1-905769-10-0

Contents

Introduction

This is a book about a major Scottish institution. From modest origins and impecunious circumstances in the late nineteenth century, the Rangers Football Club rose to pre-eminence in the twentieth. In so doing they became much more than a local football club. Indeed, they forged a reputation of international dimensions, which contributed to Scotland's national prestige. They became typical of popularly celebrated Scottish qualities: pawkishness, resourcefulness, resilience, dourness, determination, pride.

In Scottish sporting terms Rangers were unique in the extent of their growth in the twentieth century, and in their ambition. In 1929 the club opened its iconic grandstand designed by the accomplished Scottish architect and Rangers supporter, Archibald Leitch. It was a powerful statement: an aspiration to greatness and world renown, which the club has largely fulfilled. The club's Ibrox stadium, in its style and awesome size, became the coliseum of Scottish sport.

Rangers were also a mirror of their city of Glasgow: industrious, gritty, redoubtable, globally ambitious, Empire-minded. In the *Rangers Supporters' Annual* of 1954 there appears a remarkable photograph bearing a panoramic view of the city taken from the Ibrox stadium press box. As the accompanying commentary puts it: 'Dominating the foreground are the cranes . . . the shipyards, the dear Clyde, the docks, the works of all descriptions. . . . We are reminded here that without industry all would fade, spires and Stadium, all would become as a dream.' It is a reminder too that the club's greatness was won through sweat and toil and was brushed with tragedy.

However, Rangers also became synonymous in the course of the twentieth century with a Protestant religious identity. This is a matter which has to be viewed in the proper historical context of the first half of the century, when religion and denominational affiliation was important to the lives of many more people than is the case today; and much more important to ideas of Scottishness. This has to be remembered and explained with due regard for the values and circumstances of the time: several chapters in this book address this point.

The religious issue came to eclipse other factors in the way Rangers began to be perceived later in the twentieth century. The club's practice of fielding only players who were 'Protestant', albeit only nominally so in many cases, became a focus of controversy and criticism as times and values changed and such matters came to be viewed through a different prism. By the 1960s the club's all-Protestant character, in reality a phenomenon that dated only from the 1920s, was widely perceived as unacceptably discriminatory. The club's management adopted a defensive mode of response from which it has found great difficulty in emerging ever since. From the late 1960s, at least until the sensational signing of Maurice Johnston in 1989, Rangers' reputation suffered on account of the religious issue; former fans broke off their allegiances while many more from 'natural' Rangers backgrounds shunned the club and the bigotry with which it was alleged to be associated and indeed which some contended that it promoted. This theme pervades various chapters in the book, perhaps especially that of Carolyn Leckie.

Controversies over sectarianism of a religious variety have cast a long shadow and dog the club to this day, as witnessed by the recent cases brought against it and investigated by the governing body of European football (UEFA). These cases, both found to warrant punishment, have surrounded the singing of sectarian songs on the part of a section of the Rangers support. They highlight the extent of the problem the club has in transcending its past in this respect. Jonny Magee's chapter in this book explores in a scholarly fashion the tensions between tradition and modernisation in relation to Rangers. The UEFA cases may indeed constitute something of a crossroads for Rangers: if the issue is not satisfactorily tackled and resolved the club's future at the highest level of European competition may be in serious doubt.

We thus feel that this book is a timely contribution to debates about Rangers' past, present and future. Several chapters discuss the UEFA cases and their implications. Offensive songs, of course, have been symptoms for many years of a culture of sectarianism in Scotland, to which the Old Firm of Rangers and Celtic are central. The extent to which this culture has been opportunistically and fashionably indicted for all manner of ills is here well dissected by Dolan Cummings. Certainly, it might be said that the way that sectarianism has often been conceptualised as essentially a Rangers or a 'Protestant' problem is open to challenge. Hence the inclusion in the book of reflections by those like Gary Mitchell and Jonathan Watson, who have been struck by the anti-Rangers feeling in the worlds they move in; and a critique of recent 'Celtic-minded' publications, of their premises, assumptions and methods of argument. The motivation in the latter regard is to see fair play for the Rangers viewpoint so that those Rangers fans who feel the debate is stacked against them, and who feel that they alone are being 'robbed' of what they value, might become less defensive. In addition, this critique highlights questions on which many Rangers fans feel misunderstood and misrepresented as well as areas of mutual incomprehension between the two sets of fans. As such, it hopefully serves a wider goal in shifting this debate on to territory where fans of the Old Firm teams can better express the pride they feel for their respective clubs and cultures, in accordance with the times.

In Rangers' case there may be merit in looking at the way the supporters' culture around the Northern Ireland football team has radically changed in recent years. The sectarian trappings around the Northern Ireland team and its support have largely been removed without any weakening of the fans' sense of identity: quite the opposite, the Northern Ireland team has never been more proudly, loudly or strongly supported. Since many of these Northern Ireland fans are also Rangers fans, this example carries a particular significance.

Religious and political issues need to be faced. If they are examined in their proper context those who have the best interests of the club at heart will be led to appreciate how associations with certain causes and outlooks came to matter. For instance, they will be made more aware of what the Scottish–Irish links have historically produced: the two-way flows of people, the transference of folk cultures around the 'Orange and Green' causes, the politics of the Irish Question. In regard to the latter, there might be said to have been two crucial phases: first, the period before, during and after the first world war when representatives of both Rangers and Celtic assumed a high profile in public debates; and second, the out-break of the Troubles in Northern Ireland in 1969 and the impact of this in terms of supporters' songs and chants and paraphernalia and the grafting on to the Rangers and Celtic allegiances of Unionist/Loyalist and Nationalist/Republican identities refashioned and deepened by violent conflict. In the second case the phenomenon was 'bottom up' rather than 'top down'; it was disavowed by the managements of both clubs, although they arguably did little to challenge it until recently. Whatever the arguments, the Irish dimension in terms of its impact on Scottish society, and the role of its politics in shaping supporters' outlooks, needs to be explored and explained. This book may be seen as a contribution to this enterprise with chapters such as that of Chris Williamson highlighting the way the recent resurgence of Ulster-Scots culture has relevance for Rangers. We are now into a new political era in Northern Ireland and in the United Kingdom more generally; we have entered a new set of British–Irish relations and, with help, fans can take their cue from this and move away from old antipathies towards a healthier kind of rivalry.

Already, there have occurred Rangers supporter initiatives – most organised by the Rangers Supporters Trust (RST) and the Blue Order – which demonstrate an encouraging willingness to bring about change. For instance, songs about past exploits on the playing pitch, such as the momentous victory over Wolves in 1961, have been popularised to take the place of songs that have nothing to do with the team as such. The fans might build on this to celebrate other highlights of the past, such as the 1928 Scottish Cup final and the 1945 match against Moscow Dynamo (both recalled in various chapters here); the victorious Russian tour of 1962 which brought 15,000 fans to Renfrew airport in what the late James Sanderson called 'the greatest homecoming of any sportsmen to Scotland'; and, of course, the pinnacle of the European Cup Winners Cup triumph in Barcelona in 1972. Those who run Rangers and those who support them must reach a more purposeful accord in the mutual endeavour of promoting the club. It is important to lay to rest the impression that those at the top are somehow complicit in 'blanding out' or worse 'hollowing out' what the club stands for.

For such an illustrious club, Rangers have not in general been well served in respect of in-depth histories and informed commentaries. This book's ambitions are relatively modest: to convey what the club means to its fans and its place in their lives; to address debates currently swirling around the club; and to provide perspectives on the past which have relevance to its future direction. The book is composed of chapters by Rangers fans or ex-fans, with the exception of Scottish Orange Order

Grand Master, Ian Wilson, whose football loyalties lie with Hearts! The book is not an uncritical or straightforwardly celebratory volume. Rather, it seeks to highlight and explore areas of contention while attempting to redress an imbalance in the Old Firm literature. In time it is to be hoped that a definitive history of the club will accompany fresh glories on the field and new peaks of achievement. It is also to be hoped that a resolution to the controversies and tensions that currently surround Ibrox can be found. The pioneers of the Rangers Football Club and its many heroes through the years deserve no less.

HISTORY AND MEMORIES

In the Beginning

Tommy Malcolm, Ronnie Esplin and Graham Walker

The official birth of Rangers FC has long been misidentified. Many histories claim that the club was formed in July 1873. This, however, is contradicted by the early *Scottish Football Annuals* that all give the date of origin as 1872. One of them has an article, 'The Rangers FC', written by an early player, William Dunlop, under the pseudonym of True Blue. John Allan's *The Story of the Rangers*, published in 1923, was the first full-length history of the club and one of several which wrongly gives 1873 as the foundation year and an account of how the club came together that lacks firm evidence to back it up. Perhaps it was the case that the club, realising its 'jubilee' history was late, massaged the historical record. We may never know for sure. In addition, Rangers today seem reluctant to concede that their centenary celebrations in 1973 were a year too late. There is though the consolation of knowing that the club's one European trophy was won in the true centenary year, a highly symbolic matter for dedicated fans.

However, confusion about the date of the club's formation is just one of several issues of which many modern-day supporters may be unaware. For instance, Rangers were not formed as a Protestant club any more than Partick Thistle, Dumbarton or many other football clubs that emerged in the late nineteenth century, even though this was a time when some later-to-be-famous clubs in Scotland and England did spring up with church associations, and the statement of a Rangers vice-chairman in 1967 that they had begun life as a 'Presbyterian Boys Club' is therefore also incorrect and may have been an attempt retrospectively to rationalise the solidly Protestant character the club had by then acquired. Equally, few fans know that Rangers almost went out of existence before the Scottish League was established in 1890, or that the first Celtic player to score against Rangers was a former 'light blue'. In this chapter we hope to make clear the trials and tribulations Rangers encountered in the early days.

Although Glasgow Green is a focal point in the early history of the Rangers, it was in fact at another city park that the first tentative steps were taken in the establishment of the club. Four youngsters who hailed from Gareloch were walking in the West End park, discussing the latest craze to sweep Scotland: association football. The boys – Moses and Peter McNeil, William McBeath and Peter Campbell – discussed the possibility of starting their own club, enamoured as they were by Queen's Park, the pioneers of the game in Scotland. The club they formed became known as the Rangers, the name, chosen by Moses, coming from an English rugby club of the time. Thus, four boys – Moses was only sixteen and the others all under twenty – became the founding fathers of Scotland's greatest football club.

However, at this time Rangers were just one of many clubs trying to survive and prosper as football became increasingly popular. They began, like the others, by finding enough bodies to field a team. A meeting of prospective members was held, the majority of whom came from outside Glasgow, and it was unanimously decided to adopt the name of Rangers. Three nights a week were to be set aside for training although the players were often to be found on Glasgow Green six nights in the week, the sabbath being a day of rest. Within two months they had played their first game against Callender (sometimes given as Callander) FC. For this historic match Rangers drafted in four ringers: Harry McNeil (brother of Moses, Peter and William), William McKinnon, John Hunter and Willie Miller. McNeil and McKinnon were Queen's Park players while Hunter and Miller were members of the Eastern club. While the ringers stripped for action, the rest of the Rangers players performed in their everyday clothing. The game – which was played at the Flesher's Haugh section of Glasgow Green near the end of May 1872 – ended goalless.

Soon after the inaugural match a meeting of the club was convened and office bearers elected. Another match was arranged with Clyde (not the present-day club bearing that name) and an 11–0 victory ensued in a game that saw Rangers wear the light blue for the first time. Football was of course still in its infancy and there were no pavilions, dressing rooms or showers. Players changed at the side of the pitch in the manner of a modern-day pub team. In order to book a pitch at Flesher's Haugh Peter McNeil would have to arrive at noon and plant the goalposts to stake a claim to the ground. Sometimes he would arrive to find that another club had beaten him to it. But in time the club's reputation grew, and Rangers were able to command a pitch they could all but call their own. During the spring of 1873 Tom Vallance, a future captain and stalwart – and, incidentally, a portrait artist of some renown – joined the club. In the same year the first general meeting was held and new office bearers elected.

Rangers were too late in seeking membership of the Scottish Football Association and had to sit out the inaugural Scottish Cup tournament in 1873/74, but were in the draw for the following season's competition. On 12 October 1874 Rangers played their first competitive match, taking on Oxford in the first round of the Cup at Queen's Park recreation ground. The team, captained by Peter McNeil, lined up as follows: John Yuil, Tom Vallance, Peter McNeil, William McNeil, Willie McBeath, Moses McNeil, Peter Campbell, George Phillips, James Watson, David Gibb, J. Campbell. Goals by Moses McNeil and David Gibb gave Rangers victory, but they exited the competition in the next round.

However, the club was up and running, and, in 1875, Rangers moved ground for the first time, decanting to Burnbank on the south side of Great Western Road, close to St Mary's church near the Kelvin bridge. The ground was opened on 11 September by Vale of Leven, a club second only to the famous Queen's Park. In season 1876/77 Rangers moved ground again, this time across the river Clyde to Kinning Park, played their first game against the giants of Queen's Park, and reached the Scottish Cup final for the first time. In 1878 Rangers crossed the border to play matches, successfully, against Nottingham Forest and Sheffield Wednesday. Other milestones in this 1878/79 season included not only the first victory over Queen's Park but also a Scottish Cup final against Vale of Leven in which Rangers claimed they had been denied a legitimate goal and decided to boycott the replay leaving the Vale with a walkover. At the AGM in June 1879 it was declared that the club had never been in better shape; yet hard times were just around the corner.

The early 1880s proved to be a test for the young club. They lost key players like Peter Campbell and often failed to field a full team. Not surprisingly, results suffered. Tom Vallance left in 1882 and although he was to return the following year his best days were behind him. Off the field the club fell under the sway of John Wallace Mackay, an unpopular figure whose reign coincided with one of the gloomiest periods in Rangers' history. Internal strife and disputes tore the club apart, and financially matters were allowed to reach crisis proportions. Only a loan of £30 from the president, George Goudie, saved the club from extinction. On top of all this, Rangers faced an eviction notice from their Kinning Park landlords in 1884. By this time Rangers had attracted an unruly element to their support, and Kinning Park had acquired the name of one of the most disreputable grounds in Scotland.

In 1886, the controversial Mackay was forced to resign his post with Rangers, and in the following year the club moved the short distance to Ibrox Park. The ground was officially opened on 20 August by Preston North End, a crack outfit that inflicted a sobering 8–1 defeat on the hosts. The ground was supposed to hold 15,000 but many more were reckoned to have attended on this occasion. On 28 May 1888 the first match with newly formed Celtic took place and Neilly McCallum, a former Ger, scored Celtic's first goal in their 5–2 win. Rangers' line-up on the day was depleted, while Celtic's included established players they had persuaded to join them. Indeed, it is remarkable how strongly Celtic emerged from its earliest days, with a secure ground, players of proven ability and apparent financial stability. This was in stark contrast to Rangers' early experiences. Celtic also adapted more readily to the professionalisation of the game a few years later. It should be acknowledged, moreover, that relations between the clubs were friendly at least until the early 1900s.

Season 1888/89 was a depressing one for Rangers and again the club was perilously close to going out of business. However, the club struggled on and were able take their place in the new Scottish League, which was inaugurated in season 1890/91. Nevertheless, against all the odds, Rangers came agonisingly close to becoming the first champions of Scotland. The title in fact was shared with Dumbarton after a 2–2 draw in what was meant to be a decider. After nineteen years Rangers had come of age. There was no looking back, and the club would go from strength to strength. The 1890s saw an accumulation of honours, capped by a world record in season 1898/99 in which the team won every league match. In the same season the club moved to its present Ibrox home and became a limited company.

A Rangers player from the 1890s, Alexander Smith, reflected much later in the *Rangers Supporters Annual* of 1952 on the importance of the club's successes in that decade, especially seasons 1896/97 and 1898/99. He also paid tribute to the encouragement he had received from the supporters, whose reputation improved with that of the team. Smith wrote:

> I can still see in my mind's eye that wonderful procession of four-horse brakes filling the length of Buchanan Street on the evening of 1897 when we celebrated our third cup victory that season. Every brake was packed with jubilant Rangers supporters, and I still look with pleasure on a silver salver and tea service given to me one happy evening in Govan Town Hall through the combined generosity of those same Brake Clubs.

The all-conquering season of 1898/99 also saw James Henderson become the first chairman of the club's board of directors. Henderson, as his obituary (*Glasgow Herald*, 11 May 1912) informs us, went on to become a valuable member of both Govan parish council and Glasgow town council and was renowned for his deep interest in the welfare of poor children in Govan. He was replaced as chairman on his death by Sir John Ure Primrose. In his Rangers history, John Allan wrote of the latter: 'A man of many interests, and possessing that wide and generous outlook which is the foe of bigotry and crusted sectionalism, Sir John brought into football an influence that was cleansing and elevating.' In recent years, Ure Primrose's name has, by contrast, been blackened by several *Celtic Minded* writers and commentators, who seem to have tendentiously deduced from his freemasonry that he was anti-Catholic. What the evidence shows, however, is that, politically, he was anti-Irish Home Rule, having split along with many others from the Liberal Party and entered as a 'Liberal Unionist' into an alliance with the Conservatives over this highly controversial issue in the British political context of the time. In 1913 he shared a public platform with the Ulster Unionist leader Edward Carson. In so doing, Ure Primrose was simply following his political convictions in the manner of those Celtic officials of the period who espoused the cause of Irish Nationalism and were pro-Home Rule.

It seems clear, though, that increasing political tensions around the Irish Question played their part in intensifying the playing rivalry between

Rangers and Celtic, which from the 1890s was emerging as the most important in the Scottish game. However, it should not be forgotten that Rangers' early years were much more precarious than Celtic's; in fact Rangers did not attain the success and the financial security of the club which would become its great foe until it was at least twenty years old.

From Glasgow Green to the present five star Ibrox stadium – with its prize-laden trophy room inside the most famous main stand in Britain – is a long, long way. When the McNeils and the Campbells nursed their boyish dreams of crossing swords with the mighty Queen's Park and Vale of Leven, little could they imagine that a century and more on their legacy would be so spectacular and magnificent.

Other sources:

Glasgow News 1873–86, various early *Scottish Football Association Annuals*, *Scottish Sport*, *Scottish Umpire*, *Scottish Referee*, *Scottish Athletic Journal*, *North British Daily Mail* and *Glasgow Observer*.

Once a Ranger

Archie Mackenzie

My family moved from Ruchill to Merrick Gardens around 1922 because my father was transferred from the Possilpark branch of the Bank of Scotland to the branch in Paisley. We were just a couple of hundred yards from Ibrox and that's where it all began. No one before me in the family supported Rangers. My father came from the Island of Arran and my mother came from Ross-shire so they had no special football connections or interest at all. It was only when we moved parallel to Copland Road that my brother and I became fans.

I was about six or seven at that time and the great dodge then for schoolkids was instead of paying sixpence to get in to games, which we didn't have, we would go up to the turnstiles and look for a sympathetic face among the supporters going in and say 'give us a lift over'. The fellow on the turnstile would cooperate and the police knew it was going on. It was simply a generous gesture but it produced thousands of supporters in the long run. I remember the main stand opening in 1929. We had a family friend who sometimes took me in there, which was always a great pleasure.

Rangers and Celtic were already the top two teams in Scotland. Most seasons the Old Firm were the focus of football in Scotland and it's been that way since. I was aware of them splitting into Protestant and Catholic clubs because I read the papers and they said that was happening, but I didn't have first-hand experience of it and the divide then was not nearly as strong as it became. The Irish issue in the 1920s and 1930s didn't impinge on me at all; it was not a big thing to me and my friends in Merrick Gardens. My parents were good Protestant, churchgoing people and I don't remember them being at all worried about me going to the matches. There was a level of discipline and quietness that was very different from today. I was never involved in the chanting gangs nor were any of my friends.

Old Firm games were always special occasions in the Twenties and Thirties and the media encouraged it. The games were all very intense and there was enthusiasm, but there wasn't the aggro you get now. I don't think segregation was enforced: at Ibrox the Rangers fans concentrated in the Copland Road end while Celtic fans tended to drift towards the other end but I don't think it was enforced.

I wasn't at the Scottish Cup final of 1928 when we beat Celtic 4–0 but that year is marked out in my mind as the peak year for Rangers because they won the league-and-cup double.

The team two years before was the classic team of Robb, Manderson, McCandless, Meiklejohn, Dixon and Muirhead, Archibald, Cunningham, Henderson, Cairns and Morton. They are forever in my mind and I remember quite well how each of them played.

I admired Morton very much. He was a brilliant player and he was the darling of the crowds, an idol. The thing I remember about him was the 'Morton lob'. He specialised in lobbing the ball from the left wing into the goalmouth, which gave his forwards extra time to get into the penalty area and a great many goals were created in that way. There was a song at the time 'Red Red Robin' and it got changed to, 'When the wee blue devil goes bob, bob, bobbing along' after the performance of the Wembley Wizards that year.

However, the half backs, Meiklejohn, Dixon and Muirhead, were the key to the way Rangers played. Meiklejohn and Muirhead were the play-makers, they were the David Beckhams of their day and in the centre was Dixon, the defensive player. Henderson was a big strong guy, a bit like Dado Prso. He wasn't as clever as Jimmy McGrory of Celtic but he was a big factor in the team's success. Archibald and Cunningham played on the right and both were known for their rocket shots.

The players were closer to the fans then, it was an easier relationship, maybe because most of the players had other jobs as well as being foot-ballers. The Meiklejohn family had a garage just about half a mile from Ibrox and we would go down to see him helping out. The two backs, Manderson and McCandless, were both from Northern Ireland and they lived just a door or two along from us. There was no high life in those days, they were just living in a flat with two bedrooms like anyone else and you would see them out and about quite often.

Of course Bill Struth was in the background as the disciplinarian. I don't know if players would swallow his line today but it was effective then. Struth was a revered figure at Ibrox but he was no showman and I don't remember him giving interviews. You have to remember that there was no television in those days and although we had a crystal-set wireless, I didn't associate football with the radio. You had to wait on the evening papers to get the results.

I was at the Old Firm game at Ibrox in 1931 when John Thomson died. That was a great tragedy and I can still see it so clearly. It was a bright, sunny afternoon and I was at the far end of the ground from where it happened. Someone played a long ball forward and Sammy English, the Rangers centre forward, chased it and at the same time Thomson came out to intercept. There was no question of foul play at all, they just clashed and it was quite clear from English's reaction that he knew Thomson had been badly hurt and he kept signalling for the ambulance men to come over.

The whole ground went quiet except for one group of Rangers fans in the Copland Road end who started to chant something but that quickly subsided and they were strongly criticised for it afterwards. The rest of the game was played out in a kind of hush and it ended in a draw. Of course, Thomson died that night in hospital. I had a high opinion of him, he was an outstanding character. But you could say that it was the end of Sammy English's career, he never regained confidence.

There was something special about the Rangers even then and they had a Scotland-wide following. Queen's Park were also held in high esteem. They had their own unique following as an amateur club and they distinguished themselves whenever they scored. They didn't shake hands and there was no mobbing of the scorer. Their whole philosophy was that it was the team who had scored so you didn't need to congratulate anyone. It was the differentiating factor between them and all the other teams.

But there was greater respect in Scottish society in general. The Protestant–Catholic issue was there but it was a separation without it being continual agitation and there was remarkably little aggro. There were no shortages and no luxuries, people lived quietly and by and large they were well behaved and there was little scandal around.

Religion played a big part in people's lives and Sunday was a day of rest. Our family went to church twice on a Sunday and I would also go to Sunday School and that was fairly normal. We had a great respect for people like David Livingstone and Eric Liddell, who peaked round 1930. Liddell was a great hero to schoolboys like me, as well as being a great athlete he was a great Christian and he had an amazing influence. I was lucky enough to meet him when he was preaching at a church in Shettleston, which led to a funny story years later. After studying at Glasgow University, I became a diplomat and travelled all over the world. In 1981, when the film *Chariots of Fire* came out, I was staying for the weekend with an American admiral in Washington. His little grandson, aged about seven, came in and he had just seen the film. I told him that I knew Eric Liddell and that I had shaken his hand. He asked: 'Can I shake your hand?' I said 'yes' and he then dashed off to tell the admiral: 'I just shook hands with the man who shook hands with Eric Liddell.'

I moved abroad around 1939 and I have had no consistent links with Rangers or the Ibrox area since then. My parents lived there until the end of the war before they moved to Edinburgh.

I haven't been to Ibrox for several years and the players are all just names to me now. But I still keep an interest in what is going on and I still like to see them winning. There is still something there from my childhood.

Sixty Years On and Off!

George Hewitt

Tending not to dwell on how old, and arguably, decrepit I have become it only recently dawned on me that I had been supporting Rangers, after a fashion, for over sixty years. In other words I have been 'follow, following' from those far-off days in the second world war – when some of our victories were achieved by dint of winning more corners than the opposition – to the present day when even teams such as Falkirk or Dunfermline can prove to be serious obstacles to our progress.

As for becoming a so-called 'bluenose', it would appear to be a hereditary trait; thus, one of my grandfathers, my father and now two of my sons support the light blues. My father in fact could boast of having been at Hampden in 1928 for the cup final in which David Meiklejohn scored his legendary penalty against Celtic to set Rangers on their way to ending a dismal run in the Scottish Cup. Quite a year for him was 1928 since he was also at Wembley to see Alan Morton and the other 'Wizards' cast their spell over England.

Casting an analytical eye over all those years it would seem possible to identify three main phases in the fortunes of the club. Firstly, from the end of the first world war or, if preferred, winning the Victory Cup, to the mid-Sixties there was a boom period (though some might justifiably contend that this began in the 1920s). Then, secondly, for the next twenty years or so Rangers went through a sticky patch punctuated by occasional success, notably the winning of the European Cup Winners Cup in 1972. Finally, in 1986, with the arrival of Graeme Souness the club entered one of its most successful eras and there emerged some of the best sides of the twentieth century. As yet it would be premature to comment on the present century though there are worrying signs that we could be entering a downturn. Since the achievements of the Nineties must be fairly fresh in the memories of most supporters, I shall concentrate on what I can remember of more distant events.

One of my earliest recollections is the famous game against Moscow Dynamo in November 1945. The Russian side had already beaten Arsenal and Cardiff City and drawn with Chelsea before they met Rangers at Ibrox. Not surprisingly there was tremendous interest in the contest and over 95,000 spectators were reputedly packed into the ground. All I can remember is racing home from primary school on a midweek afternoon, switching on the Scottish Home Service and tuning in at the precise moment when Rangers were awarded their second penalty. An earlier one taken by Willie Waddell having been saved by the Dynamos spectacular keeper 'Tiger' Khomich, it was crucial that George Young converted this second award if they were to get an equaliser. It's a long time ago yet I still imagine I can hear the roar that signalled Young's successful conversion of the spot kick, which ensured a 2–2 draw.

Early in the second half of the Dynamo game there was an unusual incident widely reported the next day. The Russians had insisted on the use of substitutes, unheard of in British football in those days, and at one point in the second half they actually had twelve players on the field. This was quickly spotted by two of the Rangers team, Torry Gillick and Jock Shaw, who drew the referee's attention to this tactic or, perhaps, oversight by their opponents. Surprisingly, when the obituary of Konstantin Beskov – the Dynamo centre forward at Ibrox in 1945 – appeared in *The Times* nothing was said about his team's visit to Scotland or the episode with the extra player. However, after a short but amicable exchange of correspondence between the obituary editor of *The Times* and me, the record was set straight in a subsequent edition.

As a schoolboy in the 1940s and living in Edinburgh – where my father's job on the railway had taken him – I did not have very many opportunities to watch Rangers. Consequently, apart from the odd visit to Tynecastle and Easter Road (where I recall that the boys' gate had the legend 'Boys, OAPs and Soldiers in Uniform') I had to rely on the accounts of the weekend fixtures in the Sunday newspapers. Imagine my delight therefore at recently discovering in a cupboard a collection of clippings from the *Sunday Mail* and *Sunday Post*, which I had diligently filed away during these youthful years. Unfortunately these were not between the pages of *Ripping Yarns*, or, even better, *The Wizard Annual* featuring the great Wilson, but were filed in a rather uninspiring annual entitled *The Boys Book of Soccer for 1947*. Although there was a chapter on Moscow Dynamo's visit there was no mention of the game at Ibrox. However, more positively, within the book there were numerous photographs and reports of matches involving Rangers in the immediate post-war period. Here then were the jottings of journalists such as Jack Harkness, a former Wembley Wizard, 'Rex' (R. E. Kingsley) a big name in the *Sunday Mail* with his own 'club' for young fans, which I remember belonging to, and two writers, Alan Breck and Waverley, whose pen names had obvious literary associations.

'Rangers make splash hit – a glaur and glory day for the Ibrox men' wrote the man from *Kidnapped* of a cup-tie against Partick Thistle in February 1948; 'Rampant Rangers scarcely put a foot wrong' was Jack Harkness's verdict on a Ne'erday defeat of Celtic the following year. Indeed he was so impressed by the performance that he went on to suggest that the SFA should nominate the entire Rangers team to represent Scotland in the 1950 World Cup. This was a highly improbable scenario, although the situation never arose since the Scottish authorities eventually decided not to enter the tournament. Let's end this selection with the following, 'A crazy nightmare, mad fantasia, incredible caricature . . . the complete triumph of negation', which was how Waverley described a typically uncompromising defensive display against St Mirren in January 1949.

The defence in that side, which caused such dismay to Waverley, played together so often that older supporters can reel off the names as easily as their army number: Brown, Young and Shaw, McColl, Woodburn and Cox, these players were the backbone of what the press were wont to call the 'Ibrox Iron Curtain'. It was a formidable set-up that brought great success to the club in those years and lasted until the early Fifties when, inevitably, it began to disintegrate.

I can distinctly recall being at the game that heralded the departure of one of its key members: Bobby Brown. It happened at Tynecastle in September 1952 on one of those warm sunny days that sometimes occur at the start of the football season. Whether it was the glare of the sun or, more likely I'm afraid, defective judgment, the Rangers keeper had a very poor match and one that ended the career of a player who had been outstanding for both club and country. On the other hand I have no recollection of

the departure of another major figure in the 'Curtain': Willie Woodburn.
While I certainly saw him playing on numerous occasions, and greatly
admired his total commitment, until I checked my sources I had thought
his draconian sine-die sentence from the SFA was as the result of a sending-
off against Clyde at a game that I had attended in 1954. Not so. The
crucial offence whereby Rangers lost one of their greatest defenders was
perpetrated later that season while playing, of all teams, Stirling Albion.

Before fast forwarding into the Sixties – though carefully omitting any
reference to the disastrous League Cup final of 1957, which fortunately
occurred when I was furth of Scotland serving Queen and Country – one
other recollection comes to mind. In 1958 I had arranged my army leave
so that I could be home at Easter to attend the Scottish Cup semi-final
against Hibernian. The first game ended in a 2–2 draw but it is what took
place in the replay that still irks me. With only a few minutes remaining
Rangers were losing 2–1 when centre forward Max Murray seemed to
have levelled the score with a great header. But to the consternation of
the vast majority of the spectators the referee, having signalled a goal, dis-
allowed it after consulting his linesman. The Terry Butcher 'goal' that was
struck off against Celtic in the last minutes of the 1989 Scottish Cup final
could be considered a comparable incident.

The achievements of the early Sixties, when Rangers had one of their
best-ever sides, are still etched in my mind. Witnessing the destruction of
Celtic in the 1963 Scottish Cup-final replay was a particularly notable
occasion, even if I'm still convinced that an opportunity to avenge the
1957 fiasco was missed on that evening by that wonderful forward line
of Henderson, McMillan, Millar, Brand and Wilson; forty-five years hence
and the names still trip off the tongue. Again, the final a year later against
a fine Dundee team was a very close run thing, not least because I had
just been released that morning from hospital with the usual admonition
to take things easy.

However, Rangers went on to experience a recession after these triumphs,
which leads to the question of where I was on the day of the calamitous
defeat at the hands of Berwick Rangers in January 1967. As it happens,
like the Kennedy assassination, I have a pretty clear recollection of my movements on that fateful Saturday. In fact, having played rugby earlier in the
afternoon, I was participating in the customary post-match socialising in

a local hostelry while awaiting the football scores on the pub radio at five o'clock. It was undoubtedly a remarkable upset but, today, looking at what happened, it does seem that both Rangers and the media were guilty of overreacting. Certainly, it was unexpected, yet that season 'the wee Rangers' were a decent second-division team with a talented player-manager in Jock Wallace and playing at home on their own ground. These considerations make the decision – apparently on the insistence of club chairman John Lawrence – to inform two of the players, Jim Forrest and George McLean, that they would never play for Rangers again extremely harsh and unfair. Admittedly Celtic had once sacked their whole team for sustaining a similar defeat but that was in 1898 or thereabouts! Thus Rangers, in the final of the European Cup Winners Cup later that year, contested it without a recognised centre forward. In fact, many older supporters will recall watching erstwhile centre half Roger Hynd, drafted in as a striker, missing an easy chance, which might have brought the trophy to Ibrox.

While I was not present at Shielfield Park I did have the misfortune to be present at Hampden in April 1969 for the Scottish Cup final against Celtic. A 6–0 drubbing of Aberdeen in the semi-final had raised the hopes of many fans, though I remember there were concerns about the enforced absence of centre forward Colin Stein. He was a key figure but had been suspended as a result of a sending-off and his sentence was due to expire two days after the final, not much good unless there was a replay. Though it is thirty-eight years ago I can still vividly recollect standing at the Rangers end beside a boisterous band of supporters from Dalry, and watching in disbelief as Celtic took the lead in the opening minutes. The goal itself came from a corner at which Billy McNeill, the Celtic centre half and captain, was allowed to head unchallenged past Norrie Martin. It was Stein's replacement, Alex Ferguson, who had been at fault in failing to mark McNeill effectively. Interestingly, Ferguson admits in his autobiography that he was to blame for the goal. However, he goes on to attribute overall responsibility for the humiliating defeat to the game plan of the new and short-lived manager David White. The latter's tactics, according to Sir Alex, were the main reason for a dreadful performance, one that he has clearly not forgotten.

However, there were a few brighter moments during these years. Those who saw it will long remember rejoicing at Kai Johansen's long-range winner in the 1966 Scottish Cup final; likewise, a slim, 16-year-old Derek Johnstone heading the only goal against our Old Firm rivals in the 1970 League Cup final helped to lift the gloom generally prevailing at this time. Yet it was in this era that Rangers had one of their greatest successes, the winning of the European Cup Winners Cup in 1972.

Apart from reaching the final in 1967 Rangers also got there in 1961. My only rather hazy memory of that campaign is of attending the first leg of the semi-final against Wolverhampton Wanderers and of this earlier 'Battle of Britain' being played on a cold foggy March evening. For the record Rangers won 2–0 going through 3–1 on aggregate only to lose 4–1 on aggregate to Fiorentina in the final. Happily the outcome in Barcelona in 1972 was to be different.

Various attempts at winning tickets for Barcelona all came to naught though I did manage to see the warm-up friendly at Love Street against St Mirren – not much of a consolation. Thus, on the evening of the game, my only way of obtaining a progress report was by dashing out from the evening class where I was teaching and switching on the car radio. There was, incidentally, no live coverage because of some typically fatuous decision by the SFA. Nonetheless, a couple of days later, I got an eyewitness account from one of the janitors with whom, as a fellow Bear, I was on good terms. He had been at the Nou Camp, seen the whole match and taken part in the mêlée thereafter. This, at least according to my source, was largely caused by the heavy-handed behaviour of the Spanish police.

This European triumph was thirty-five years ago but, sad to relate, has with one exception never looked like being repeated. Instead, despite frequently qualifying for Europe it has been a case of enduring an endless catalogue of defeats from Continental sides usually far more accomplished than Rangers. Only in season 1992/93 were things a bit different when, with the likes of Durrant, Goram, Gough, Hateley, McCoist and McCall, Rangers were only denied a place in the final of the new Champions League as a consequence of the alleged chicanery of Bernard Tapie, the egregious owner of Marseille FC. On a personal level there was one memorable incident during this campaign, which occurred during the group game against FC Bruges at Ibrox, just after Scott Nisbet scored his bizarre winner. The noisy celebrations that ensued as the ball swerved past the bemused Belgian goalkeeper caused my wife, who had momentarily left the room, to turn back hastily, trip on the stairs and break a bone in her right foot.

If there was no significant success in Europe in the latter part of the twentieth century, there was plenty at domestic level. I could go on at some length but perhaps the best approach would be to give a short selection of snapshots from my memory bank. There was Graham Roberts's first game for Rangers against Dundee United in late 1986 when he showed the commitment and determination that played such a big part in winning the league title later that season; that wonderful volley by Ray Wilkins which started the 5–1 rout of Celtic in 1988; the even-more-powerful strike by Jorg Albertz against the same opponents about a decade later; those marvellous performances by Andy Goram in so many games against Celtic in the Nineties; Mark Hateley's marvellous header to open the scoring in the league decider against Aberdeen in 1991; Paul Gascoigne's brilliant hat-trick against the same opponents in 1996; Brian Laudrup's outstanding skill on so many occasions during his all-too-brief stay at Ibrox.

Reading over this list it occurred to me that many supporters would if asked compile similar ones. Indeed, two of my sons did the same exercise and produced results remarkably like my own. For what it's worth I shall add on their behalf: 'Terry Hurlock winning every 50–50 challenge'; 'John Brown scoring and vaulting the advertising boards at Parkhead'; 'Kuznetsov's thunderbolt in a New Year's game against Celtic'.

Unfortunately our record so far in the twenty-first century has not been too inspiring. However there has been some success both in both the championship and the Scottish Cup. The 'Lovenkrands final' was certainly a special day while of course there were also those exciting down-to-the-wire triumphs: the first of these, the 6–1 defeat of Dunfermline on the last day of the 2002/03 season, even caused one leading Celtic player to advance conspiracy theories. Seems a bit paranoid, yet I must own up to having similar feelings in 1986 when Celtic took five goals off a St Mirren side containing several ex-Parkhead players to win the league on goal difference from Hearts. Then there was 'Helicopter Sunday' in May 2005, when Motherwell's last-minute defeat of Celtic saw the league trophy airlifted from above Fir Park, where it had seemed destined to go, to Easter Road where Rangers had beaten Hibernian. As the legend on the photograph displayed on our kitchen wall notes, 'the helicopter is changing direction'.

Nowadays, while I might sip my coffee from my Rangers mug, adjust one of my plethora of club ties and scrutinise my team calendar I'm seldom to be found at Ibrox since I have largely become an armchair supporter. Yet, just occasionally, I seem to hear the plaintive voice of the late James Sanderson. In addition to writing a regular newspaper column, Sanderson was also the host of a radio phone-in during which he frequently punctuated the exchanges with the immortal question: 'And were you at the game?' Well, on a Saturday in March 2007 I made the effort to give a positive response to Jimmy's query.

It was a beautiful spring afternoon and, on leaving the car in Bellahouston Park, the view of the stadium from that distance was inspiring. There was also the welcome absence of those noisome rufflans wanting paid 'to watch your car, mister' who infest other parking spots. Reaching the ground, I was duly impressed with the statue to John Greig rightly honouring the victims of the Ibrox disaster. Likewise, I was very pleased to be taken by two of my sons to the section of the main stand – the 'Stefan Klos panel' to be precise – with the commemorative brick to which they had fairly recently subscribed on my behalf. Again, the chit giving the elderly and infirm access to the elevator worked smoothly enough while I also felt that a free pass to a prominent lap-dancing club was, considering my advancing years, quite flattering.

On the other hand there were some less attractive aspects of my visit. For instance, there are those semi-derelict, dilapidated houses adjacent to the main stand reminiscent of a street scene in Berlin at the end of the second world war. Surely the club can put pressure on the local authority and clean up one of the main approaches to the ground? As for the catering facilities they seemed as dire as they were on previous visits, with the same unhealthy food and drink (non-alcoholic of course). To be fair I'm also aware from past experience that more upmarket and edible meals are available in the various private boxes within the main stand. Finally, the seating available, even in the club deck, seemed designed for hobbits and could teach some budget airlines a thing or two about squeezing in their customers.

As for the game itself, it was, I'm afraid, pretty depressing. Sadly, it was one of those all-too-frequent days when despite their opponents, Inverness Caley Thistle, being reduced to ten men for most of the game Rangers could still only manage a draw. Little evidence here then that the recent return of Walter Smith had made any significant difference. If anything, what my trip to Ibrox underlined was the depth of the current crisis. The basic problem is clearly a financial one. For whatever reason, there is obviously very little cash available to attract worthwhile players. Consequently, any hope of significant progress in Europe would appear remote while success in the Scottish Premier League has become increasingly difficult.

'The way forward' I shall leave to those with much greater knowledge and insight than myself of the internal workings of the club. Interestingly, the scurrilous but amusing fanzine *Follow Follow* (*FF* 187) devotes much space to an examination of the problems at Ibrox. None of it, incidentally, reflects very favourably either on the chairman David Murray, or the board. However, could it be that Rangers in the sixty years I have briefly touched upon have reached the zenith of what can be realistically expected of them? This might well be the case especially if they and Celtic remain thirled to the Scottish league.

Yet I am reluctant to end on a negative note. Among my Rangers memorabilia I recently rediscovered a report in the *Glasgow Herald* of 7 May 1973 by football correspondent Ian Archer of that year's Scottish Cup final, in which Rangers beat Celtic 3–2. The following extract seems a more upbeat way in which to end this brief memoir:

> On Saturday night the Scottish Cup lay in the boardroom at Ibrox, taken there from Hampden Park by a Rangers team who knew that history demanded heroics and tradition some tangible evidence of their glories. It was their first triumph since 1966. In their centenary year, the club brought back Scotland's most famous trophy to their own impressive building and there the champagne flowed. Moses McNeil, that Victorian oarsman from the Gareloch who stopped rowing long enough to found this Glasgow institution, would have loved and understood every minute of it all.

Great stuff. They don't write columns like that any more!

He Who Laughs Last, Laughs Longest

Ronnie Esplin

In the late 1960s and early 1970s, Roseberry Street in Oatlands may have been just another run-down tenement area of decaying post-war Glasgow awaiting renovation but it was the ideal place for a wide-eyed youngster intrigued by the vagaries of Scottish football. Clyde's Shawfield stadium was a mere fifty yards away from our room and kitchen, Hampden Park was two miles south via Polmadie Road and Celtic Park was two miles in the opposite direction. Junior side Glencairn's dilapidated Southcroft Park was a mile up Glasgow Road and, for good measure, Roseberry Park, the home of school and youth-cup finals, was a long goal-kick up Rosyth Street.

And in my formative years, before we decanted to Cambuslang and the sheer decadence of an inside toilet, I gratefully and voraciously imbibed every kind of football on offer. The Bully Wee's part-timers – such as Dom Sullivan, Harry Glasgow and Eddie Mulheron – were in stark contrast to Jock Stein's sides, which had Scottish, and at times European, football, firmly by the throat. The Scottish and League Cup competitions, Junior Cup finals and Scotland internationals, which were played at the ageing national stadium, offered the chance to see the likes of Bobby Moore and Bobby Charlton, the occasional unknown Dumbarton and Partick Thistle player as well as the famous Willie McCallum of Cambuslang Rangers.

But despite my location and the choices on offer, I was, in fact, a Rangers fan. The Jesuits at Ibrox had captured me long before the age of seven and that's where I preferred to go, jumping a bus along Caledonia Road to the St Enoch underground where the claustrophobic subway sped noisily to Copland Road. My earliest memory of the whole Old Firm palaver was as a six-year-old, then living in Blantyre, when I ran into the neighbour's packed house announcing to all and sundry that in support of my new-found friend Stevie Miller, I had become a Celtic fan. The chorus of disapproval that my naïve proclamation provoked – most vociferously and most crudely from a couple of men that I didn't even know – hastened me back out with my bottom lip trembling to tell my mate that I had reconsidered my gesture of friendship.

Social workers, and my parents, may want to look away now but between the ages of eight and nine, and I have checked with record books, I attended at some of the biggest games ever played in Scotland – on my own. If my dad was too busy or I couldn't muster any like-minded friends, I would nip over to Shawfield, not such a great adventure admittedly, but, much more irresponsibly, I would also sneak away to Hampden, Celtic Park or even cross the city to Ibrox. More often than not, however, there would be a little group of us from Oatlands (none of whom, incidentally, were Clyde fans despite our proximity to Shawfield) who would seek out the excitement of live football in a football-mad city. Unlike the present day, a lack of cash was no barrier to attending matches for those still at school. I don't recall paying into many games until I was a teenager. I had perfected the art of lingering close to the turnstiles and targeting the kind/drunk punter before pleading in time-honoured fashion, 'Gonnae gies a lift o'er Jimmy.' The buzz of planting your feet on the other side of the turnstile knowing you were in for free was addictive.

It would be disingenuous though to claim that we were serious students of the game. Much of our time at Shawfield was spent scavenging empty 'ginger' bottles from the feet of supporters so that we could return them to the kiosks for a few pence. Occasionally I would notice that Sullivan was far too good to be a Clyde player or that most of the Bully Wee fans seemed to be pensioners. We drew some withering glances bounding up Aikenhead Road ahead of the Scotland versus Portugal friendly with a popular gang chant of that era amended to suit the visit of the Black Pearl to the national stadium, although I can't recall if he actually played:

> Standing at the corner swinging a chain, along came Eusebio and
>   asked my name,
> I kicked him in the balls and kicked him in the head and now
>   Eusebio – is dead.

It didn't catch on.

The 1970/71 Scottish Cup campaign marked some new landmarks in my football journey. My first visit to the main stand at Ibrox was with my dad to see Rangers beat Falkirk 3–0 in the third round. Willie Henderson's brand new and overly long white laces, which were wrapped round his black boots like a bandage, captivated me from my front-row vantage point, as did the man beside me who kept rasping 'go on the wee barra' whenever the Rangers winger scampered down the right wing.

The goalless semi-final against Hibs at Hampden inspired a memorable 'Rangers Are Rubbish' headline from then Easter Road manager Dave Ewing. I recall the tangible hostility from the Rangers fans at the replay driving Willie Waddell's side on to their 2–1 victory. I was part of another huge crowd at the other semi-final replay between Airdrieonians and Celtic, which, after a 3–3 draw in the first game, the Parkhead side won to set up another Old Firm final. I listened to Derek Johnstone's late equaliser on the radio at home in the first match and vowed to sneak up to the replay. However, for the first time, I could not smuggle myself in to the national stadium and as I loitered outside with only rosette sellers for company, the roars from the Celtic end told me the game had gone their way before I trudged off home.

By the time my dad and I walked over to my first Old Firm derby at Parkhead on 3 January 1972, I probably knew the route every bit as well as him. I witnessed Celtic beating Finnish side KPV Kokkola 9–0 in a 1970 European Cup tie, and through the fog of time I'm sure I recall Willie Wallace scoring against Dundee from my vantage point in the Jungle. But I definitely remember John Connolly grabbing the winner for St Johnstone in a shock 1–0 victory for the Perth side, which probably clinched his move to Everton. And the New Year dander through Dalmarnock was not to take in my first Old Firm encounter. I have vague recollections of a League Cup section match earlier in the season, in which Old Firm debutant Kenny Dalglish scored a penalty in a 2–0 win at Ibrox, although my first meeting with him remains crystal clear. Soon after he had burst on to the scene I was walking up to Wolseley Street primary school when Dalglish stepped out of a car and handed an old woman waiting at the kerb a huge bag of Celtic strips, presumably to wash. I asked, moronically, 'Are you Kenny Dalglish?' to which he replied, 'aye' before getting back into his car. As it subsequently transpired, it was one of my more fruitful exchanges with the great man.

I was probably oblivious to the fact that Rangers went into the traditional New Year meeting seven points behind league leaders Celtic, who were heading for the seventh of their nine league titles in a row or that Rangers were in the midst of their European Cup Winners Cup run that ended in triumph in Barcelona when they beat Moscow Dynamo in the final. [1] The signs, as they often did at that time, pointed to a Celtic win. Willie Waddell's men had to rely on a last-gasp goal to beat Partick Thistle on New Year's Day at Ibrox while Jock Stein's side rattled seven past Clyde at Shawfield without reply. [2] The start of our journey to Celtic Park that dull January day was strangely quiet. There were no other fans around as we made our way between Richmond Park and Shawfield stadium, other supporters appearing only as we neared the ground. A chance meeting with my Uncle Jimmy Campbell from Blantyre resulted in a spare ticket being produced for my dad, I, of course, being lifted over.

As the supporters buses emptied, fans piled towards the turnstiles fuelled as much by optimism as by the contents of their carry-outs. We got into the ground relatively early, which meant that we avoided the stampede of police reinforcements after 'hundreds of ticket-less fans tried to storm the gates'. [3] And, as tradition demanded, I was shepherded down to the front of the terracing, where other youngsters, and one old lady wrapped up warm with a 'dress' Rangers scarf, jockeyed for a decent view of the match through the static policemen on the cinder track.

So there I was, three months shy of my tenth birthday and filling up with wonderful anticipation as kick-off approached and the discriminatory chants around the ground grew louder. Between 66,000 and 70,000 fans were present, depending on which account you believe, although anyone who ever occupied the Rangers end during an Old Firm game at the old-style Celtic Park would verify that head counting wasn't a Parkhead strong point. With a Rangers scarf round my neck for the first time inside Celtic Park, the stadium appeared more foreboding, more menacing. My previous visits, I convinced myself, had been mere reconnaissance missions. I was now part of a blue army in enemy territory, a superior green enemy that had won most of the battles over the previous five years and indeed, uniquely, three times at Ibrox within a four-week period earlier in the season. The goal nets and crush barriers were coloured a different, darker green than is associated with the club nowadays, although I am not sure if the silver goalposts, or those little triangular stanchions where Bobby Lennox once struck the ball with a powerful drive, were yet in place. When the teams emerged, and the blue jerseys bolted towards us through the bedlam, I wouldn't have wanted to be in any other place in the world.

Celtic took the lead through Jimmy Johnstone after thirty-five minutes and two-thirds of the ground exploded. I can just about remember the Celtic winger stooping to head Harry Hood's quickly taken free kick past Peter McCloy. As the distant celebrations continued, and I wondered if I was set to watch Rangers suffer another Old Firm defeat, the old lady turned and exclaimed above the din, 'Don't worry boys, he who laughs last, laughs longest.' It was the first time I had heard that saying and I was only half sure what it meant. And I had no idea it would come true that very afternoon.

The *Daily Express's* John Mackenzie claimed the first half had 'more skill than anyone has the right to expect from an Old Firm game – and much of it from Rangers' [4] but when my dad came down to check on me at half-time, there was little sense of satisfaction around. The second half remains mostly a blur but I do recall the feeling of time running out and an anxiety slowly infiltrating the Rangers support as they contemplated yet more Old Firm depression. But, with nine minutes to go, Colin Stein equalised, leaving an indelible image in my sub-conscious.

Newspaper reports of the goal are sketchy, indicating that most reporters had probably missed the preamble. It appears that from either Dave Smith or Willie Mathieson's through ball, both Stein and Willie Johnston found themselves in on goal with the Celtic defence missing. Jim Blair of the *Evening Times* claimed that keeper Denis Connaghan, who was making his Old Firm debut, 'should have stopped Stein's scoring shot'. [5] However, that's not how I remember it. The build-up was too quick to take in as the ball flashed around the pitch but the final seconds remain framed forever in delicious slow motion. Suddenly Stein is boring in towards goal from the left and in an instant the volume is turned up.

We stretch on tiptoes to see if he can get his shot away before a tackle comes in but Stein, despite being full of bustling power and aggression, seems to take an age to unleash. The ball travels a few more agonising yards towards the six-yard box and still nothing. But then he just fucks it past a flailing yellow jersey and into the corner of the net. As a fearsome noise splits the sky I experience my first adrenaline rush. I'm drowning in a bear hug from a beery-breathed stranger who had been ten yards behind me five seconds ago. I break free and look further up the terrace for my dad and uncle Jimmy, to share the delight, but to no avail. It's pandemonium. I'm exhausted and exhilarated. The old lady is being buffeted around but appears to be safe. I've witnessed my first Rangers goal against Celtic. I'm enjoying the greatest feeling in the world in the greatest game in the world. The old lady in front of me, my fellow schoolboys around me and the men at my back. We would not be moved, not by the Hibs, the Hearts nor the Celtic and that's what we bellowed into the winter air. He who laughs last ya bass!

However, the intoxicating camaraderie I felt with my fellow Rangers fans was less inclusive than I had been led to believe. As far as football was concerned, the west of Scotland could not be neatly divided into blue on the one side and green on the other; it was much more complicated than that. I discovered that, in the Protestant community, social-class divisions were often more important than those forged by religion, while the opposite was usually true among Roman Catholics. I recently took part in the latest in the long line of documentaries commissioned by foreign film companies, which try to unravel the complex layers of the Old Firm. In this French effort, called *Glasgow Colours*, two primary-school boys talk about 'Catholic and Protestant' schools with specific reference to Celtic and Rangers, perpetuating the myth that the education system in Scotland represents two sides of the same Old Firm coin. [6] The Holy Trinity in Scotland that is Celtic Football Club, the Roman Catholic Church and the Catholic education system has been enduring. Contrary to what some of the more rabid Rangers fans believe, Catholic schools do not promote bigotry, but, in the west of Scotland at least, they do produce an endless stream of Celtic fans. A schoolboy friend, Chris Griffin, told me how the headmaster at his primary school in Easterhouse burst into the classroom after hearing the draw for the 1970 European Cup semi-final shouting, 'Boys, we've got Leeds United!' My own experience as a parent, witnessing as I have, for instance, a move to introduce 'The Fields of Athenry' on to the curriculum and a Henrik Larsson painting project, shows little has changed in thirty-seven years. When I took my son up to the first night of training with his youth team – a de facto primary school team – resplendent in his Real Madrid strip, twenty-one out of twenty-three of the other boys had Celtic strips on. There is nothing conspiratorial about it; that's just the way it is.[7]

Non-denominational schooling offered me a somewhat different experience. If Protestantism was a sensitive subject among teachers at Cathkin High in the mid-Seventies, and it most certainly was, then the subject of the Rangers Football Club was, for the most part, strictly taboo. The club had become the unacceptable face of Scottish sport and, for many, a blight on Scottish society. The high-profile hooligan problems at friendly matches in Manchester United in 1974 and Aston Villa two years later, in the wake of the trouble at the 1972 European Cup Winners Cup final in Barcelona, had tarnished the club's reputation. Rangers' sectarian signing policy, which came in to the public spotlight after Villa, was equally to blame for the club's fall from grace.

Housemaster, geography teacher and erstwhile Jordanhill rugby player Ian 'You are nothing but a shower of bloody Orangemen' Gray, personified the swathes of Protestant middle-class professionals who were contemptuous of Rangers. The mention of the club elicited head-shaking to such an extent that I'm sure only his bull neck prevented self-decapitation. That one of the school's many rugby-orientated teachers sneered at Rangers is perhaps no real surprise, especially given that he subsequently became an SNP councillor. Nor was it any surprise that the English teacher, Mr McLean, who proudly wore a hammer-and-sickle badge on his lapel, and his political beliefs on his sleeve, found the remnants of Empire that lingered at Ibrox repugnant.

However, maths teacher Gordon Scott, who gave his time unselfishly to take our school team – not all of whom were Rangers fans, incidentally – was similarly unimpressed by the team of choice of many of his young charges. Notwithstanding the off-field problems at Rangers, the treble came to Ibrox twice during our time at Cathkin High, yet we were given no encouragement to look to Govan for inspiration. Once, as he drove a few of us home after a Saturday-morning match, we tried to get him involved in our discussion about the Rangers game that afternoon. 'What are you going to watch that rubbish for?' was the exasperated reply. Former teammate John Allardyce remembers the animosity his affections for Ibrox evoked:

Unlike many Roman Catholic schools, where teachers were open about supporting Celtic, it was never really encouraged to follow Rangers at Cathkin High and you could find yourself in trouble for any football chants. I can't remember even one teacher admitting to being a bluenose. I do recall Mr Scott on many occasions making comments and shaking his head when we mentioned that we followed Rangers. I think his team was Hamilton so maybe he was like the followers of many provincial clubs, who disliked both Rangers and Celtic.

Another ex-pupil, John McKillop, recalls:

Being a Rangers fan was frowned upon, definitely. Not being good enough for the football team, I decided that rugby would be my chosen sport. One Saturday I should have been reporting to Mr Gray at 9 a.m. outside the PE department. However, on the Friday evening I was offered a ticket for the Aberdeen versus Rangers game the next day so there was no contest. But what a roasting I got on the Monday. Talk about the hairdryer; Sir Alex Ferguson had nothing on Mr Gray. He gave me three of the belt no less for letting him and his rugby team down, telling me I was low life. There ended my rugby career.

In short, Cathkin High was not a breeding ground for Rangers fans. And if I need reminded of how little influence non-denominational schooling in the 1970s had on forging or reinforcing its pupils' football allegiances, I only have to glance down from my press seat at Celtic Park to see our season-ticket-holding-former-school-team goalkeeper. Old Firm fans also have differing relationships with what is perceived to be 'their' churches and church leaders. I have noted how the local priest would enthusiastically support the club of his flock, 'let's hope we get a good result this afternoon' while the only clerical champion for Rangers that I can recall was the Reverend James Currie who was a lone, and sometimes misguided, voice in his support for the Ibrox club in the 1970s. In the main, leaders of the various Protestant churches – notwithstanding the club's unofficial chaplain Stuart McQuarrie – are still conspicuous by their absence at Ibrox.

Indeed, many claim that in terms of providing leadership to their natural congregation, they are simply conspicuous by their absence. In fairness, this antipathy is reciprocated. Most Rangers fans, especially those who proclaim loudest their Protestantism, seldom darken a church doorstep outside the services associated with hatches, matches and dispatches.

Celtic and Rangers fans also display marked political differences. The Celtic support (and the Catholic population) is solidly Labour, and the Catholic Church is cognisant of the power that comes from having such a large block vote. The late Cardinal Thomas Winning, a Celtic fan, tormented the Labour Party when their policies were not to his liking, thus earning the tag of Scotland's most powerful unelected politician. In recent times Bishop Philip Tartaglia, among other church leaders, has also flexed his Catholic muscles in the political ring. In a scathing attack on Labour Party candidates in Paisley he said: 'They could field almost anyone and expect Catholics to vote for them because they always did in the past.' [8] Conversely, Rangers fans (and Protestants) are spread much more evenly around the political spectrum. Graeme Souness's dalliance with Margaret Thatcher in the late 1980s, as the club embarked on an unprecedented spending spree, served only to encourage hatred of Rangers on a Scotland-wide basis and fostered the idea that the club was full of Tories. However, Ibrox fans are, in the main, happy to keep football and politics separate. [9]

The age-old sectarian issue that has bedevilled the Ibrox club is coming to a head, and not before time. UEFA panicked the club in 2006 by imposing a fine after finding Rangers fans were guilty of discriminatory chanting during a Champions League clash with Villarreal. To yet another round of condemnatory statements from the club were added yet more anti-sectarian initiatives. A *Wee Blue Book* was published containing suitable songs and the club began working even more closely with the Rangers Assembly and the Rangers Supporters Trust, among others, to get to grips with the problem before the threats of bans and points deductions became a reality. Anti-sectarian messages are boomed out to supporters before games at Ibrox; there is now no ambiguity as to where the club stands with regards the bigotry issue.

However, a by-product of this bright, new, blue future has been the intensification of existing tensions between some fans and the club. In addition, a clearly defined split emerged within the Rangers support

41

causing tensions between the doves and the hawks, which were again revealed at the start of the 2007/08 season in, of all places, Inverness. Days after yet another anti-sectarian initiative, Follow with Pride, was launched, Rangers fans were criticised for the add-ons to songs sung at the Tulloch Caledonian Thistle stadium during a 3–0 victory. It was clear that there remains a section of fans which prefers songs about the Ulster Volunteer Force and the Young Carson Volunteers to traditional ditties like 'Follow Follow' and 'Every Other Saturday' and they do not intend to be moved, regardless of how much it harms the club. One RST representative told me about their attempts to re-educate the fans: 'We are getting there. Just give us time.' However, time could be running out.

The drive to make sense of the complex attitudinal and cultural complexities at Ibrox continues, but, on the face of it, traditional rivals Celtic have no such problems. With a few notable exceptions, Celtic writers and commentators have been kind to their club, preferring to nurture the fans' traditional persecution complex than to offer critical examination. Catholics in Scottish society were discriminated against and even the most ardent bluenose now accepts that. However, there is a literary strand at Parkhead – epitomised by the likes of James MacMillan and some of the contributors to the *Celtic Minded* tomes – that will not allow the Protestant population, and especially anyone connected to Rangers Football Club, to discard their hair shirts. The rantings of composer and Celtic fan MacMillan, including his infamous 'Scotland's Shame' speech in 1999, was a classic case of crying wolf once too often. And in reading many of the articles in the *Celtic Minded* books, one is reminded of the *Monty Python* sketch in which four Yorkshiremen try to 'one-up' each other as their nostalgic accounts of deprived childhoods become increasingly outrageous and absurd. For Python's poverty, read anti-Irish, anti-Catholic and anti-Celtic. However, in addition to wallowing in endless self-pitying claims of persecution by Protestants, and endless squeals of societal bias towards Rangers, a startling lack of humility shines through. Among a plethora of pomposity, my favourite is a line in the piece by Andrew Milne, 'Being Celtic Minded', which boasts that 'Celtic is much more than a football team . . . it is part of humanity's history of survival.' Put that in your pipe Barcelona! [10]

While serious social commentators and academics sent MacMillan packing with his tail between his legs, Joseph Bradley (university academic and editor of both *Celtic Minded* tomes) continues with his burgeoning 'Rangers and Protestant bad – Celtic and Catholic good' cottage industry. [11] For the sake of historical accuracy, if nothing else, their conclusions should be challenged. Of course some people are bigoted. Three hours after the botched terrorist attack on Glasgow airport at the end of June 2007, our taxi driver kindly offered his solution to the increasing security tensions in modern-day Britain: 'We should do something radical, like send all the Asians back.' He compounded his racist views by complaining about the influx of Eastern Europeans into the country's hotel and leisure industries, and how that development had led to complaints from tourists. I immediately thought of MacMillan et al and their claims that Irish Catholics remain discriminated against in Scotland. Was the taxi driver's rant a microcosmic example of the indigenous population railing against incomers? MacMillan and his acolytes, however, would have been interested, one presumes, in the fact that the taxi driver was Irish and he was taking us through Dublin city centre, yards from its iconic post office, when he let rip with his invective. Having travelled to the fair city the day after visiting the Dunbrody Famine Ship in Wexford, the irony of the situation was neither lost on me, nor on my companion, an unreconstructed Irish Nationalist. [12] The success of the Celtic Tiger is being underpinned by cheap Eastern European imports, a development that is not finding acceptance by all in the Emerald Isle. So can we look forward to MacMillan making an 'Ireland's Shame' speech any time soon?

We should not be complacent about sectarianism in Scotland but neither should we get hysterical. By and large we all rub along together just fine. I watch football through different eyes these days, with a clarity that comes with no longer being a fully paid-up member of the Follow Follow brigade. Celtic versus Rangers is not the greatest game in the world any more, if it ever was. However, on those occasional moments of nostalgia, when I picture Stein powering his way through on goal, I think of that wizened old lady who shared that special moment at Celtic Park with me and how her utterance, 'He who laughs last, laughs longest' turned out to be absolutely right. With a minute to go, Jim Brogan popped up with a header to give Celtic a 2–1 win. The laughing stopped, at least where I was standing.

Still, you can't have everything.

Notes

[1] I attended every home game of the campaign and no football fan over forty-five years of age can forget the night of 19 April 1972 when the semi-finals of the European Cup and the Cup Winners Cup took place in Glasgow, 150,000 fans splitting themselves unevenly between Ibrox and Parkhead. Rangers, kicking off earlier against Bayern Munich, beat the German club 2–0 to go through to the final 3–1 on aggregate while at the other end of the city, Dixie Deans wrote himself into the history books for the wrong reasons by missing the vital spot kick in the penalty shoot-out that allowed Inter Milan to beat Celtic. Heady days indeed.

[2] For a game that was an all-ticket sell-out, the Old Firm match was still advertised in the *Daily Express* whose readers also learned that it would cost them sixty pence if they wanted a stand seat to watch Partick Thistle take on Airdrie at Firhill and twenty pence to watch Queen's Park versus Brechin at Hampden. The teams at Celtic Park: Celtic: Connaghan, Hay, Brogan, Dalglish, McNeill, Connelly, Johnstone, Lennox, Deans, Callaghan, Hood. Sub: McGrain. Rangers: McCloy, Jardine, Mathieson, Greig, Jackson, Smith, McLean, D. Johnstone, Stein, MacDonald, W. Johnston. Sub: Conn.

[3] *Daily Express*, 4 January 1972

[4] *Daily Express*, 4 January 1972

[5] *Evening Times*, 4 January 1972

[6] *Glasgow Colours*, released 2007. It is a typical Old Firm documentary that highlights the differences between the clubs, ignoring the relative peace in which both clubs co-exist. Television companies like Sky and ESPN have made documentaries about derby games in places like Greece, Turkey and the Baltic States, which put the Old Firm derby in context.

[7] To indicate the more enlightened days in which we live with regards the Old Firm, the team received and accepted an invite to tour Murray Park near the end of season 2006/07.

[8] *The Scotsman* 13 September 2006. Tartaglia was appointed Bishop of Paisley by Pope Benedict XVI in 2005.

9   This was the conclusion in my first book *Down the Copland Road* (Argyll, 2000).

10 *Celtic Minded 2*, p 124.

11 To gratuitously add to my co-editor's stinging critique of MacMillan and some of the contributors to the *Celtic Minded* books would be like getting down on your knees to head the ball over the line when your team is 9–0 up.

12 The incident later that evening, when the Irish manageress of an O'Connell Street pub had to ask the Irish bouncers to put an end to the incessant 'Ooh ah, up the RA' chants from a bunch of Scottish Celtic fans, which threatened to ruin the traditional Irish entertainment, raised another chuckle.

Jim Forrest's Goals and Other Reflections

Graham Walker

My earliest memories involving Rangers are of the football scores being read out on *Scotsport* and my delight if they had won. I was around five years old. I'm not entirely sure why the club was already in my heart: my father supported Hearts and my mother and older brother had no real interest in the football. Much of it probably stemmed from being taught to sing 'Follow Follow' by our downstairs neighbour and bluenose, David McLeay. 'Up the stairs, doon the stairs we will follow on' he sang to me as I marched 'up and doon' the stairs of our Pollokshaws tenement building. The name itself – the Rangers – magically enthralled me, as did the royal-blue shirts which by then sported the neat white V-neck.

By the age of seven I was attending matches at Ibrox, lifted over the turnstile by my father who was admitting me, probably not without reservations, to an intoxicating spectacle of vast terraces and tumultuous noise. From the first moment I was hooked, feeling weirdly secure among the roaring, cursing mob, the men in their weekend suits with beer cans and bottles sticking out of every pocket. However, it was two successive League Cup finals at Hampden – late in 1963 and 1964 – that brought the greatest thrill of those early times and provided my first real idol. Jim Forrest, a young centre forward who had just broken into the team, scored four in a 5–0 victory over Morton in the first of these games. I watched exultant at the King's Park 'Celtic' end behind the goal which they all, plus another from Forrest's cousin Alex Willoughby, went in; there were 105,000 at Hampden and such experiences simply never leave you. The following year I was back to see Forrest score the goals – at the same end – which put paid to Celtic in a 2–1 win. I cheered wildly as Jim Baxter tossed the wide-lugged cup high into the air at the end.

That was my first Old Firm game and certain factors compel me to dwell on it. My father was working a Saturday day shift at the *Daily Record* and I was taken to the match by my Uncle Adam, a lifelong Celtic fan, a Catholic and a Dunkirk survivor. He and my dad's sister Isa formed a 'mixed marriage' in the euphemistic parlance of lowland Scotland where divisions between Protestants and Catholics were slowly revealing themselves to me as intriguing. By the time of this cup final my uncle and I had established a significant bond around our Rangers–Celtic rivalry, although it must have still required some forbearance on his part to have to accompany someone clad in a red, white and blue tammy. He took me to the small enclosure below the main stand, technically in the Celtic half, although as neutral a position as could be found. Just before kick off my maternal grandfather materialised. A dead ringer for James Cagney, he was a Rangers man and a member of Thornliebank Orange Lodge. His brother had been killed in the Great War. He too was a typical Glasgow character, a pavier with the city council, and a wind-up artist bursting with patter. The teams lined up and the national anthem started. 'Sing up son!' my grandfather enjoined, as my uncle stayed mute. 'I don't know the words', I replied, mesmerised by the ritual's dramatically divisive impact on the Hampden crowd.

After the game the three of us walked over to Pollokshaws Road and the Bay Horse pub. I was left standing outside for what seemed like an age while my grandfather and uncle slaked their thirsts. Later in the evening, in my uncle and aunt's home in Pollokshaws, I devoured the match reports in the pink *Times* and green *Citizen*. My parents had joined us by this time. Then my uncle, upon reading the same papers, observed that the Celtic chairman Bob Kelly had claimed that a shot on goal by his team had crossed the line before being retrieved by the Rangers goalkeeper Billy Ritchie and that the referee had unfairly deprived Celtic of a goal. We had been aware of some drama and controversy at the time but had not been sure about the details. However, I remember clearly my uncle's sense of injustice retrospectively imposed. It was, in fact, my first exposure to the by now much-discussed phenomenon of 'Celtic paranoia', an engrained folk memory of perceived ill treatment at the hands of match officials and the governing body of Scottish football. As several newspaper photographs were to indicate the following day, the ball had not crossed the line and the referee had been correct. Significantly, Kelly had not even waited for such evidence to prove or disprove his allegation.

As the years have passed I have been forced to listen over and over again to the outrage of Celtic fans about this goal chalked off or that penalty denied, as if theirs was the only club to be affected by bad decisions. I remember not so long ago, when I should surely have been doing something more important, sitting down to compile a list of dodgy decisions suffered by Rangers in Old Firm games and building myself up into a lather of indignation and, in the manner of my uncle, the conviction of having been the victim of a history of injustice. And as for all the officials being freemasons and/or closet Rangers fans, I had to laugh when I read former Celtic player Brian McClair's admission that a linesman had openly celebrated with him at Love Street in 1986 when news of Dundee's goals against Hearts came through and confirmed Celtic as champions.

The rawness of the emotions at that Old Firm League Cup final hit me like a tank. Subsequently, as I grew up in a housing scheme to which we moved when Pollokshaws was subjected to a disastrous programme of urban redevelopment, I became accustomed to the social and cultural realities of religious divisions. These were by no means barriers to Protestant–Catholic friendships or, as noted, marriages. Rather, they were nods to history and the past's power still to guide behaviour and attitudes, and to fashion a sense of belonging which was coherent and meaningful precisely because it was specific and tribal. The position of the churches in the community was still a prominent one, albeit that they had begun a steep decline. In the 1960s the vitality of church-related activities and associations, even in working-class areas, was an important factor in perpetuating a sense of Protestant or Catholic identity. Rangers and Celtic, Orangeism and Hibernianism, formed for many a layer of passion and commitment on top, and a token of extra involvement and loyalty. In the world in which I grew up Protestants and Catholics could be close, intimate and, on many levels from political leanings to humour, indistinguishable. Yet the distinctive categories took root in our minds; separate schooling could only have contributed to that. And the suppressed tensions could erupt at given times – most obviously at Old Firm games. Meanwhile, the recrudescence of the Irish troubles at the close of the 1960s brought more into the light the tangled roots of Scottish sectarianism. Scotland was not of course to go the way of Ulster during the following generation; the fear of such a fate was perhaps the strongest reason for this good fortune, but it should not be forgotten that in contrast to Northern Ireland, Protestants and Catholics in Scotland lived and worked together and often married one another. Religious tensions were significant and their causes complex and debatable, but the amount of social and cultural interaction provided crucial civic ballast.

Looking back I can see that the place I hailed from, Pollokshaws, was in many ways emblematic of the issues I'm trying to discuss and tease out.[1] A weaving centre since the mid eighteenth century, Pollokshaws developed into a multi-industrial burgh in the Victorian age and was subsumed into the city of Glasgow in 1912. Like its surrounding places – Barrhead, Thornliebank, Renfrew – it attracted a large volume of Irish immigrants, both Catholic and Protestant, during the nineteenth century, and became notable for its concentration of churches of virtually every Christian denomination, for its range of political activity, and, notwithstanding a strong local temperance movement, for its pubs.[2] As well as the mainstream British political parties the 'Shaws had a branch of the United Irish League in the late nineteenth and early twentieth century, part of a mass Irish Nationalist movement. At the same time the burgh boasted seven Orange lodges, which in 1905 came together to build a hall in Barrhead Road.[3] This hall with its peculiar name fascinated me as a child, standing as it did across the road from our own Pollok Church of Scotland, a congregation which previously had been Pollokshaws Pollok United Free Church and before that Pollokshaws Burgh United Presbyterian.[4] Beside where we lived in Greenbank Street had stood for years a rather ramshackle Gospel Hall.

Indications of the strength of Orange and Green party feeling in the history of the 'Shaws can be detected in a variety of sources. An Orange song – 'Pollockshaw Heroes' – dates to 1852, evidence of a significant Protestant-Irish settlement long before the better-documented arrival of thousands of Protestant immigrants to shipbuilding areas of the Clyde later in the century. The song announces:

The place we have planted our colours
They are taking deep root in the soil

In a few years they'll bring fruit abundant
And doubly repay our toil
And when on the bright sun of summer
The colours will bear a good hue
So we are the Pollockshaw heroes
That love to wear Orange and Blue.[5]

In 1875 the centenary celebrations for the great Irish National leader Daniel O'Connell involved a large procession through Pollokshaws, which was led by several Catholic priests. One of them, a Father Munro, urged his listeners not to be influenced by 'false Protestant leaders or renegade Irishmen', an apparent reference to the Home Rule leadership of the time.[6] In 1922 the local newspaper described the spectacle of the 12 July Orange Walk in the area, which involved the local lodges with their brethren from Thornliebank, among them my grandfather.[7] He indeed walked each year, a ritual as scrupulously observed as his attendance at every Rangers home match for decades. My mother's grandfather, on her mother's side, John Smith, was also an Orangeman. By all accounts, and certainly in our family folklore, he was a true gentleman, and a good neighbour in his Harriet Street tenement block to 'Mistress Callaghan', an Irish woman of firm Catholic and Nationalist convictions who lived across the landing. Civilities were carefully preserved and protected in the midst of often bitter differences.

In that same year of 1922 the Pollokshaws paper reported on the unveiling of the Thornliebank war memorial which, like the one in Pollokshaws bearing the name of my grandfather's brother Henry, still stands today. The report stated that 'perhaps the largest assembled crowd ever seen in Thornliebank showed up'. Among them were ex-servicemen's organisations, the Boys Brigade, the Scouts and the Freemasons. Wreaths were laid by both the Orange Order and the St Vincent de Paul Society.[8] This was, probably, an occasion which reverberated most strongly in the Protestant community, yet certainly not exclusively so. Sacrifices made in wartime, economic privations in peacetime and a fast-developing popular culture of football, cinema and dancing were just some of the things that breached sectarian divisions and fashioned a common set of experiences which balanced the continuing tensions and at times friction.

Above all, perhaps, there was the factor of working-class consciousness, which strengthened politically in the early twentieth century. Pollokshaws was the birthplace of Scotland's most celebrated socialist icon, John MacLean. As I was growing up I heard him spoken of almost reverentially, not least by my Labour-minded father. Along with the officials of his engineering union, he helped to collect the funds to pay for the memorial cairn to MacLean which was erected in 1973. The inscription read: 'Famous Pioneer of Working Class Education. He forged the Scottish Link in the Golden Chain of World Socialism.' At the unveiling of the cairn various groups from the nether world of the Scottish Left appeared, some displaying their support for the 'Irish struggle'. This did not go down well with many of the locals. My Aunt Isa – reporting on the event to my father who had not been able to be present due to work – commented angrily that 'those wereny our people'. The remark stuck with me and I've analysed it often subsequently. Who were and weren't 'our people'? I don't think the answer is straightforward. Isa might have wished to distance herself from the Trotskyite hangers-on and the Scottish Republicans; she undoubtedly would have wanted nothing to do with those whose support for the Irish cause clearly endorsed the then murderous campaign of the IRA. A working-class suspicion of better-off agitators telling them what to think and to do seems likely to have been part of her reaction. But the 'our people' whom she clearly believed should have been central rather than peripheral to the event were the ordinary folk born and bred in the 'Shaws like her, for whom MacLean's reputation transcended political sectarianism. There may have been some residual Protestant or Orange-flavoured resentment over the display of Irish Nationalist and therefore Catholic emblems, but she had married a Catholic and was raising a son as one. MacLean's support for James Connolly, the Irish (though Edinburgh-born) socialist republican executed after the Easter Rising of 1916, would not have been something she or the majority of 'Shaws folk would have known about or absorbed.

My father too talked mainly about MacLean's work for the working class, his stress on education and his fight for better conditions. MacLean's militancy was admired – and my father cut his own political teeth in the hotbed of the engineering apprentices' strikes of the late Thirties – but the world of socialist theory about imperialism was, well, another less-relevant world. Over the years, in the course of my academic career, I have studied the development of the Scottish Labour movement and the life and work and ideas of John MacLean; I've learned and sung the ballads about him; and I've cherished the quirky connections that I might claim to have with him. These include my paternal grandfather's employment at Lockhart's Pottery in the 'Shaws following his previous job at the same firm in Bo'ness; MacLean's father moved from Bo'ness to the 'Shaws for the same reason, a job at Lockhart's. MacLean lies in Eastwood cemetery where my own bluenose grandfather, and the grandmother who died before I was born, are buried. MacLean was a great man who served a magnificent challenge to the capitalist system of the day. Yet socialism itself did not have all the answers.

Class loyalties ran alongside religious ones. They sometimes blended and sometimes clashed. My father, affected like most by Orange and Green antagonisms, nonetheless found himself in regular conflict with those paragons of Protestant working-class respectability: the factory foremen. His time at Dalglish's in Pollokshaws featured many a run-in with the foreman and the bowler-hatted and stiff-collared boss himself. My father wanted to get taken on at Weir's in Cathcart and he did so after being spoken for by another neighbour, Hughie McPhee, a Catholic married to a Protestant. My bluenose pal David from our close also worked in Weir's and was a strong trade unionist. Just as my uncle Adam introduced me to the ear and nerve-shredding experience of an Old Firm encounter, so as a younger man did he take my teenage father to see the legendary Benny Lynch fight at Shawfield; Lynch's appeal effortlessly spanned Glasgow's sectarian boundaries, even when, at Celtic Park, he fought Jimmy Warnock from Belfast's Shankill Road. Adam also on one auspicious occasion mischievously fixed up my dad to play a trial with Maryhill Harp. My father, desperate for a game, agreed only to find when he got there that the opposition was the local Maryhill Juniors and that this derby was of a decidedly Orange versus Green nature. Wearing his green-and-white strip he endured torrid abuse of – it has to be said – Ibrox vintage, for this was the Thirties when some Rangers players and officials spoke at Orange functions, and the heyday of the original 'Billy Boys' gang. It was in this era that members of the latter gang would stand at the Copland Road end of Ibrox bellowing Orange songs.[9] And, of course, it is precisely these songs, and the ones in praise of these same Brigton desperadoes, which have landed Rangers in trouble some seventy years later.

When Aunt Isa died in 1983 my father and I went to tell one of her oldest friends, Kate Ward, by then a widow living some fifteen floors up in one of the multi-storey blocks in the 'Shaws. The sorrow slowly turned to happier reminiscences and my father urged me to get Kate talking about 'Meek's penalty'. Kate and her late husband had been Rangers stalwarts since the early 1920s and her fondest memory – like that of many older fans of the time – was of the 1928 Scottish Cup final when the club ended its twenty-five-year-long 'hoodoo' of failure in the tournament with an emphatic 4–0 triumph over Celtic. The old lady described as if it had happened the day before, the agonisingly nervous wait for the Rangers captain Davie Meiklejohn to strike home the opening goal from the penalty spot. I could virtually taste the relief and the joy of the moment when 'Meek's' shot hit the net. But Kate and her husband were also working-class Tories – or 'Unionists' – as they were then known. They frequented the 'Unionist Rooms', just off Shawbridge Street, and went to meetings to hear the extreme Protestant ranter of the inter-war era, Alexander Ratcliffe. For them, religion and a sense of patriotism which conjoined Scottish and British loyalties trumped the politics of class interest; not that they were in any way ashamed of where they came from. Kate was a reminder in the 1980s of what then and since seemed barely believable – the superior political strength of the Conservatives and Unionists in Scotland from the end of the Great War to the 1960s, give or take the odd blip. One factor in the Unionists' success was the way that religious divisions could override those of class especially in economically straitened times when rumours were rife about the 'other side' exercising undue influence. As a Revd R. F. Whiteley was reported to have said in 1931 in the Pollokshaws Orange Hall on Barrhead Road:

> They lived in difficult times, difficult because of the lack of employment, and he would speak a word to any who had influence in that connection that they would not forget their brethren of the Orange Order, because they knew only too well that those of the other side had their passwords and such like which they could well use, so it was necessary for

Protestants and Orangemen to defend themselves and to see that they got a fair chance in any work that was available.[10]

Heroes like Meiklejohn to the Rangers faithful were followed in the post-war era by other illustrious names from the club's hall of fame: George Young (revered by my grandfather), Willie Waddell, Willie Thornton, Willie Woodburn, Jock 'Tiger' Shaw, Billy Simpson, all of whose exploits were related to me by relatives and family friends. My father did his best to compete with hosannas about Hearts' 'terrible trio' of Conn, Bauld and Wardhaugh. By the time I was inhaling the unique Ibrox atmosphere the great line-up of Ritchie, Shearer, Caldow, Greig, McKinnon, Baxter, Henderson, McMillan, Millar, Brand and Wilson was at its peak and the feeling of being part of it was simply glorious.[11] But it came to a premature end that 64/65 season when the League Cup proved to be the only trophy we would capture. First Henderson went missing for months with bunion trouble, then Baxter broke his leg in our quest for the European Cup. Their replacements – Craig Watson and Wilson Wood – are remembered only by Rangers diehards. The team slumped in the league, finishing an embarrassing fifth (not quite as embarrassing as our rivals, who were eighth) and crashed out of the Scottish and European Cups at the quarter-final stage. Baxter missed the big clash with Inter Milan, the kind of game in which he would have revelled – witness his imperious display later that year for Scotland against Italy at Hampden. The season served as an early warning to me of the trials ahead as a devout follower of a football team. Nevertheless, for all the disappointment, I could reflect that my idol, Jim Forrest, ended the season with an astonishing fifty-seven goals. Not even 'Super Ally' McCoist, later on, would match that. Forrest's total included goals against Inter Milan home and away as well as five in a match against Hamilton Accies. Along with John Greig it seemed that this lethal striker would underpin our future return to pre-eminence.

But Rangers were to be distinctly out of tune with the second half of the Sixties, both on and off the field. The club came to be identified with a way of life now threatened by a counter-cultural movement that sought to liberate people from traditional forms of authority and their value systems. More specifically, Rangers' by now well-established practice of signing only Protestant players had exposed it to the critiques of a new generation conscious of discrimination and civil-rights struggles around race in the USA and South Africa. More and more the Orange anthems sung at Ibrox seemed to defy the spirit of the times, while crude chants about the Pope forced some erstwhile fans to distance themselves. Elements in the Rangers support became notorious for their hooligan behaviour, although it needs to be kept in mind that this was a time, notwithstanding the 'peace and love' mantras, of spectacular violence involving youth gangs in Glasgow.

The social and cultural dynamics and tensions of this heady period have been well caught in novels and films. Of these, mention might be made of Alan Spence's writings and Gillies and Billy McKinnon's film *Small Faces* for the way Glasgow and Rangers are situated in treatments of the era. Both in Spence's work[12] and in *Small Faces* Rangers are part of the representation of an urban-working-class reality whose time-battered outlook collides with the growth of new, more expansive and revolutionary and anarchistic currents of thought, albeit fuelled by an emerging consumer culture and possibly deceptive.[13] The very idea of belonging itself is called into question as something restrictive and oppressive. Some of the characters in Spence's *Magic Flute* novel, or in his luminously insightful short stories, feel a compelling need in a time of new opportunities to move on from, in this case, their Govan working-class environment; some feel a sense of identification with it which precludes thoughts of alternatives. The struggle was clearly that of Spence himself and it is notable that he should reflect much later on the way that his travels and his own personal intellectual and creative journey, while leading him wittingly to try to reject Rangers and what the club appeared to stand for, could not remove the attachment which had been forged in boyhood.[14] In *Small Faces* the eldest of three brothers, Bobby, is a prominent member of a local gang, taciturn, brooding, inarticulate and heading for a tragic end, with the same Rangers photos on his bedroom wall which I had on mine. Alan, the middle brother, is a budding artist, opening himself up to the promise of the era, with posters of Che Guevara on his wall. The youngest, Lex, is drawn to aspects of the lives of both, although is clearly portrayed as a free spirit destined eventually to break out of the circle of family feuding, emotional dependency, machismo, atavism and tribalism. That said, the film-makers give him the name – Lex MacLean – of the famous Rangers-supporting comedian of the time whose jokes about the team were an antidote to the dourness of those who ran and spoke for the club. Interestingly, Lex the comedian's Sixties record, 'Every Other Saturday', has recently been revived at Ibrox in an effort to get the fans to stick to exclusively football-related songs. Indeed, Lex's mantle has been inherited by comedian Andy Cameron, who has been to the fore in this effort.

Both Spence and the McKinnon brothers treat sympathetically those of their characters who embody the cultural conservatism and the specificity of the identity they are born into, and the question arises as to what should be held onto and preserved and made compatible with greater freedom for the individual. There is in fact a very Scottish drama being contemplated: the lure of the tribe and the security and the romance of a collective sense of belonging pulling against the urge to dissent, to 'split' (such a very Sixties word for something with such a history in Scotland), to be different. Spence's work, and *Small Faces*, speak to me in dramatic language I feel I am almost programmed to understand, immersed as I once was in the culture they address and still am in the fortunes of a football team whose symbolism runs so deep in the city and the nation's consciousness.

My 'Spencean' dilemmas came later during the 1970s and 1980s when Rangers' signing policy and many of the fans' knee-jerk politics in response to badly understood events in Ulster made life difficult. There was never any question of changing my allegiance; I was much too steeped in the club's history and folklore. In addition, the experience of supporting the team in the dedicated fashion I did in the Seventies served only to make the bond between us imperishable. I attended the Ibrox-disaster match in 1971 and researched and wrote about it much later[15]; I roared the team round by round to the European Cup Winners Cup final in Barcelona in '72; clad like so many others in Levi Staprests and an Arthur Black shirt, I was in the middle of the mass delirium engulfing the Rangers end when the ref's whistle ended the '73 Scottish Cup final and left us 3–2 conquerors of Celtic – my 'Meiklejohn moment' came when the ref walked to our keeper Peter McCloy and took the ball off him to signal that it was all over; and I celebrated long into the night – and the following summer – when we clinched our first league title in eleven long years at Easter Road in '75; and much, much more.

But, equally, I became increasingly dismayed by the club's apparent willingness to be tied to particular aspects of its past and of its 'staunch

Protestant' image. For me Rangers were more than that, and if there should have been no shame in standing for a particular identity there was certainly the disgrace in allowing the club to be portrayed as discrimina-tory, bigoted and reactionary in the way it bumblingly and disingenuously responded to its critics. The club, like the Ulster Protestants, was finding it problematic to construct a positive vision of the future that would build on life-affirming aspects of history rather than those which backed it – and them – into a cultural and political cul-de-sac. Later on, in the 1990s, in my adopted city of Belfast, I'd watch the twelfth of July parade each year and observe the always substantial Scottish presence and, sentimentally, the bands from Thornliebank. I was aware of how much these Ulster-Scottish links meant to those participating, and to those cheering from the pavement, and part of me was similarly moved. On the other hand, as I watched the Orange Order self-destruct and damage the broader cause of the Union I could not but hear echoes of Rangers prior to what quickly became known as 'the Souness Revolution'.

The sports writer Hugh McIlvanney remarked at the time that Rangers fans tended to celebrate the reputations of the 'hard men' who had worn the club colours: Woodburn, Davis, Shaw, Shearer, Greig. He went on to say that they had got another in Souness and that their world would never be the same. This has proved very true, but, with the exception of a few, Rangers is still the world to these fans. For me, the signing of Mo Johnston in 1989 was liberating, and I don't think I was by any means alone. At a stroke the club had stepped out of the shadow of that part of its past (and part of not much more than half of its past) that was holding it back.

Dilemmas, controversies and problems of course remain. Many Rangers fans now complain that any song or chant in praise of the traditional image of the club is considered fair game for the forces of political correctness and those who make a career out of a supposed campaign against sectar-ianism. Their defensiveness can be understood and maybe sympathised with in certain cases – it is often a reaction to an agenda set by the Celtic-minded[16] – but it remains dangerous to the health of the club. The issues need to be faced up to openly and radically. It is important to feel that you can be passionate about your club and its history, and, certainly, I don't think I could have tried to understand and comment on important matters such as the Irish troubles without the intensive feelings of the

JIM FORREST'S GOALS AND OTHER REFLECTIONS

kind experienced in supporting Rangers. Nevertheless, it behoves us all to resist the descent into intolerance and the attractions of a defiance which can only be futile. There is too much at stake for our club.

Jim Forrest was kicked out of Ibrox following the team's calamitous defeat by Berwick Rangers in the Scottish Cup in January 1967. He, along with George McLean, was made the scapegoat by a traumatised management.[17] It was a scandalous way to treat one of the most promising young players to have pulled on the jersey, and Forrest arguably never recovered. Rangers were to rue his absence a matter of months later when they went down narrowly to Bayern Munich in the final of the European Cup Winners Cup. Sometimes, much later, when enthralled by the wonderful Michael Mols in the days before his tragic injury, I caught glimpses of Forrest: something in the style of running and in those tidy, emphatic finishes.

In an interview with my co-editor for another book, lifelong Rangers fan Stuart Daniels of the Kinning Park supporters club commented on the thrill of seeing some veteran players paraded at Ibrox. 'I thought to myself', he went on, 'What is nine in a row, it's nothing, if you could bring some of these greats back, the Davie Coopers, the Davie Meiklejohns and the Jock Wallaces, just to see them walking down the tunnel. Seeing old Tiger Shaw coming out, wee Shearer coming out, that's what being a bluenose is all about, people around you, kith and kinship you know, the memories came flooding back.' [18]

I think that puts it perfectly, but I would still add something – Jim Forrest coming down that tunnel.

Notes

1   For another such place – Bridgeton – see the entertaining memoir of his ministry there by Revd. Bill Shackleton, *Keeping It Cheery: Anecdotes from a Life in Brigton* (Glasgow: Covenanter Press, 2005); and Hugh Savage's grittier *Born Up A Close* (Argyll: Argyll Press, 2006). Both these books are better and more important than their hackneyed titles suggest. See Savage's comments on working at Ibrox and encountering the legendary Bill Struth, pp. 141–4. For an insight into 'mixed marriage' in Glasgow working-class life in the 1950s see Meg Henderson, *Finding Peggy* (London: Corgi, 1994).

2   See Ian R. Mitchell, *This City Now* (Edinburgh: Luath, 2005), chapter 1.

3   A. McCallum, *Pollokshaws Village and Burgh 1600–1912* (Paisley, 1925), p. 140.

4   The church records are in Strathclyde Regional Archives CH3/1171.

5   Song contained in 'The Poet's Box' collection in Mitchell Library, Glasgow.

6   *North British Daily Mail*, 9 August 1875.

7   *Pollokshaws News*, 14 July 1922.

8   *Pollokshaws News*, 19 May 1922.

9   For a scholarly account of this subject see A. Davies, 'Football and sectarianism in Glasgow during the 1920s and 1930s', *Irish Historical Studies*, Vol. xxxv, no. 138, November 2006.

10 *Belfast Weekly News*, 26 March 1931.

11 See Bob MacCallum, *The Best of the Blues* (Edinburgh: Mainstream, 2001). It has to be noted that this actual line-up did not play together as often as is commonly believed, Caldow's leg break in 1963 allowing Provan to take over at left back, and McMillan often giving way to McLean.

12 See especially *Its Colours They Are Fine* (Edinburgh: Salamander Press, 1983), and *The Magic Flute* (Edinburgh: Canongate, 1990).

13 In this connection see another work set initially in the Protestant working-class west of Scotland with Rangers and Orange Order dimensions to it: Stuart Christie, *Granny Made Me an Anarchist* (London: Scribner, 2004).

14 See his article 'Carrying the torch for my first love', *Sunday Herald*, 2 May 1999.

15 'Death on Stairway 13', in R. Esplin (ed.), *Ten Days That Shook Rangers* (Ayr: Fort Publishing, 2005).

16 See chapter in this book on the 'Celtic-Minded' outlook.

17 See C. Williamson, 'A Blot on the Landscape: the Sacking of Scot Symon', in Esplin (ed.), *Ten Days* . . .

18 R. Esplin, *Down the Copland Road* (Argyll: Argyll Publishing, 2000), p. 181.

POLITICS, RELIGION
AND CULTURE WARS

From Turnstile to Press Box

Graham Spiers

I have always loved football. I played the game since I was three, then at school, then at university, then for various amateur teams, before time and fate decreed that, like all ex-players, I had to face being 'put out to grass' and to content myself with playing 'fives'. I adored the game and used to shudder sometimes at the thought: imagine a football-less universe. Life just wouldn't seem worth it.

And, amid it all, the team I loved was Rangers. I can't remember exactly the first time I stepped inside Ibrox stadium. In that way in which every football fan has a kaleidoscope of memories about following football or a particular team from infancy, I have teeming images and memories of watching Rangers as a child, but being able to place them in chronological order is another matter. The first of my two-hundred-odd visits to Ibrox as a kid and a teenager must have been, I think, in either 1969 or 1970. Funnily enough, when the question has come up in pub chatter with friends I have remained convinced my first-ever Rangers match was against Ayr United at Ibrox, in which Willie Waddell's team won 3–0 or 4–0 and in which a youthful Alex MacDonald played. I've checked the Rangers records for this match and have found that they beat Ayr 3–0 at Ibrox on 17 January 1970, so maybe this was my first match. Such blurred, imprecise memories are surely the way of most fans.

My love of football was passed on to me by my dad, a former amateur player himself and someone who, despite becoming a Baptist minister, by all accounts had a bit of a nasty streak as a striker with, among other teams, Hawick Royal Albert. Looking back, going to games at Ibrox on a Saturday for us seems to have been every bit as religious a rite as going to church the following day. Going to the football became an essential part of my life and, I guess, from about the age of seven, Ibrox became my regular home.

The things I remember about the stadium as a kid are those fantastic aspects that strike every impressionable youngster: the smells, the atmosphere, the vast steps – vast at least in the eyes of a child – climbing up and into the old oval arena (as it was). Every week this was a sight which utterly captivated me: reaching the top of the staircase at the Broomloan Road end and then taking in the great scene, the green pitch, the gathering crowd. As I write about this now I can actually feel again that strange thrum of excitement which was mine more than thirty years ago. Not for a first time I wish somebody by now had invented a time machine – it would be amazing to go back to those days and step inside the old Ibrox once more.

Rangers matches, scenes and incidents all stick out vividly and yet in a chaotic jumble. For example, I was at the '5p game' played against Arsenal at Ibrox in August 1973 to celebrate Rangers' centenary (in the wrong year) when a crowd in excess of 70,000 turned up and, at the Broomloan Road end at least, there was a worry at one stage of dangerous congestion. That night sticks in my mind for one particular reason: I lost my dad in the throng for about twenty minutes which, for a ten-year-old kid (and especially a little nerd from Bearsden), was pretty worrying. In the circumstances I also did something that night to rectify the situation which was totally unlike me at the time and has proved totally unlike me ever since; I used some gumption to make my way to our regular spot on the terracing – the second aisle down at the top of the Broomloan steps and then about two-thirds of the way towards the front – to find my way back to my parent.

I remember, too, the Rangers–Ajax match of 1973, again, for totally spurious and almost inconsequential reasons. By this time Quinton Young was playing for Rangers and, as a winger myself as a kid, I was modelling myself on his (admittedly slightly portly) style, just as before him I had previously tried to emulate His Eminence, Sir William 'Bud' Johnston (the self-made master of diplomacy and on-field peacekeeping). In that Ajax match at Ibrox – and get this for inconsequential recall – Derek Johnstone did something that has stayed in my mind to this day. Trying to spring the offside trap as Ajax defenders rushed out, Big Derek took the ball on his chest and then lobbed it high in the air – almost like a rugby league up-and-under – and darted behind the out-rushing Dutch defence to have an effort on goal. For some reason that piece of play intrigued me and, in the moments following it, a debate took place between my dad and I as I tried to understand what Johnstone had been doing. (DJ, do you even remember this moment in your life . . . it lasted precisely five seconds?)

During the years that I regularly visited Ibrox between 1969 and 1984 – at which point I left Glasgow to go away and study – for me the great seasons were around the mid-1970s, by which point Jock Wallace was beginning to perfect his vice-like grip on the club. My recollection is that, between 1973 and 1975 in particular, teeming crowds rolled up to Ibrox – by this I mean audiences of 60,000 for league games against the likes of Hibs, Hearts, Aberdeen and Dundee – and made for a thrilling experience for a young kid. I'm pretty convinced that an edition of the *Rangers News* of around this time carried a feature about the swollen Ibrox crowds, pointing out that Rangers at the time were attracting among the best attendances in Britain (perhaps this was slightly earlier, maybe 1973/74). For instance, during this time I remember being at a Rangers–Dundee match on a Sunday when around 65,000 turned up. Of course, for various reasons, the audience downturn in Scottish football was only two or three years away, but, in the mid-1970s, the spectacle at Ibrox was pretty special.

I was also at the New Year Old Firm derby of 1975 and, once again, due to the process of a football lover's random recollections from childhood, I recall this match for totally spurious and almost weird reasons. For one thing, Rangers won 3–0, which had rarely been the case against Celtic in the league in the years building up to 1975. Secondly, the Ibrox pitch that day was like a ploughed field, and even though I have subsequently seen footage of that match on video – when I instinctively shouted out: 'I was at that game!' – I can still picture the state of the pitch in my mind's eye. But the third, and most peculiar reason of all for remembering that 1975 game, is to do with my old man's well-meaning but totally naive protectiveness as a parent.

Despite having watched Rangers almost week-in and week-out for years, this match was still my first Old Firm experience in the flesh. (By this stage I was twelve years old and, prior to that ripe age, my dad had decided that the Glasgow derby was no place for a young child.) So what happens, after all this parental concern, when I do get to go to an Old Firm game? I go with my Rangers scarf on, accompanied by my dad, to the exact same spot we occupied every week – the second aisle down from the top of the

Broomloan steps, two-thirds of the way to the front – slap-bang in the middle of the Celtic support.

Apart from the murky weather, a beanpole Ally Scott running loose like an unkempt giraffe and Tommy McLean's extreme 1970s-style of crossing a ball – a floating, almost wafting delivery to the far post – I have one other memory of that afternoon. When Rangers scored their first goal, and despite being absolutely hemmed in on all sides by Celtic supporters, I instinctively jumped to my feet and yelped my delight. This was followed by a swift, numb realisation on my part that there was a gloomy silence all around me. There was some grumbling, but I've never forgotten what then occurred. Amid the stirring a compassionate Glasgow voice behind me said: 'You shout for your team, son . . .'

If you were a 1970s fan of Rangers the roll-call of names that comes to mind is quite colourful. There were the obvious names and faces; indeed, I can still reel off the first regular Rangers team I ever watched (and you have to reel this team off in the 1970s style, which means it comes in peculiar stanzas, almost with musical breaks for punctuation): 'McCloy, Jardine and Mathieson . . . Greig, Jackson and Smith . . . McLean, Conn and Stein . . . MacDonald and Johnston.' That last bit then became 'MacDonald and Young'; and then there were further variations such as 'McCloy, Jardine and Miller'. But Peter McCloy, Sandy Jardine, John Greig, Colin Jackson, Tom Forsyth, Alex MacDonald, Tommy McLean, Derek Johnstone and Derek Parlane were all pretty much the backbone of a Rangers team which, for me, seemed to endure for years and years.

I was there the drizzly Ibrox day John Greig gave a blatant V-sign to the Rangers fans in the old centenary stand – the punters had been giving him some fearful (and totally well-earned) stick. When I first went to Ibrox my recollection is that the main singing section of the Rangers fans came from that covered terracing area opposite the main stand: it was only when it was transformed into the centenary stand – and they were benches, not seats – that the choristers moved round to the Copland Road end. Anyway, by the time the centenary stand was up and running it brought with it another scam for those of us at the uncovered Broomloan Road (or Celtic) end. If it started to rain – and certainly whenever it pissed it down – as a kid you could run round the terracing to a side gate and get in to that new seated area. I had done just that the day Greig gave us his V-sign. Again, I can't remember the day or specific match, but I can picture Greig doing it like it was yesterday, because it happened during an incident of play right in front of me. By about 1976, and after fifteen years at Rangers, Greig was starting to toil on the field and more than a few fans used to get on his back. On this particular day he was having a nightmare and, for an umpteenth time, had just been dispossessed of the ball. The play continued and broke towards the touchline by the centenary stand, and when Greig chased his opponent and came towards us, the growling of the fans increased. Suddenly – and almost involuntarily – he gave us a Harvey Smith: a swift and well-designed two fingers. To this day I can still remember about thirty Rangers fans around me rising from their splintery pews and, reciprocating Greig's greeting, shouting: 'Aye, and up you too, Greig!' (Over the years I have once or twice mentioned this incident in diary columns in newspapers and John Greig is quite touchy about it. On one occasion he phoned me up out of the blue and, in that almost morally aggrieved voice that to me has an Edinburgh background shot through it, he whined: 'I've never had a cross word wi' the *Glasgow Herald* in thirty years and suddenly you're writin' something aboot this . . . you've just made it up!' I said to him: 'John, for God's sake . . . why would I make up something as daft and inconsequential as this? It's funny, it's totally unimportant and it happened over thirty years ago. Get a grip.')

Other Rangers players, though, to me as a kid, stood out as special. Johnny Hamilton, while singularly lacking in pace, was still a gifted and imaginative midfielder, and it was beyond my comprehension as a child how Rangers managed to get Hamilton 'free' from Hibs (I always thought players cost 'a fee'). Then there was the perennial substitute – and perennial trier – Jim Denny, forever recalled in the famous Ibrox exclamation of 2.59 p.m.: 'Christ, Denny's playing!' Then there were more elusive and more fleeting players – Ian McDougall, Eric Morris, Alex O'Hara and others – who came and went at this time (in truth they 'went' more prominently than 'came'). McDougall – again off the top of my head – was a decent, industrious player who had an excellent game at Parkhead against Celtic (circa 1975?) and yet quickly disappeared over the horizon. Other players I vaguely remember – Davie Armour, Richard Sharp, Gordon Boyd, Chris Robertson – had come through the club's ranks but could never truly penetrate the steely body-politic of the Rangers first team of that time. All I remember about Eric Morris was that, in the *Rangers News*, it said that he came from Irvine Meadow, which I imagined at the time would be some sort of leafy, floral-lined arena (I now know better). From memory O'Hara left Rangers and went to both Partick Thistle and Morton – I can't remember which first – but he, too, shared with Denny the famous distinction of being recalled by exclamation, as in: 'Christ, O'Hara's playing!'

From this tapestry of memories growing up following Rangers it is also impossible – indeed it would be blasphemous – not to recall The Girvan Lighthouse. Peter McCloy was everything as a Rangers goalkeeper – a hero, a villain and a total haddy. Indeed, I have only ever heard the term 'haddy' being used so passionately and distinctively in the context of McCloy. For a while in the mid-1970s – and as insulting as it seems to say so – Rangers played with Derek Parlane and Derek Johnstone up front (or some such combination which might also involve Ally Scott or Martin Henderson) and Big Peter's only instinct was to hoof the ball high into the clouds, whereupon, about two minutes later, it would land on Parlane's head and be headed backwards towards the opposition keeper. I remember one game in particular at Ibrox when this tactic seemed to recur and recur – McCloy bashing the ball into the sky and Parlane doing nothing except heading it backwards to the opposition keeper – until one punter beside us shouted: 'Peter, for Christ's sake, gonnae vary it!' My other memory of McCloy is of him enacting his stock phrase – 'like a coo going down to its bed' – while losing a goal against Falkirk at Ibrox. For obvious reasons I can't remember the Falkirk scorer but I can still see McCloy failing to make the save: both he and the ball seemed to travel in slow motion as the shot wafted past him and McCloy dived to the ground in four considered and distinct instalments.

Everybody knows Rangers have been dogged by the bigotry problem. I was at Ibrox the rather dramatic day in the mid-1970s when Willie Waddell solemnly walked to the centre circle before a match to make a public announcement to the effect that Rangers would no longer be anti-Catholic in its signing policy. (I can still picture Waddell stepping up onto a small box – supposedly a podium – with a microphone to hand and wearing his thick-rimmed glasses – and a Rangers top? – to make his pronouncement.) When you consider that that day was over thirty years ago, and in 2007 Rangers were still mired in the bigotry issue and UEFA punishments, you realise the depth of the problem.

Part of the problem lies in the rather vague and poorly defined 'traditions' of Rangers. Some of the more zealous Rangers fans – and even Martin Bain, the current Rangers chief executive – have spoken of the 'traditions' of the club, yet the term is undefined, unfocused and lacking in historical veracity. By 'the Rangers traditions' I think some supporters like to propose, with a certain vague authority, a Rangers FC with clear historic roots as Protestant, Unionist and – whatever this next bit means – being against Fenians. The problem with this is that, any time you speak to a Rangers FC historian, they assert that much of this is more a modern flight of fancy than any actual representation of history. I once spent an afternoon putting this dubious 'Rangers tradition' to the test by asking whether the various great and shaping figures of Rangers' past were zealously Protestant or pro-Unionist in this way. The co-founding Moses McNeil, for instance: using the historian's method of understanding (rather than just groping in the dark), could he be said to have been renowned for his commitment to Protestant theology and the Union? Or the great and patriarchal Bill Struth, one of the shaping figures of Rangers FC: was Protestantism important to him, and, similarly, the Union? Whenever you ask a club historian about this they reply 'no-one knows, there's no evidence' yet today some Rangers fans like retrospectively to assert that all this was definitely the case. Ronnie Esplin is a fellow Rangers diehard from youth, and today a football reporter for the Press Association: he, too, believes that Rangers' history is sociologically and politically too varied and mixed to make clear assertions about 'the Rangers way' in the sense that some supporters try to do. In this context, one problem Rangers have is that Celtic's roots, in contrast, are utterly clear and distinct: Catholic, Irish and with evident cultural and political resonances. Rangers, in its history, has no such clarity, which has forced some contemporary supporters to clutch hopefully at historic branches (and mainly those which, as they see it, can then depict their club as being in clear cultural opposition to Celtic).

In more recent years it has been a regret of mine – even if it has sometimes caused me mirth as a journalist – to see the image of Rangers and the reputation of a small group of Rangers fans slide towards incurable paranoia. When I was a kid watching the club, and later as a teenager, I am convinced that none of this siege-mentality was ever apparent around Rangers (indeed, it was held to be the exclusive right of Celtic). Yet the way in which supporters groups like the Rangers Supporters Trust and certain websites have almost single-handedly turned some Rangers fans into the Most Offended People Ever (MOPE) really has taken the biscuit.

I genuinely like the RST. In media circles they have been jokingly referred to as 'the paramilitary wing' of the Rangers fans for their frequent and perennially doomed guerrilla assaults on newspapers and media outlets (the RST, I think I'm correct in saying, accounts for the decline in sales of just about every newspaper in the Western world as being down to their boycotts!). The rank and file of such groups tend to be decent bunches of lads but the problem the RST has had is in one or two conspiracy-obsessed characters among its leaders. Amid a series of wacky outbursts against the press by the RST, my own favourite moment remains the time late in 2005 when the redoubtable Trust, having dreamed up yet another wheeze about the media having it in for Rangers, issued a press release in which they condemned me for being 'Celtic-minded' (I'd obviously been hallucinating about being a Rangers supporter) and urged 'all right-minded Rangers fans' to boycott my newspaper of the time, *The Herald*. (The RST had developed a voracious appetite for newspaper boycotts – they've certainly seen off *Le Soir* in France, a paper that has simply died on its feet.) But my favourite part of this outpouring was when the RST, simply unable to resist entering the realm of fabrication, condemned me for having referred to Rangers fans as 'vile troglodytes' in a match report. (That's right . . . vile troglodytes!) Helpfully, the RST even inserted a publication date on which this (non-existent) phrase was said to have been written by me. Enjoying hamming it up, one or two media colleagues were much amused at this allegation. It actually became quite surreal – though the RST hadn't meant it this way – to picture yourself sitting in a press box under pressure of deadlines at games and writing: 'Rangers neatly worked the ball forward and, following a lay-off from Novo, Prso walloped the ball home. Behind the goal it sent the vile troglodytes into raptures. . . .' At *The Herald* at the time we actually thought of trying to use the expression in a genuine match report, so preposterous was it. Needless to say I had never used such an absurd description in any report covering Rangers, and to this day I'm not sure where the RST boys got the idea from. But it did give me much fodder for columns – as did the rest of the MOPE's endless persecution complexes and myriad boycott suggestions – during the duller football months.

The media – television, radio and newspapers (across all of which I enjoy spreading my tentacles) – and groups like the RST and the Rangers Supporters Assembly enjoyed much debate as the bigotry problem at Ibrox ended in the UEFA humiliation of Rangers in 2006. The problem – bigotry – was and remains a complex issue. Resolving the problem can sometimes be hindered by over-simplistic arguments on the Scottish sports pages, where the issue, if anything, is exacerbated. The bigotry problem is also hindered by the persecution mentality of groups like the RST, who like to pretend there isn't much of a problem to solve in the first place, and that it is all the fault of the media. None of these aspects are helpful in curing the bigotry ill, and yet, even so, I believe much progress has been made in recent years.

In the bigotry saga I also came to appreciate anew one particular aspect: the power of the media. Before the Rangers–UEFA case I hadn't fully realised the power of the press and in particular – if you are capable of writing well and writing polemically – the power of a newspaper columnist. Down the years I'd heard much tosh about 'the power of the pen' and I had more or less ignored it. But the Rangers case of 2006 taught me that it was true. In truth, it was media reporting and comment that brought Rangers to book over bigotry: it was the influence of certain columns in *The Herald* and elsewhere that made UEFA act. And when Rangers finally did respond, having been punished by UEFA, it was effectively only at the point of a bayonet – do something or else! When I look back now, if it was a battle between a group like the RST and the media over the reputation of Rangers, there was always only going to be one winner. As a columnist on a respected newspaper you really can have a remarkable influence.

In regard to the Rangers–UEFA business, people occasionally tell me of ludicrous notions and theories being posted about me on fans' websites: everything from 'bringing Rangers down' to 'instigating the UEFA prosecution' to goodness knows what else. Mercifully for me, a broader and more intelligent coalition of football supporters will view such hysteria with a wry smile. And I'm afraid that, while I may, like other people, have exerted an influence through what I wrote in columns, the truth of my 'involvement' was much duller. As a journalist covering Rangers I was duty bound to report and investigate UEFA's prosecution of the club in 2006. I also, by chance, happened to know a behind-the-scenes figure at UEFA from years back, who suddenly found himself in 2006 being told to take up the Rangers case by their disciplinary committee. Every journalist dreams of having a mole in the right place at the right time, and, journalistically, I simply got lucky in terms of UEFA and Rangers – I had someone who leaked juicy details to me all along the way. I'm sorry all this caused some of the conspiracy theorists to go slightly berserk. I've learned by now that, if you are a football pundit with a prominent place in the media, you simply have to live with misapprehensions and distortions of what you believe or stand for, made by certain people for mischievous ends. I'm not sure how many 'vile troglodyte' farces I've been subjected to, but it's been a lot! What seems to happen is, someone makes something up, and before you know it there is foaming outrage on a website. Well, that's fine. Life is too fulfilling and too enjoyable to worry about any of that. More to the point, if some people get a kick out of pursuing such theories then, as ludicrous as they might be, I'm quite happy for them to derive a certain satisfaction from such exercises. I'm comforted, as I say, by the knowledge that the wider coalition of more intelligent supporters see these for what they are.

Though I enjoyed the boisterous debate and bobbing and weaving amid the endless boycott threats of groups like the Rangers Supporters Assembly, I was still shocked at how far the bigotry issue went when I went down to Ibrox one night in November 2004 to meet certain members of that race known as the Most Offended People Ever in the flesh. At that meeting there was a healthy representation of the permanently aggrieved RST in attendance, and I asked the gathering if they wouldn't mind if I recorded our Q and A session. There were a few strange grumblings at this, but, as it was an open forum, the idea was eventually accepted.

I had always noticed how, when it came to it, the RST had always indulged in a certain foot-dragging when it came to specifically condemning bigotry. (And I mean here *specifically* . . . the RST indulged in a certain vague or woolly condemnation of bigotry; the problem they had in specifically condemning dirges like 'The Billy Boys' was that too many of their board members openly liked the song and approved of it.) To back this up, on the tape-recording from that meeting with the fans I can be heard having the following conversation with one member of the RST. The subject had wandered on to the vexed theme of another favourite chant at Ibrox – 'Dirty Fenian Bastard' – which was especially popular whenever Martin O'Neill or Neil Lennon was in town. The RST member seemed overly keen to defend the chant:

Spiers: 'Do you think the chant "Dirty Fenian Bastard" is unacceptable?'

RST: 'It depends on the circumstances . . .'

Spiers: 'Okay, well in which circumstances would you regard it as acceptable?'

RST: 'Well, you give me a set of circumstances for it, and I'll answer you . . .'

Spiers: 'But I can't think of any circumstances in which it would be fine. Can you?'

RST: 'Eh . . . come back to me in two or three minutes . . .'

Two or three minutes later the RST member came back with the following answer: 'Okay, so take out the word "bastard" . . .'

From such an exchange you got the gist of the problem at Rangers in the troubled years following 2005/06: if official and allegedly 'leading' supporters groups were quite keen to defend such chants, then what chance was there? I had a similarly fraught exchange on the BBC one evening with another leading Rangers supporters club member, in which trying to get him to admit to and condemn the bigoted chanting at Ibrox was like trying to pull teeth. Songs such as 'The Billy Boys' – and this strangely-cherished term of abuse, 'Fenian' – became chants and phrases almost to die for among certain Rangers zealots. It was – and remains – an embarrassment to any decent-minded Ibrox fan, of which there are multitudes. Rangers have a fantastic support, which is evident to me time and time again, and I have come to realise that a few in the RST, and some of the website zealots, together represent only a small, festering rump of that support. The wider Rangers fan base that I have known for thirty years is simply driven by a love of football, not half-baked or ignorance-stewed politics. Not only that, but Rangers today, like most clubs, have a new generation of fans, who are college or university educated, and have little time for all the nonsense.

To me the most recent seasons following my old club as a reporter have been a mixture of trouble and farce. At games with Rangers we've had the bigotry problem; moments of hooliganism such as in Villarreal; the embarrassment of those daft Nazi-like salutes and Lord knows what else. Off the pitch, meanwhile, with the paranoia in some quarters becoming rampant, it genuinely became hard to believe that seemingly everyone – the SFA, the Scottish Executive, the media, various radio stations, UEFA, Interpol, the United Nations – could all have it in for Rangers in the absurd way that some groups would have us believe. I genuinely wish Rangers had avoided the reputation for paranoia which, for one hundred years, was meant to have been the exclusive right of their great rivals.

In the debate over bigotry I think we are witnessing a raging against the dying of the light among some of these supporters. In twenty years' time I can't believe some of these songs or chants will be defended by Rangers supporters, let alone be bellowed from the stands. And I truly believe that Rangers will come good again, though it will require a change in the club's ownership and financial structure.

The World of the Celtic-Minded

Graham Walker

Since the advent of devolution to Scotland in 1999 there has been more public discussion of the topic of sectarianism in Scotland than for at least the previous half-century. The smaller political context created by devolution has led to the issue being scrutinised as part of a broader project of national re-evaluation and renewal. There has been a readiness to own up to past sins, the best example being the Church of Scotland's apology in 2001 for the inter-war campaign conducted from within its ranks against Irish Catholic immigrants to Scotland. Controversies over schooling, Orange and Republican parades and, above all, the Old Firm's role in the persistence of sectarian attitudes and conflict, have absorbed political energies and focused media attention as never before.[1]

One of the catalysts for all this was the intervention of the classical-music composer and avid Celtic fan, James MacMillan, who in August 1999 alleged that Scotland was 'endemically' sectarian. For MacMillan this meant simply that Scotland was an anti-Catholic society. His speech anticipated the opening of the Scottish Parliament and may well have been intended to serve a political warning: 'hands off' Catholic schools. The then head of the Catholic Church in Scotland, Cardinal Thomas Winning, who at the time predicted that Catholicism would be Scotland's sole faith in the future, soon proved himself an astute manipulator of the Scottish media and a daunting opponent for Scottish Executive ministers. He was to cause them untold trouble, for example, over their attempt to rid Scotland of the hangover from the Thatcher years concerning the teaching of homosexuality in schools (Section 28). After that bruising encounter there was no likelihood of any Scottish minister or party taking on the Catholic Church over the position of its schools. That position, of course, is one of full state funding in a context of unfettered Church control over the teaching of the curriculum and the appointment of teachers. Criticism of these arrangements is routinely denounced by the Catholic Church as bigotry in another guise. Subsequent controversies over schooling have centred on attempts by the Executive to create a number of shared-campus schools, which have met with resistance from the Catholic Church. The considerable political influence exerted by the Catholic lobby in post-devolution Scotland – far outpacing its Church of Scotland counterpart – has recently received scholarly attention.[2]

A similar sense of political mission has informed the publication in recent years of two volumes entitled *Celtic Minded*. [3] Edited by Joe Bradley, these books set out to link celebration of Celtic FC to ventilation of grievances of a social, cultural and political nature, and to the assertion of an Irish Catholic identity which the books' contributors, among them James MacMillan, believe is marginalised in Scottish society. The books constitute an attempt to intervene in the developing public debate on sectarianism and to construct a case for Celtic as the victims of the phenomenon rather than in any way part of the problem. Conversely, the blame is put on Rangers or on the historic prejudices of Protestant Scotland, which are believed to have shaped the club. Indeed, many of the *Celtic Minded* (CM for short from now on) authors wish to re-define the issue of sectarianism as racism: specifically anti-Irish Catholic racism. Parts of Scotland's past, such as the Kirk's inter-war campaign, are thus pressed into service ostensibly to prove that the country is, to use Bradley's word, 'hegemonically' racist in this sense. The *CM* volumes are certainly testimony to a fan base which is much more pro-active and 'savvy' in the arts of political propaganda and public relations and more adept at hitching itself to fashionable discourses than its counterpart across the football divide. Moreover, Bradley's enterprise has certainly shaped the contours of the sectarianism debate as it relates to football. As such, its assertions and arguments deserve critical scrutiny.

Although, as mentioned, there has been a remarkable growth in public discussion about sectarianism, the phenomenon itself is rarely defined satisfactorily. Glib definitions about religious conflict have tended to take the place of proper debate over its many aspects and causes. The tendency in the political and media coverage of sectarianism has been a reductionist one. As the anti-sectarian campaigner who forced a change in the law on the subject, the MSP Donald Gorrie, admitted, sectarianism 'is a convenient shorthand term to cover a complex issue, which is partly religious, partly historical, partly political and racial'. [4] Where the complexities have been taken into account, in recent scholarly work and in a Glasgow City Council Report, the conclusions have been at variance with the claims of the CM lobby, whose analysis is grounded in another form of reductionism, namely that sectarianism is simply anti-Irish Catholic racism.[5] So the first objection Rangers fans would have to the CM enterprise concerns the flip and facile way in which the sectarian issue is framed and presented as purely an anti-Irish Catholic phenomenon, a 'hurdle' in the words of Herald journalist and CM contributor Hugh MacDonald to the acceptance of that community.[6] For many, and by no means only Rangers fans, the claim that Irish Catholic identity and culture are not acknowledged is frankly mystifying. It is a culture recognised, for example, in official campaigns celebrating cultural diversity in Scotland much more substantially than Irish Protestant identity.[7] The kind of Irish cultural activities which are the subject of James MacMillan's contribution to CM volume 2 are widely admired in Scotland and are indeed commonly viewed as bringing Ireland and Scotland closer; this is evident in the attention paid to such festivals as the annual 'Celtic Connections'. Irish Catholic identity is a cultural plus in contemporary Scotland – witness the testimonies of recent immigrants to Scotland from the Irish Republic [8] – while the most visible product of Irish Protestant influences, the Orange Order, is ritually vilified in the Scottish media. An anthology of writers in Scotland from an Irish background, published seven years ago, featured only one from an Irish Protestant background.[9] Clearly there are minorities and there are minorities.

For many Rangers fans it is their club and the popular associations it has historically held which are increasingly marginalised and traduced in contemporary Scotland. To these fans the claims of the CM seem totally at odds with new political and cultural realities. A sense of Scottishness which draws on Protestant religious identity is now decidedly at a discount, and anyone attempting to advertise such an identity is likely to be dismissed as a bigot. Against this set of perceptions the idea, propounded tirelessly in the CM volumes, of Rangers as the 'establishment' club, provokes outright derision and incomprehension. Similarly, the CM line of argument, rehearsed to the point of tedium, about Celtic fans having 'to keep their heads down' on account of their 'unacceptable' identity is bewildering. When has a support as raucous and 'in yer face' as Celtic's ever kept its head down? Given the reaction to setbacks on the field of play of some members of that support – which have involved attacks on the homes of referees and opposition players and even chairmen (Hugh Dallas, Jorg Albertz, Nacho Novo, John Yorkston) – perhaps it is those who upset Celtic who have greater cause 'to keep their heads down'.

Apart from strictly football issues, the 'keep your head down' thesis sits very awkwardly with, for instance, a recent report by the Medical Research Council in Scotland, which found that Catholic schoolchildren possessed greater self-confidence than their Protestant counterparts and were less likely to be 'picked on'. [10] In the view of many Rangers fans it is their allegiance which has more often to be kept quiet for fear of being interpreted as sectarian or bigoted. Stephen Ferrie, in *CM* volume 1, advances precisely this Rangers-establishment/Celtic-downtrodden typology with reference to Scottish writer Alan Spence's 'play', *The Magic Flute*, and the cultural norms of 'Sunday School, Boys Brigade, Orange Marches and Rangers matches' that are featured in it. Firstly, Stephen, *The Magic Flute* is a novel not a play – did you really read it? Secondly, the novel is set in the early 1960s: things have changed and we don't live in that world any more. Third, the cultural activities referred to were typical of the west of Scotland Protestant working class, not the 'establishment'. [11] In his landmark 1970s television drama *Just Another Saturday*, Peter McDougall may be suggesting that lads like his main character are dupes, but equally he shows awareness of the Orange Order's appeal to working people in circumstances where it assumes significance as an identity marker and as a phenomenon, like Rangers, which is disowned by polite Scottish society.

Bradley and co. write as if nothing has changed since the 1930s. No acknowledgement is made of the epochal cultural transformations of the late twentieth century or even of gestures such as the apology of the Kirk in 2001. Moreover, they propagate bad history. Particular parts of the past are selected and woven into an uncomplicated narrative of anti-Irish Catholic prejudice in Scottish society. There is no sense of interacting forces in this kind of history, no appreciation of political, social or cultural dynamics.

There is also of course no real sense of perspective or proportion or proper context. To take again the episode of the Kirk in the inter-war period: this was part of a wider picture in which we must also consider the massive level of (overwhelmingly Protestant) emigration from Scotland; the impact of the 1918 Education Act conferring full state funding on Catholic schools and the coincidental loss of educational influence on the part of the Protestant churches; the prejudiced outbursts of certain Catholic prelates; the Catholic Church's inflexibility on issues such as mixed marriage; severe economic recession; the legacy of the tragic losses sustained in the Great War; and those many Protestants within the Kirk, and without, who fought against such scapegoating.[12] The campaign, in short, was the result of a number of developments, it did not just spring from primordial prejudice, and, not least, it did not succeed in its aims. In this connection, it is also time that a rest was given to the assertion that there were more anti-Catholic societies than Catholics in late eighteenth century Glasgow. This has peppered many a Celtic-minded polemic over the years and it is trotted out routinely to 'prove' that anti-Catholicism is something innate in the Scottish psyche. However, the apparent source for it [13] is unreliable and anti-popery was as much political as religious; the Vatican was at the time a genuine political power. Wolfe Tone was as anti-Catholic as his Scots contemporaries.

That history is not the strength of the Celtic-minded – notwithstanding their preoccupation with it – is further indicated in an interview with the writer Des Dillon, another in Bradley's line-up. Here, Dillon dutifully parrots the 'more anti-Catholic societies than Catholics' gag before delivering himself of the following: 'Protestants were sent from Scotland over to Ireland causing segregation and bigotry over there and then that culture came back over to Scotland with the shipyard workers and the Protestants that came in during the famine and we just imported it wholesale.' [14] How will that do for a summary of four centuries of Irish–Scottish relations? Well, for the Celtic-minded we have to conclude that it will do very nicely since it parcels everything up neatly as the fault of the nasty 'Prods'. And, given that Dillon's theatre work is being used as an educational aid in the current Executive-endorsed anti-sectarianism initiatives, it is not unreasonable to deduce that his travesty of an historical assessment is all too easily accepted by mainstream opinion in Scotland.

Clearly, Dillon is unaware of the two-way traffic in peoples between Scotland and Ulster that long pre-dated the Reformation and the later Plantations. Neither does he seem to grasp that the influx of Scots to Ulster which really made the difference regarding the development of demographic patterns and social, religious and political divisions came, not via the London government's official plantation schemes of the early seventeenth century, but during the mid-to-later part of that century.[15] Many of these migrants were fleeing 'the killing times' in Scotland and political and religious persecution. Their story was thus not dissimilar to that of the mass migration of Irish people to Scotland in the wake of the Famine in the nineteenth century. Both peoples moved because of threats to their survival. The Scottish Presbyterians who settled in Ulster then suffered civil disabilities as Catholics did; they too were disadvantaged by the penal laws of the Anglican Ascendancy. Indeed, such discrimination and persecution forced many thousands to seek a new life in America during the eighteenth century and eventually to support American independence against British rule. It was all a bit more complex than Dillon suggests. However, in a world where the sectarian frothings and historical illiteracy of Des Dillon appear to be taken seriously is it any wonder that Rangers supporters perceive the odds to be stacked against them? For Rangers fans a double standard is in operation in relation to sectarian controversies: Celtic fans mouthing abuse such as 'Orange bastards' is regarded as acceptably political or 'a bit of craic' while Rangers fans supposedly deal in a repertoire of straightforward bigotry and racism.

The *CM* appetite for victimhood – paraded in page upon page of these two books – is matched only by a delusional self-righteousness. This is exemplified by Richard Purden's contribution to the second volume, which is entitled 'Something About Us'. Quite. Purden proclaims the Celtic fans' solidarity with the oppressed and the marginalised, but it very quickly becomes apparent that those genuinely victimised and neglected in Scotland or elsewhere matter much less to him than the cheap thrill to be had in identifying his football team with them. Purden is typical of those Celtic fans – Coll and Davis's smug contribution in *CM* with its risible reference to a 'moral theology' around Celtic is another example – who are pleased to trumpet their club's charity work and their fans' supposed politics of compassion and vaunted stance against injustice.[16] Other clubs and their fans prefer just to get on with it. It is truly hard to suffer the conceit of people like Purden who think that their self-regarding politics makes them and their football club 'special'. It's easy to talk a good game Richard. Oh, and since you casually append racism to the Rangers fans' list of sins can I just take this opportunity to remind you – and the whole *CM* cast – that your co-supporters in 1988 staged Scottish football's worst display of racist bigotry against Mark Walters. Given this, and the breathtaking attempts wilfully to rewrite the history of that shameful episode, you might think that Celtic fans would learn some humility.

However, of the *CM* team it is Willy Maley who is the star striker in the sectarianism-equals-racism campaign. Although a witty and engaging writer, Maley's approach reveals most tellingly the ahistorical and disingenuous core of the *CM* world view and the self-serving character of its analysis. In his contribution to the second volume – a somewhat truncated version of an essay which appears in a prestigious Irish journal[17] – Maley indulges in some trademark vilification of Scotland: a 'stiflingly singular' place in which anti-Irish racism ('hibernophobia') is traced to 'Scotland's complicity in the subjugation of Ireland'. So far so congenial for the *CM* audience, reared as they are on the Des Dillon school of history. But wait, on inspection it appears that Willy has excised an entire part of his argument published for his readers in the salons of Dublin from his *CM* piece. Since this part is about anti-gay prejudice can we infer that either Willy or editor Joe, or both, were rather unsure about how it would be received? After all, another *CM* contributor and former colleague of Maley's, Patrick Reilly, is a staunch supporter of the Catholic Church's stance on gay issues, such as civil partnerships and gay adoption, and was fully behind Cardinal Winning's opposition to the scrapping of Section 28. A blast – such as Willy's in *Field Day Review* – against the anti-gay agenda may not have been comfortable reading for Patrick or, it might be surmised, for the bulk of the Bradley book's target audience, who would be loath to admit gays to their victims' club.

But let's move on to look at what Willy says. He refers to James MacMillan's lecture and the controversy it generated; he then quotes the non-sequitur comment of novelist and MacMillan cheerleader, Andrew O'Hagan, that following the debate over sectarianism the 'Scottish clergy' began to denounce homosexuals. O'Hagan, like Maley, is a scalding critic of 'stiflingly singular' (for which read Protestant) Scotland and someone who feels as victimised on account of his religion and identity as the *CM* authors. He is also a writer who is able to say without a trace of irony that in attending a Catholic school 'we felt sectarianised and proud of it'. [18] For O'Hagan and Maley it is imperative that anti-Catholicism in Scotland be linked to other forms of prejudice, in this case homophobia. 'Hibernophobia', writes Maley in *Field Day Review*, 'and homophobia are part of the same lattice work of discrimination based on a crippling notion of what it means to be Scottish – straight, strong, Protestant and pure. Real Scots don't have Irish origins. Real Scots don't have same-sex relations.' So, it's all the Prods' fault again. Except that in the real world – not Planet O'Hagan or post-colonial Possil – the 'clergy' were Catholic. As a scholar has recently pointed out, the Church of Scotland's stance on Section 28 was 'relatively positive', and it continues to take a markedly more liberal line on gay-rights issues than its Catholic counterpart. [19] It was not a Protestant clergyman who labelled homosexuals 'perverted'; it was Cardinal Winning. As has become customary, those like Maley who are desperate to invoke the spectre of a repressive Protestantism in contemporary Scotland have to fall back on the 'Wee Frees', a by now tiny congregation utterly without power or influence in Scottish life. The supposed dead hand of Calvinism on Scottish society or the long cultural shadow it allegedly casts, a theme laboured by James MacMillan, gets the blame yet again. Conveniently, bigotry and sectarianism conform to notions of bleak and joyless Calvinism. The *Celtic Minded* writers fixate on, and are happiest with, this caricature of Protestantism in Scotland. Des Dillon, in a recent interview on Celtic TV, spoke contemptuously of the 'Wee Frees' and their 'wooden benches' and their supposed lack of imagination. [20] And their Gaelic language and culture Des? Better not go there lest you find that life is a bit more unpredictable and mixed up than you thought; we wouldn't want to disturb our neat wee parcels of heroes and villains would we? Dillon, O'Hagan, Maley and others are quite simply not interested in the realities of Protestantism as a faith or with its cultural diversity in Scotland; they are indifferent to the varieties of Protestantism and have no respect for them. They wish to collapse these varieties and the whole range of Protestant opinion from fundamentalist to liberal into a usable stereotype. They are engaged in a narrowing down of the sectarian debate to ensure that the perpetuation of sectarian attitudes is identified with one side only.

To return to Maley's disquisition on homophobia in Scotland. He acknowledges that Catholic clergy have engaged in gay-bashing although he disingenuously gives the impression that they have been less to blame than their Protestant counterparts. However, he has a ready-made excuse for these Catholic clergy: they have joined in the scapegoating of gays because 'that's how it works in the world of divide and rule'. This is Willy putting on his post-colonial theory straitjacket. He has a mechanical explanation for everything. If confronted with something awkward like the spiritual leaders of the supposedly oppressed community actually oppressing others then just add that magical ingredient – post-colonialism – and it all becomes comprehensible. Cardinal Winning was thus so in thrall to the cultural power of Calvinism that he could not resist the urge to do a bit of oppressing of his own!

As has been pointed out by historians as distinguished as Nicholas Canny, post-colonial theorists like Maley have no respect for the past.[21] They deal in frozen categories: the 'colonisers', the 'colonised', the 'subject people'. As Stephen Howe has observed, their 'cultural reductionism' is as crude as the economic reductionism of the worst kind of Marxist.[22] They are totally uninterested in historical variety, complexity or heterogeneity. Colonialism is advanced as the explanation – or the excuse – for everything. In *CM* volume 2 Bradley parades something called 'The Coloniser's Breastplate', which lists the different sorts of repression suffered by the victims of colonialism whom he appears to define as Irish Catholics both in Ireland and Britain. What seems to be implied here is that hundreds of years of history conform to the model of a colonial elite dictating to a dispossessed people. This really is a view of history on a par with the *X Files* or the conspiracy theorists of 9/11. After entertaining us with his sleight-of-hand polemics, Maley states: 'Nationalism, revisionism and post-colonialism are three of the major preoccupations of modern Irish studies. Scotland appears not to have got past the first post.' Scotland has less to worry about than Maley implies. In fact Willy is being disingenuous again: he and many of his 'postcolonial' colleagues are really old-fashioned Nationalists and they despise the revisionists. Indeed they railed against revisionism for daring to disturb the 'natural' order of the traditional Nationalist historiography of Ireland. Postcolonialism, certainly as Maley practises it, is simply Nationalism tarted up for a date with academia. Maley aspires to be Scotland's Terry Eagleton, and it is he and his ilk who have never got past the first post.

It is hard to resist the conclusion – and I won't bother – that Maley and Bradley are essentially Irish Nationalists with a hatred for what they perceive as Protestant Scotland's part in the 'subjugation' of Ireland. This agenda informs pretty much everything they commit to print and precludes any serious engagement in historical inquiry. They are 'culturists' who are unashamed to make use when the occasion demands of class rhetoric; but it is no accident that the CM analysis should surface at the moment of the left's decline and the fracturing of Labour politics. The CM agenda is a reflection of the replacement of a once-dominant class narrative with one centred on ethnicity and race, with the triumph of 'identity politics'. For decades the Scottish Labour movement pulled off the considerable feat of persuading Protestant and Catholic workers to transcend sectarianism; they did not expunge it and can indeed be criticised for not trying hard enough to do so. Nonetheless, they came up with an alternative to it in the political sphere, and they campaigned with remarkable success around issues of working conditions, housing, health and unemployment. They inherited the radical liberalism of Victorian and Edwardian Scotland, which gave them a firm foothold among Protestants, and they appealed successfully for Catholic support in the new age of (near) universal democracy following the first world war. In both cases they were successful largely in spite, not because, of the socialism of many of the movement's leading figures. They succeeded because they exploited a deep-rooted sense of egalitarianism and ethical consciousness in Scottish society. Their crusade against the Lords and Lairds, and latterly the factory bosses, chimed with a very Presbyterian repudiation of oligarchy, authoritarianism and unearned privilege. Their pragmatism facilitated a concordat with the Catholic Church; doctrinaire socialism was eclipsed by compromised policies on sensitive moral issues and, arguably, education. The Scottish Labour story is now heading for a sticky ending. Of course, there have been the effects of the withering of class as an organising concept in people's lives, the 'Americanisation' of us all, the impact of the fall of Communism between 1989 and 1991. Yet, significantly, there has also been the rise of identity politics, pushed ironically by those from the community that has been a pillar of Labour's political edifice in Scotland.

The CM arguments involve mechanical assumptions about the continuation and perpetuation of sectarian or racist attitudes from the past and about the unchanging nature of such prejudice. They glide over in particular the complex dynamics of the tensions within the working class of west-central Scotland and their historical development. Bradley and co. have succeeded to an alarming degree in lulling opinion-formers into an acceptance that sectarianism and racism are necessarily synonymous. They are not: everything depends on context. The Kirk's campaign of the inter-war years certainly had a racist element. Yet the bulk of Rangers–Celtic antagonism is hard to label 'racist'. [23] It is a two-way rivalry the intensity of which can be found in many parts of the football world; both sides give as good as they get in terms of the lexicon of abuse and the ludicrous caricaturing and mythologizing of the enemy. Sectarian attitudes can spring from many sources and it is necessary to try to distinguish between those which are formed out of fear and feelings of being under threat from those which are closed to any just and fair treatment of people of a different creed. Much of this behaviour is of a ritualised kind which carries no significant conception of 'the other side' as somehow inferior or less human. Even sectarian discrimination can be the result of a desire to help 'one's own' rather than do down the other side. It is now politically incorrect to dismiss some sectarian behaviour as 'banter' but we should, nevertheless, keep in sight the socially beneficial role of such banter on many occasions and its proven capacity to keep sectarian asperities within certain bounds.

Rangers fans bridle at the constant barrage of opinion which, despite the obvious mutual hatreds, lays the blame for sectarianism solely or mainly at their door. They accuse the anti-sectarian pressure group, Nil By Mouth (NBM), as being far more orientated towards the condemnation of Rangers and their fans, and judging by their publicity, mission statements and interventions NBM seems indeed to have been guided by the assumptions and conceptualisations of the Bradleyites.[24] Do NBM, and Bradley and Co., accept that terms like 'Orange bastards' and 'hun scum' are sectarian? If so, do they, then, following their own precepts, consider them racist? This is to say nothing of explicitly anti-Protestant sentiments to be heard in several songs sung by Celtic fans ('Roamin' in the Gloamin'; 'North Men, South Men') and the reference to Rangers fans as 'animals' in the popular version of the official Celtic song.[25]

Songs are of course another hobby horse of the *CM* contributors. In the first volume Patricia Ferns argues for her right to sing songs about 'the core identity of the club and its support'. Significantly, she then goes on to mention pro-IRA songs such as 'The Boys of the Old Brigade', and waxes apoplectic about being asked to refrain from singing them by Celtic officials. For Ferns these songs represent 'a national and cultural struggle'. Some might say that it is a struggle which has divided Ireland far more deeply than London rule ever did, and has involved some of the bloodiest atrocities ever committed in Irish history – and committed, moreover, against people supposedly considered fellow Irish men and women. What Ferns and, presumably, Bradley and the bulk of the *CM* authors uphold as songs dear to Celtic, others view as hymns in praise of sectarian murderers. No *CM* contributor – with the honourable exceptions of Eddie Toner, Michael McMahon MSP and Tony Roper – seems perturbed about songs and chants giving succour to those Republicans who committed such deeds as Enniskillen, Teebane, Kingsmills, the Shankill Road, La Mon, and Darkley. The latter, to take an example, involved Republican gunmen shooting dead three worshippers at a Pentecostal church in 1983 and wounding several others. Apropos James MacMillan's absurd notions in the first volume of *CM* about Irish Catholics and Celtic FC being metaphorically feminine and being 'rogered' by Maley's 'straight, strong' Protestants, what precisely was feminine about Darkley, James? How do the murders and stabbings of Rangers fans over the past few years fit your fantasy? [26] Some Celtic fans – and the tendency is clear in the *CM* books – display both ignorance and sectarianism in their insistence that it is Celtic fans alone who have been the victims of such Old Firm-related violence. [27] Ferns even has the brass neck to say this about the IRA slogan *Tiocfaidh ar la* (Our Day Will Come): 'Sure it has a political resonance but it seems to me that the phrase also encapsulates something that any football team might aspire to: namely success.' So, if Rangers fans argue that the use of 'No Surrender' is simply an injunction to the team not to give up, we should expect to be taken at face value by the media and our opponents? Aye right!

It becomes clear through Ferns's piece – and others such as those by Brian Warfield and Aiden Donaldson – that the Irishness which the CM project is most concerned to celebrate and affirm is in fact that of the Republican armed struggle. Since victims of IRA violence include Scottish soldiers and Ulster people with Scottish family connections, is it surprising that much opinion in Scotland will be hostile to the glorification of bombers and assassins? I may add that it is no less hostile to Loyalist killers on these counts. There is, among many Celtic cheerleaders, a categorical refusal to face up to the reality of the IRA campaign as a grubby sectarian war of attrition that got nowhere. And as for the IRA's supposedly inspiring history, does that include the collaboration with the Nazis in the second world war? Go and read up on Sean Russell bhoys and ghirls. While you're at it read up on Arthur Griffith, founder of Sinn Fein, who wrote in 1913 that no Irish Nationalist should regard a Negro as his equal.[28] Do some reading about anti-Semitism in Nationalist Ireland.[29] People who sing about Thompson guns, broad black brimmers, and raids on police barracks, and who bellow the militaristic and chauvinistic 'Soldier's Song', have no right to lecture others about the songs they sing. These are the songs sung at Celtic Park, not 'She Moved Through the Fair', 'Danny Boy', 'Galway Bay' or 'The Mountains of Mourne'. It is songs of hate, and this includes 'The Fields of Athenry' with its infamous add-ons, which are at issue. It is, in short, about anti-Britishness rather than pro-Irishness.

It may also come as unwelcome news to the Celtic-minded that their expressions of a deeply tribal Irish Nationalism are widely discountenanced in the Republic of Ireland today. In February 2006 a proposed march to draw attention to the plight of victims of IRA atrocities was prevented from taking place in Dublin by an angry mob that rioted and fought running battles with the Gardai. The result was looting and mayhem and the exposure of the so-called Republicans as sectarian bigots. The Irish press's response was interesting. It was widely reported that the shirt of choice of the rioters was the Celtic one, prompting the pressure group Sport Against Racism Ireland (SARI) to write to Celtic Park pointing out that the use of Celtic colours by 'extreme green nationalist thugs' brought the club into disrepute. [30] The Irish popular music magazine, *Hot Press*, then entered the fray with an article entitled 'CeltThick'. This piece referred to the 'hardcore' Celtic fans as 'deeply prejudiced and sectarian, they are as close as we have to football hooligans and (ironically) the British National Party'. The author then went on to claim that they peddled 'a uniquely Irish fascism'. [31] Remember Celtic-minded people, this was the Republic of Ireland press, not the 'racist' Scottish Protestant one. As was also pointed out, the rioters had no understanding of what Republic-anism ought to mean, an ideology of universal citizenship rights to unite Catholic, Protestant and Dissenter. In reality, Irish Republicanism has never been about that since the late eighteenth century, and the Celtic fans were simply expressing the often anti-Protestant and always anti-British character of the movement just as they regularly do in a football context. Asked to respond to criticism of the Celtic fans' behaviour in Dublin, Bradley declared that it was unfair that the club had 'to continually combat such connotations'. 'These perceptions', he went on, 'can be used as a stick against the club by people who want to change things about Celtic and their fans that they don't like.' [32] Yes, Joe, change the fans' predilection for singing songs which celebrate a murder campaign. Bradley wants it both ways: he wants Celtic's Irish identity to be cherished and promoted know-ing full well that for people like Ferns this means being able to sing what she likes; and on the other hand he wants to argue that the Celtic supp-orters' culture is beyond reproach. Those who rioted in Dublin, it may be suggested, would be among those most enthusiastic about the *CM* books Bradley has put together. [33]

Bradley's books actually betray the rich variety of Irish experience. Their claims and grievances revolve around the expression of one brand of Irishness. Does Patricia Ferns speak for the whole Irish community in Scotland? Does Bradley? Of course not. The diversity of political view-points within the Irish community in Scotland during the actual period of their settlement and since has been lost in the din of a one-note whine. Who precisely is the butt of the anti-Irish racism referred to? Apparently, just Catholics; Bradley in the first volume remarks that Irish Protestants assimilated 'easily'. I sometimes wonder why I bothered researching the Poor Law records of nineteenth century Glasgow to bring to light the considerable evidence of Irish Protestant poverty and destitution. [34] What about Catholics of Irish descent in the highest echelons of the Scottish establishment – such as in politics, the law, education and the media? Have they joined the 'hegemonic' and 'racist' forces ranged against their own people?

Bradley and co. refuse to engage with opposing points of view. They simply ignore the research findings of academics like Steve Bruce, Michael Rosie, Ian Paterson, Lindsay Paterson and Christina Ianelli, which make it difficult for them to sustain their claims. [35] They have nothing to say about such a salient feature of Scottish society as intermarriage between people of different faiths. When, as Bruce points out, almost half the marriages involving Catholics under thirty-five that take place in Scotland are 'mixed', how can the case for saying that an anti-Irish Catholic racism is so dominant be sustained? How do claims of racism stack up in a situation where some of the most fervent Rangers and Celtic fans and exponents of Orange and Green political cultures are products of mixed marriages? How in the light of this can Catholics in Scotland be seriously regarded, as Irene Reid in *CM* volume 2 suggests, as 'the other'? There is simply too much social (and other) interaction between Protestants and Catholics in Scottish society to make such terms mean-ingful. The segregation there is, it might be said, has largely been at the behest of the Catholic Church with its rigid stance on schooling. Incidentally, Irene, how do you account for the fact that Rangers fans in the past did not engage in any special vilification of other Irish Catholic Celtic players such as Pat Bonner, Anton Rogan, Neil Mochan or Charlie Tully? Indeed, Tully guested for Rangers in a friendly during the 1950s. Have you really studied how Neil Lennon behaves when he and Celtic are not getting their own way? Were you simply unaware, or did you choose not to mention, that he was reported for spitting on a Rangers supporters' scarf during the Old Firm game, which ended with the gratuitous and inflam-matory display of defiance on the part of Lennon and his manager? Why is it that the numerous attacks by Celtic fans on Rangers players in public over the last few years have been deemed less newsworthy than attacks on Lennon? Why, on the issue of the ill-treatment of players, have Celtic fans reserved their worst abuse for Rangers players from a local Catholic (and presumably at some point) Irish background, namely Mo Johnston, Neil McCann and Chris Burke? It surely can't be anything to do with sectarianism, sorry racism? The Celtic fans condemnation of the so-called 'treachery' of these players betrays their own profound sectarianism. Conversely, why have such players been so readily accepted by Rangers fans – and yes, that includes Mo Jo – if they are such a bigoted and racist bunch?

Let me finish with some comments on the recent controversy surrounding the highly talented young Celtic player Aiden McGeady and his decision to play international football for the Republic of Ireland and not Scotland. For Bradley, writing in *CM*'s second volume, this is further clinching evidence of anti-Irishness in Scotland. Certainly, it seems to be the case that there is in Scotland a wide sense of resistance to the notion that any other identity than Scottishness should be given priority in a sporting context on the part of those born in Scotland. Yet the hostility to McGeady's choice of the Irish Republic would be magnified many times in the as yet hypothetical case of a high-profile player choosing England in such circumstances. Anti-Englishness, it can be claimed, runs far deeper than anti-Irishness, even in 'Protestant Scotland'. The *CM* people really need to ponder the implications of this. It might also surprise them to hear that I think McGeady's critics are wrong. He and any other player in a position to make a choice should be allowed to do so in accordance with whatever they deem to be the relevant factors. If that means that they feel their primary identity is Irish (or anything else) rather than Scottish then so be it. The more we transgress the spurious 'natural laws' and 'blood and soil' logic imposed by nations, nation-states and borders the better. All nationalisms are in my view problematic and all the better for being diluted. However, two observations might be made about this. First, the evidence so far suggests that there are very few in Scotland who feel their primary identity to be Irish despite the best efforts of people like Bradley to influence the responses to the recent census in order to highlight the Irish community more clearly. Second, a somewhat ironic point: those urging the Irish in Scotland to assert their Irishness should logically concede the right of those in Ireland who consider themselves British or Ulster-Scots first and Irish second to so proclaim and consequently defend. Somehow, I doubt if this is what the *Celtic Minded* cultural warriors, post-colonial theorists and politicised football fans have in mind.

Notes

1   For attention to the problem at the level of the Scottish Executive see the report of an Executive committee published in 2002, *Tackling Religious Hatred*.

2   See Martin Steven, 'The Place of Religion in Devolved Scottish Politics', *Scottish Affairs*, No. 58, winter 2007.

3   J. Bradley (ed.), *Celtic Minded: Essays on Football, Culture and Identity Vols. 1 and 2* (Argyll, 2004 and 2006).

4   *The Herald*, 8 January 2005. Gorrie's efforts succeeded in adding a penalty for certain offences if a sectarian motive could be proven to have been part of the crime.

5   For scholarly commentaries see S. Bruce et al, *Sectarianism in Scotland* (Edinburgh, 2004), and M. Rosie, *The Sectarian Myth in Scotland* (Basingstoke, 2004). The Glasgow City Council report was published in 2003 and was entitled *Sectarianism in Glasgow*.

6   *The Herald*, 25 November 2006.

7   See *The Herald*, 18 November 2002; also entry for 'Irish' on Scottish Executive website re 'onescotland'.

8   See *Irish Times*, 7 June 2006.

9   J. McGonigal et al (eds.), *Across the Water* (Argyll, 2000).

10 Reported in *The Herald*, 20 October 2003.

11 See Bill Murray's comments on *The Magic Flute* in his *The Old Firm* (2nd edition, Edinburgh: John Donald, 2000), p. 295.

12 See Rosie, *Sectarian Myth*, chs 5–9 for an illuminating discussion of this period in all its controversial aspects. See also Bill Murray's discussion of 'The Catholic Church and the Secular State' in his *The Old Firm in the New Age* (Edinburgh: Mainstream, 1998), pp. 200–2.

13 'Senex' (Robert Reid), *Glasgow Past and Present vol. 2* (Glasgow, 1884)

14 *Irish Post*, 27 August 2005. The interview was conducted by *Celtic Minded* contributor Richard Purden.

15 It should also be pointed out that many Scots Protestant migrants to Ulster were massacred by Catholics in 1641 or forced to return to Scotland.

16 See points made about Celtic's mission statement of 1996 in Bill

Murray, *The Old Firm in the New Age*, pp 141–4. As Murray observes, Celtic's founders were primarily concerned to keep Catholics in the faith and did not encourage mixing with Protestants.

17 W. Maley, 'A Letter From Glasgow: Where the Streets Have No Shame', *Field Day Review*, No.2, 2006.

18 See interview in *The Drouth*, spring 2005.

19 Steven, 'The Place of Religion'.

20 The programme – *Booked* – was shown on 22 January 2007.

21 Quoted in S. Howe, *Ireland and Empire* (Oxford, 2002).

22 Howe, *Ireland and Empire*, p. 109.

23 See Murray, *The Old Firm in the New Age*, p. 200.

24 NBM has also been reluctant to entertain discussion of the role of segregated education in the persistence of sectarianism.

25 See Celtic fans website 'The Huddleboard' – 'Hating the Orangies online since 1999' – for frequent posts of a sectarian nature. On 8 September 2006 there was a defence of the use of the word 'animals' in the Celtic song 'Hail Hail'.

26 It is also interesting in relation to MacMillan that a music critic has pointed out that he has exposed himself to the charge of insensitivity regarding Jewish religious beliefs. See Michael Linton, 'Sacred Fanfares', *First Things* No. 106 (October 2000).

27 Rangers fans were murdered in incidents which either occurred around Old Firm fixtures or were reported as having an Old Firm context in May and June 1999, August 2000, November 2000 and October 2003, and were the victims of stabbings and life-threatening assaults in incidents reported in February and May 2001, May 2002 and November 2004.

28 See Griffith's preface to the 1913 edition of John Mitchell's *Jail Journal*, reprinted in the 1983 edition published by Sphere Books.

29 See RTE programmes entitled *Ireland's Nazis*, scripted and introduced by Cathal O'Shannon and broadcast in January 2007. On 'The Huddleboard' website on 10 January 2004 there was a host of anti-Semitic and sectarian posts and pro-Nazi messages. There was also reference to 'a pure Irish Celtic race'.

30 *Observer*, 5 March 2006.

31 *Hot Press*, 22 March 2006.

32 *Sunday Times*, 5 March 2006.

33 Also worth mentioning in this regard is the story reported in the *Drogheda Independent* in 2006 about the promising young Irish footballer who was offered a trial by Rangers. Attacks on him and threats against his family forced him to decline the offer.

34 See G. Walker, 'The Protestant Irish in Scotland', in T. M. Devine (ed.), *Irish Immigrants and Scottish Society* (Edinburgh, 1991). See also the forthcoming work of the historian Geraldine Vaughan.

35 Bruce et al, *Sectarianism*; Rosie, *Sectarian Myth*; I. Paterson, 'Sectarianism and Municipal Housing Allocation in Glasgow', *Scottish Affairs*, No. 39, Spring 2002; L. Paterson and C. Iannelli, 'Religion, social mobility and education in Scotland', *The British Journal of Sociology*, Vol. 57, No.3, 2006.

Confessions of a Justified Rangers Supporter

Dolan Cummings

Hullo, hullo, we are the Billy Boys
Hullo, hullo, you'll know us by our noise

On 3 May 2007, Rangers FC were fined 12,000 euros by UEFA for the behaviour of their fans at a UEFA Cup tie in Spain. The home club Osasuna were judged to have been responsible for some minor crowd trouble, having botched the security arrangements, and were fined nearly four times as much. Rangers' fine was widely seen as punishment not for fighting but for singing.

In fact, the offence had come to light well after the game, when somebody posted footage on the website YouTube of Rangers fans waiting to be escorted from the empty stadium after the game. Tina Turner's 'Simply the Best', a traditional favourite with Rangers fans, was playing over the stadium public address, and some of the fans were singing the almost-traditional alternative lyrics, answering Tina's 'I call you when I need you, my heart's on fire', with, 'Fuck the Pope and the IRA!' By any objective standard, this was a peculiar thing to do. To anyone familiar with Scottish football, however, this behaviour warrants little more than a roll of the eyes. Rangers fans are well known for banging on about such things, and however offensive it might seem, wise observers know better than to take it seriously.

Wise observers are becoming a minority, however. The unspoken convention that sectarian songs are ignored at football matches has been undermined in recent years, and haughty disapproval has given way to censoriousness. Efforts to eradicate sectarian songs and chants from football are part of a wider cultural shift in British society, a growing concern with language and attitudes that are deemed offensive, irrespective of whether they have any practical bearing on society. There has been more and more hand-wringing about this in the media, and summits and campaigns sponsored by the government, churches and football clubs themselves. But the attempt to articulate the problem in the bureaucratic terms required by European football's governing body has thrown the question into relief.

The issue was first brought to the attention of UEFA's Control and Disciplinary Body in 2006, when somebody complained about Rangers fans singing the song 'Billy Boys', with its infamous lines, 'We're up to our knees in Fenian blood/Surrender or you'll die', at an away tie against another Spanish team, Villarreal. On that occasion, the fans were eventually declared not guilty of something called 'discriminatory chants', on the grounds that 'supporters have been singing the song "Billy Boys" for years during national and international matches without either the Scottish football or governmental authorities being able to intervene. The result is that this song is now somehow tolerated.' [1] UEFA's mandarins, meeting in the sedate Swiss town of Nyon, could not see why, if sectarianism was as much of a problem as the song suggested, nothing had been done about it before. They responded with the bureaucratic equivalent of a Gallic shrug. That said, they were soon pressed into reconsidering their judgement and eventually fined Rangers.

The issue refuses to go away not because UEFA bureaucrats are espe-cially worried about it, then, but because sectarian songs and chants continue to generate anxiety in Scottish society, even if critics find it hard to express exactly what the problem is, beyond the blunt charge that these songs are offensive. Certainly the problem has proved unamenable to bureaucratic language. The notion of 'discriminatory chants' is so odd that I can only do it justice in two distinct phases. The first is to make the seemingly pedantic point that the whole purpose of football chanting is to 'discriminate' between your team and the opposition: us and them. This is true whether the discrimination takes a 'sectarian' form, or an entirely innocent one: 'Come on, Rovers!', or more risqué, perhaps, 'Stand up if you hate Man U'. There are those who find the whole business of football partisanship rather distasteful, but it is not discrimination in this sense that most people are worried about.

Second, then, presumably the concern is that the discrimination is not primarily about football, that 'discriminatory' attitudes or prejudices are being imported from wider society into football, and that they are being perpetuated through football. In the case of Rangers, this would mean that as the songs are 'anti-Catholic' they have a detrimental effect on Catholics. The model here is clearly racism, which was widely apparent in British football as recently as the 1980s, and was indeed an expression of a wider social problem. Now, the slogan, 'Fuck the Pope and the IRA', like much of the Rangers repertoire, certainly does refer to religious and political aspects of British history, and especially the conflict in Northern Ireland. There is no doubt that the traditional following for Rangers in Scotland and Northern Ireland is Protestant, and that the football rivalry between Rangers and Celtic FC, whose following is traditionally Irish Catholic, has always been coloured by sectarianism.

The assumption, then, is that the behaviour of the Rangers fans in Spain was an expression of deeper social tensions analogous to racism, and likely to exacerbate those tensions. The basic argument of this article is that this assumption is false, the analogy with racism is inapt, sectarian singing does not harm Catholics or anyone else, and thus the attempt to stamp out sectarianism in football is unnecessarily illiberal and ultimately infantilising.

All in the game

When I was young, I had no sense:
I bought a flute for fifty pence.
The only tune that I could play
Was 'Fuck the Pope and the IRA'

The association between Rangers Football Club and sectarianism is undeniable, and seemingly as unvarying as the song suggests, but it is also hard to pin down, and its meaning has in fact changed considerably over the history of the club. The clearest expression of sectarian thinking on the part of the club itself was its historical reluctance to recruit Roman Catholic players. Significantly, this was not a founding principle of the club, but rather something that was established informally after the first world war, as an influx of Irish Catholic labour hardened sectarian feeling among the club's working class Protestant following. No doubt the partition of Ireland a few years later did little to heal the divide. Sectarianism in football was thus a reflection of sectarianism in wider society.

The eventual signing of Maurice Johnston – not just a Catholic, but a high-profile former Celtic player – did not of course put an end to sectarianism, but it did send a powerful signal that things were changing; much more so than later attempts to prohibit offensive songs. It is poignant that this happened in 1989, the same year as the collapse of the Berlin Wall. (The former event was considered so cataclysmic by some that observers in Glasgow might have been forgiven for thinking it precipitated the latter.) The objection to Catholic players coincided almost exactly with what the historian Eric Hobsbawm called 'the short twentieth century', the period between the first world war and the fall of Communism, a period defined by mass political movements of left and right, which framed and shaped other conflicts. It is not fanciful to suggest that the end of the Cold War, by transforming the political landscape globally, really did contribute to the peace process in Northern Ireland. That process has not ended sectarianism, but it perhaps took some of the heat out of the sectarian rivalry in football, especially in Scotland.

In any case, the whole world was changing at the end of the twentieth century; and Scotland with it. 1988 saw the Glasgow Garden Festival, located a stone's throw from Ibrox on a site once occupied by docks, and symbolising both the demise of the city's heavy industry and the hope of something new. In 1990 Glasgow was European City of Culture and Margaret Thatcher was ousted from government (her legacy well and truly established). Scottish society had not simply moved on from the days of sectarian discord when Rangers had discriminated against Catholics; it was entering a completely different era. By the time Rangers were chasing nine-in-a-row in the mid-1990s, sectarian songs and chants in football were no longer a reflection of sectarianism in wider society, but *the only significant form of sectarianism* to be found in Scotland.

When the composer James MacMillan gave a speech at the 1999 Edinburgh Festival about anti-Catholic bigotry, 'Scotland's Shame', he made a point of highlighting the 'totemic significance' of Rangers FC. Indeed, if he had failed to do this, nobody would have known what he was on about. There is no significant anti-Catholic discrimination in jobs or housing, no segregation except through voluntarily chosen and apparently benign Roman Catholic schools, and no sectarian violence apart from those few assaults (deplorable as they are) associated with football.

MacMillan made much of the misbehaviour of Donald Findlay QC, who had just been forced to resign as Rangers' vice-chairman after being filmed singing the old favourites at a party to celebrate the club's Scottish Cup triumph. Findlay was not just a senior figure at Rangers, but a leading advocate, prominent Tory, and unmistakeable (if lopsided) pillar of the Scottish establishment. For MacMillan, no doubt, this showed that sectarianism was rife at all levels of Scottish society. In fact, the response to Findlay's behaviour was more indicative of prevailing attitudes to sectarianism. As soon as footage of his performance at the cup party was sent to a newspaper, his position at Rangers became untenable. An anonymous crowd singing sectarian songs was one thing: no respectable member of society could or can be associated with this kind of behaviour without losing respectability. In reality, the Scottish establishment, the political and cultural elite, abhors sectarianism and any expression of it, however trivial. Indeed, the cultural elite – people like MacMillan – often seem to despise football fans who sing sectarian songs rather more than those fans hate their rival fans, and certainly with more seriousness.

The question of whether sectarianism is a problem beyond football is complicated by the attitude of the clubs: both Rangers and Celtic – whose fans used to, and occasionally still do, sing IRA songs – regularly insist that sectarianism is a wider social issue, deeply rooted in Scottish society. Indeed, it is in the interests of the clubs to say so. The truth, that sectarianism is more or less limited to their supporters, in and around their grounds and others where they play, seems to put rather a burden on them. To argue, as I have, that sectarianism is actually not much of a problem at all, is not an attractive option to the clubs precisely because they are, first and foremost, businesses and not political organisations. They are in no position to challenge prevailing ideas about sectarianism: this would court controversy, which is exactly what they want to avoid. Thus, it suits them to read from the well-worn script according to which the problem is deeply rooted in society and we must all play a role in tackling it. I should note in passing that you can say that of just about any social problem today without fear of contradiction.

Rangers chairman David Murray was closer to the mark when he described the troublesome element among the Rangers support as 'ninety-minute bigots'. This was an echo of the Scottish nationalist politician Jim Sillars' complaint after his failure to get re-elected in Govan in 1992, that the Scots were 'ninety-minute patriots' who would support the national team at football, but did not have the courage of their convictions. Tellingly, the weight was on the 'ninety-minute' part, the point being that all their shouting and singing counted for nothing. The same is largely true of the apparent bigotry of Rangers fans.[2] After the game, Rangers fans continue to fraternise with Catholic friends, colleagues and indeed family. If thousands of Scots really did want to be 'up to our knees in Fenian blood', or even considered themselves to be in competition with their Catholic neighbours, as they once did, Scotland would be a very different country.

The lure of offence and the reaction against it

You are a Fenian, a Fenian bastard
You're only happy on giro day
Your maw's a stealer, your da's a dealer
Please don't take my hubcaps away

Of course, the fact remains that sectarian songs and chants are plainly offensive: that is their very purpose. It could be argued that this alone is a sufficient reason to ban or seek to eradicate them from football, though in the case of the Rangers fans singing in the empty stadium in Osasuna, for example, it is not at all clear exactly who was actually 'offended'. But even if we accepted that clamping down on such behaviour was a legitimate enterprise, it would be hard to draw the line between sectarianism and other forms of offence. After all, the giving and taking of offence is an integral part of football even in cities untouched by sectarianism. The journalist Mick Hume has described football as 'the home ground of the id', where people are free to abandon the normal standards of polite society and vent their frustrations at the opposing fans. While there is a notional sectarian division between Liverpool and local rivals Everton, there is a much greater rivalry between Liverpool and Manchester United, which is based solely on football. Fans of those clubs have to find ways to abuse and offend one another without recourse to sectarianism – with reference to everything from historical disasters to the sexual proclivities of players' wives – but there is no more love lost between them than between fans of Rangers and Celtic.

Every so often there is controversy about opposing fans making hissing noises when they play Tottenham Hotspur – this is meant to evoke the Nazi gas chambers, in a bid to upset the north London club's traditionally Jewish support. It is shockingly offensive, and reliably provokes outrage in the media, but nobody seriously thinks it reveals an undercurrent of anti-Semitism in British society, or that the fans who do this are actually Nazi sympathisers. They are more often described simply as idiots, but what's important is that it is generally understood that it would be foolish to respond by launching a major campaign against anti-Semitism, and trying to persuade fans to abandon offensive ideas and opinions that they don't actually hold anyway. Football is not a reliable barometer of political feeling in wider society.

The situation with Rangers is admittedly different in that there is a history of sectarianism in Scottish society, and some of the fans do claim to take seriously the prejudices expressed in the songs. But this is a shrinking minority that cannot by itself account for the persistence of apparent sectarianism in football. This has gone from being an expression of a wider social phenomenon to a particular form of a very different phenomenon which is peculiar to football, that is, deliberate offensiveness. It is particularly well-suited to this purpose precisely because it has an authentic history that makes people nervous. Of course, it us understandable that people feel distaste: the history of sectarianism is a bloody and sordid one, and it is right that we are generally disapproving of sectarian language and behaviour, forbidding it in schools and so on. But it is a mistake to continue the pursuit into the deliberately irrational and often daft world of football.

It is important to recognise that today's 'anti-sectarianism', with its focus on football, is not a continuation of progressive political opposition to sectarianism any more than 'sectarianism' itself is a continuation of reactionary political ideas. Rather, it is an overreaction to offensiveness in football per se, in the context of a society that is increasingly ill at ease with unregulated expression of any kind. Sectarianism is simply a convenient focus. Ironically, the increasing publicity surrounding sectarianism in football only increases its potency as a means of giving offence, perhaps even enhancing football's status as a 'counter-cultural' realm of irrational passion in an increasingly anxious and fastidious society. Certainly, I have to confess that the notoriety of Rangers has always been part of the appeal for me, and my own experience may shed some light on what that notoriety means to fans today.

'No-one likes us, we don't care'

Build my gallows, build them high
That I might see before I die
The Antrim glen and the hills of County Down
And see again the lights of home

I can't claim to be a typical Rangers supporter; far from it. Though I grew up in a notionally Protestant family in Glasgow and even attended the Boys' Brigade for a few years, I was never interested in football as a boy, and those friends I had who were supported the local team Partick Thistle (often seen as a refuge for middle-class fans put off by the sectarianism of the Old Firm, but I'll come back to that). I went to a genuinely non-denominational school, attended by good numbers of Muslims, Hindus and Sikhs as well as Catholics and Protestants. It never occurred to me to ask what religion the Chinese kids were.

Several of my classmates did support either Rangers or Celtic, generally in accordance with their religion, but this never seemed an important divide in the school; when there was talk of gangs, these were geographical rather than sectarian, which generally seems to be the case in Glasgow. Some of the boys in my first-year class adapted the Rangers song 'Billy Boys', singing 'We are the 1B boys', but they included at least two Catholic Celtic fans. The other song they sang a lot was the theme from the cartoon *Thundercats*. I do remember a boy being made to replace the cover of a textbook, having drawn a Red Hand of Ulster on his original cover, and another boasting about singing 'Up the 'RA' (IRA) while out with his stepfather, but that's about it.

My interest in football came several years after leaving school, when I was living in a flat, still in Glasgow, equipped with Sky Sports, which in tandem with the new Premiership was transforming English football, flooding the game with cash and glamour. English football's reputation for hooliganism was by now a thing of the past. I adopted Blackburn Rovers, possibly because their manager Kenny Dalglish was one of the few Scottish footballers I remembered from childhood (he also happened to be a Celtic legend, but I probably didn't even know that). They won the league. Then Rangers signed Paul Gascoigne from Lazio, and my new interest in football combined with a mischievous streak to make me decide to follow the Ibrox club.

I was used to mixing with people who considered Rangers to be almost satanic. Hostility to the Old Firm, and Rangers in particular, is part of the make-up of respectable society in Scotland. This is partly to do with sectarianism, and partly because of the perception that both clubs are vast money-making machines, profiting from sectarianism and keeping a stranglehold on Scottish football; there are often murmurs about corruption, even. The fact that Rangers had just won seven consecutive championship titles (in the midst of their record-equalling nine-in-a-row campaign) was almost as offensive to this mindset as the sectarian association.

For me, then, there has always been a certain contrarian element to supporting Rangers. While my particular background is unusual, however, I would suggest that there is something contrarian in the support even of more traditional Rangers fans. Whatever the prejudices of the liberal middle class, and whatever impression they may sometimes themselves give, Rangers fans are not, as a rule, stupid. They are all too aware of the club's unpopularity in wider Scottish society, and as often as not wear this as a badge of honour. It is not that Rangers fans cling to bigoted attitudes *in spite* of widespread disapproval, but increasingly that apparent sectarianism is a kind of two-fingered salute to the censorious critics.

Often this is done with surprising good humour, such as when, during the short Rangers career of French goalkeeper Lionel Charbonnier, it was discovered that the words of 'The Sash' could be sung to the tune of 'The Marseillaise'. There are also frequent jokes among supporters acknowledging wryly that some of their favourite Rangers players are Catholic. Nacho Novo, who, as the song reminds us 'said no to the Provos' (turning down a move to Celtic) is of course a Spanish Catholic, and thus, according to looser definitions, a 'Fenian'. While never the classiest of players, however, Novo was always the type who 'played for the jersey', and thus endeared himself to the supporters. The recognition that Catholics can be good Rangers players does not make 'sectarianism' disappear in a puff of good sense, however, precisely because apparently anti-Catholic attitudes are not based on a political or religious worldview, but more often simply express identification with Rangers, albeit in characteristically bad taste.

Looking to the future

Follow, follow,
We will follow Rangers
Up the Falls, Derry's Walls
We will follow on . . .

Fuelled by official anti-sectarianism, however, this contrarianism can take on an exaggerated and very childish quality. One of the Rangers songs I do find embarrassing is sung to the tune normally used for 'Can you hear the [eg. Celtic] sing? No-o, no-o!' It goes 'We are not sectarian, no-o, no-o', with the punch line after two-and-a-half repetitions, 'We are UVF!' This is embarrassing not because it invokes a paramilitary organisation, but because it does so purely for the shock value. Even by the standards of football songs, it is utterly puerile. The fans who sing it have nothing whatever to do with the UVF; for the most part, they are not even remotely sympathetic to it, assuming they even know what it is, or was. But they know it's outrageous, or more accurately naughty, to invoke it. The effect of campaigns against sectarianism in football has not been to civilise, but to infantilise.

This is especially true when official anti-sectarianism is endorsed by the club itself. It is understandable that Rangers FC should seek to distance itself from some of the unsavoury behaviour of its fans, as any club would, regardless of whether the offensive behaviour was considered sectarian or not. Initiatives like Pride over Prejudice, launched in 2003, are well-meant, but there is a danger that they take sectarianism too seriously. And the club's *Wee Blue Book* of approved songs is surely the stuff of satire; it's hard to say whether the reference to Chairman Mao's *Little Red Book* is deliberate or not, but it is unmistakeable. In reality, songs and chants are the product of years of tradition, memory and banter among fans, not club diktat. It is ironic that, while the 'authenticity' of 'real fans' is highly prized in football generally, and often counterposed to the sanitised and commercialised character of football in the age of Sky Sports, Rangers songs are considered a little *too* authentic, the fans a little *too* real.

Official anti-sectarianism neither challenges prejudices (which are far less widely or strongly held than is supposed), nor encourages more mature or civilised behaviour. If anything, it fuels elite prejudices about the uncouth and unwashed masses in the stands. And since it ends up treating fans as children, it is not surprising that some respond by behaving as such. In many respects it is analogous with bans on smoking. The world would certainly not be worse off if no sectarian songs were sung at football matches, any more than it would be a worse place if nobody smoked, but something is lost when these things are achieved through coercive measures imposed by the authorities. Significantly, this was not the experience with racism: for all the high-profile campaigns to 'kick racism out of football', it is the fans' own distaste for racist chants etc that leads to an informal self-policing. 'Sectarianism' is taken less seriously, because it is simply not regarded as a real and pernicious force in society like racism is. What self-policing does now happen with regards to sectarianism is very much in the spirit of 'don't get the club into trouble', rather than genuine moral disdain.

The club often portrays the association with sectarianism as a barrier to progress for Rangers. Now that UEFA has been convinced to take an interest, there is talk of national football associations being required to dock points from clubs whose fans indulge in 'discriminatory chanting'. It should be emphasised, though, that UEFA has had to be cajoled into taking this seriously; its bureaucratic procedures seeming more potent than woolly campaigns or the clumsy (not to mention wildly inappropriate) criminal law as a means of shutting up the crowds. More generally, it is argued that if Rangers FC is to become the kind of top-table European club the fans want it to be, and perhaps even to play in the English Premiership, then outmoded and inappropriate songs and attitudes will have to be left behind. But this has things the wrong way round. Rangers is a football club and its progress depends primarily on success on the pitch.

To take a lesson from history, the important thing about the Graeme Souness 'revolution' at Ibrox was not simply that he left behind the parochialism that had dogged Rangers – by signing first a number of English players and then the iconic Mo Johnston – but that in doing so, he brought about a lasting reversal of the club's football fortunes. Indeed, for Souness, the point about Johnston was not simply that he was a high-profile Catholic, but that he had been expected to rejoin Celtic: his unexpected capture was a major psychological blow to Rangers' biggest rivals in football. Souness's manipulation of sectarian expectations was reminiscent of Jock Stein, the legendary Celtic manager, who once explained that given a choice between two players of equal talent, he would always take a Protestant over a Catholic, knowing that Rangers would be unable to recruit the other. Like Stein, Souness never forgot that he was running a football club, not a heritage organisation or a museum.

It so happens that the Frenchman, Paul Le Guen, who had a short and ill-fated spell in charge in 2006, was Rangers' first ever Catholic manager. That was of much less interest to the fans or anyone else than the promise, based on his success with Lyon, that he would take Rangers to a new level by transforming the culture of the club and the way the team played. We will never know whether he might have succeeded if given more time and backing. In any case, the barrier he faced had little to do with the fans, who were by no means unanimous in siding with the Scottish players when they seemed to be resisting the new manager's methods. Perhaps the problem was a lack of sophistication on the part of those players, perhaps Le Guen was simply too authoritarian in his efforts to change the culture (as another Catholic, former club captain Lorenzo Amoruso put it, rather prosaically, if a player is used to eating brown sauce, you might as well let him go on having it).

The important point, though, is that the cultural change needed if Rangers are to progress is one on the training ground and the pitch, not the stands. The songs may well make less and less sense the further the team progresses in Europe, but frankly it's up to the fans to work that out for themselves. For a time during the nine-in-a-row campaign, it seemed that the unpopularity of Rangers had more to do with the club's success than the association with sectarianism. As with Manchester United in England at the time, disdain was heavily tinged with envy. Those of us who enjoy the fact that 'no-one likes us' look forward to more of the same. True Rangers fans, the vast majority, want to see the team win and the club flourish no matter what. Those who are more interested in railing against Catholics than watching the game can come to their own conclusions.

In the late 1990s I worked part-time in a petrol station. When I first met the woman who worked the night shift she asked what team I supported. When I told her Rangers she grinned, and immediately informed me that she used to be in a band. For a few moments I wondered what kind of band, and what this had to do with anything, before it dawned on me that she meant an Orange band. Unlike me, she had been a 'proper' Rangers fan, born and bred, and in the Orange Lodge. Except that she wasn't a Rangers fan at all: she had changed her allegiance in 1989, in disgust at the signing of Mo Johnston. Now she supported Partick Thistle.

Notes

[1] Reasons for Rangers decision, UEFA website 13 April 2006.

[2] While observers often note with shaking heads that several Rangers songs commemorate the Battle of the Boyne, which was fought over three hundred years ago, nobody seems to mind that 'Flower of Scotland' commemorates a battle fought nearly seven hundred years ago. In fact neither song is sung for political reasons. Historical allusions aside, both are essentially football songs.

Rathcoole Ranger

Gary Mitchell

My wife, Alison, started screaming, 'He's hitting our car. Gary, he's on top of our car. The car's on fire.' Panic tore my eyes from the television screen and instinct picked me up from my seat and ran me towards the front door. My father, Chuck, who was watching television with us in our living room, followed me. My wife continued to watch the horror of our property being attacked through our living-room window as I tried to open the door. It was double locked, for safety, and I had to rush to the bedroom in our bungalow to get my keys from the coat that I had carelessly thrown on the bed earlier that evening.

'They are at the door, Gary,' Alison screamed, 'they are trying to get in.' My hands trembled as I selected the appropriate keys and returned to the front door and I felt a rage pushing adrenaline through my body and an uninvited urge to hurt entered my heart. Anger clouded my senses and I tried to scan my house for weapons in my imagination but there was no time; I had to get that door open and meet the attackers head on.

Alison passed me in the corridor carrying our little boy Harry towards the back door to make their escape. Two windows popped and she grabbed the telephone from the wall and dialled 999. My father was inside the front door, eagerly waiting to help me defend our property.

When I opened the front door and ran outside my car was on fire and my alarm was ringing loudly but nobody was there. My wife later informed me that they had parked their getaway car at the bottom of the driveway and made good their escape before I could unlock my door.

My head was light and my stomach churned. Alison was screaming from behind our house and I began to run back to her. When the car exploded she threw herself on top of Harry to shield him from harm. I heard him ask Alison if he was going to die and through trembling lips she tried to reassure him and convince him that he was going to be all right.

Watching this scene unfold shook me in a way I hadn't thought possible. I picked them both up from the ground and held them in my arms and thanked God that we had survived. Harry was crying and shaking. His body was icy cold as he stood in the garden in his pyjamas, his tears masked by rain streaking down his face, and he looked up at me and demanded, 'Don't let them kill me, daddy.'

The fire brigade arrived. Fire-fighters tackled the blaze as we recounted the details of the attack to the officer in charge. When the fire was out the four of us stood in the garden waiting for what seemed like an eternity for the police to arrive.

My mum, Sandra, was with her siblings in my late grandmother's house in Rathcoole. My grandmother's body had been returned to her home and the funeral arrangements were being discussed when news of another attack on a member of my family reached her.

A few doors away from where my grandmother's body lay in her coffin in her house my disabled, pensioner uncle Geordie had come under attack at the exact same time that we had. His home was attacked by three car loads of masked men who informed him that he had four hours to get out of Rathcoole or be killed.

Rathcoole, for those who don't know, is a Loyalist housing estate just north of Belfast and for years it has been notable for high levels of para-military activity. Having recently survived a quadruple heart bypass it was hardly surprising that Geordie collapsed under the pressure of this incident and had to be rushed to hospital immediately.

Similarly, when I relayed this news to his brother Chuck, the stress and strain of our situation also proved too much for him and he felt faint and disorientated. We took him inside to wait for the police not realising that later that night Chuck would also find himself in intensive care.

Reliving the full devastating effects of this night over and over again has since made me feel terrible and ashamed because I allowed my instincts to rush me out of the house to confront the attackers. In hindsight I wish I had reacted like my wife. I feel a great deal of pride knowing that her instincts drove her towards safety rather than danger like mine.

I am ashamed to admit that I regretted locking my front door so well and that my mind was overwhelmed with a primal desire to wreak violence on the perpetrators. It is an ugly and regrettable admission that I felt cheated of an opportunity to hurt these people. I have sickened myself with thoughts of revenge ever since. I now thank God that He prevented me from getting through that door and also because I got an earlier flight home from London that day than I was booked on or I wouldn't have been in the house at all and my wife and little boy would have experienced this horrific ordeal alone.

Harry's eighth-birthday party had to be cancelled and Christmas was impossible. We had to rent temporary accommodation and continued to pay a mortgage for a bungalow we were not allowed to return to.

My brother Stephen is a Reverend and it is often to him that we would turn for support and luckily he always produces the words we need to help us find the strength to keep going in the faith. Did I mention he was a Rangers supporter? I often feel that his life is similarly conflicted to mine as he stands in his pulpit wrestling with demons and angels. I know of the inner turmoil that he suffers as a Rangers and Manchester United supporter.

That relationship would need a full chapter by itself. I often think of him with a beautiful Rangers angel on one shoulder urging him to do the right thing and that nasty, ugly Man U devil atop his other shoulder suggesting it is all right to cheat to win. That's a battle I don't envy him.

My grandmother's funeral was marred by the fact that we needed a police escort. The proceedings had to be altered against the dying wishes of my grandmother. Sadie always wanted to be buried from her home but instead we had to have the ceremony at a funeral parlour on the outskirts of Rathcoole. This added to the trauma and misery for the whole family.

The sad, depressing fact is that I have always known that within our community of ten thousand in Rathcoole, amongst the decent and respectable people, there have always lurked a dozen or so scumbags who have the capacity to take out their own frustrations on a seven-year-old boy and two disabled pensioners. They attacked my family because of what they'd heard about my plays, but if they think their actions will create an impotence in my work they are sadly mistaken: my weapons are not baseball bats and petrol bombs, they are words, and I have an abundance of them.

I am determined and resolute that long after the thuds of the baseball bats, the sparking of the flames and the exploding of the petrol bombs have been silenced my words will echo strongly and vibrantly in the hearts and minds of the millions of people around the world I have touched and had the privilege to entertain.

At this point it would be a reasonable question to ask what this story has to do with Rangers and why it should be in a book about Rangers. The answer is contained in what I omitted from the story. The people who attacked my house hid their faces behind Rangers scarves just like the men who attacked my Uncle Geordie's house. One man told Geordie the Mitchell family had four hours to get out of Rathcoole or be killed and he was wearing a Rangers top (probably counterfeit). The lad who shouted 'one Mitchell dead' at my grandmother's funeral was also wearing Rangers clothing as were the lads loitering around outside the funeral parlour making insulting gestures, trying to provoke a reaction, chanting and singing Loyalist songs.

These men and boys are no more Rangers supporters than they are Loyalists because while they were hiding their faces behind Rangers scarves the very team they claim to be supporters of were playing their most important match of the season on television in the living room of the people they attacked.

My wife has a history of screaming – when she sees a spider for example – therefore over the years, particularly when Rangers are playing live on television, I have developed the ability to block out her voice. Somewhere in the background of course my brain will still scan her words and decipher the code before returning the signal to my brain and engaging the appropriate response. This process will at best take me to full time or half-time and at least get me up until the ball goes out of play. Recent technological advances have now made it possible to pause a live football match with your Sky+ remote control but I find that, other than fast-forwarding the half-time commercials, I would rather not use it during a live Rangers game.

Particularly on a night history could be made. Rangers were as close to qualifying for the last sixteen of the Champions League as they had ever been or in fact as any Scottish club had ever been. So tonight the game had my complete attention. My father, Chuck, had been relegated to watching Liverpool in the bedroom but had decided to join me in the living room instead and my wife was supposed to be in the kitchen making something but had decided to keep Chuck company. Other possible intrusions had been minimised and so I felt completely relaxed and enthralled. Then came the screams.

Normally, I suppose I would have reacted faster; I suppose any husband would have reacted faster even if they did think it was going to be a false alarm but not me and not tonight. No, my brain very slowly ran the words over and over again but then Rangers surged forward and I think the message my brain sent me was, 'He's hitting the bar. Gary, they're on top, Rangers are on fire.'

I agreed with the sentiment of this wrongly decoded message and was glad that my wife had entered into the spirit of the occasion. I smiled a self-satisfied smile to myself and leaned forward in my chair, closer to the television, trying to suck in the atmosphere, but something was disturbing me, nagging at my subconscious mind.

A little voice piped up, 'Gary, your wife knows absolutely nothing about football. You married her for her looks, remember? She doesn't know what a bar is and couldn't possibly ever offer an opinion as to whether or not Rangers were on top and certainly would never, ever use the expression Rangers are on fire!'

Panic tore my eyes from the television screen and instinct picked me up from my seat, now I was really understanding what my wife was saying: somebody was on top of my fucking car and it was on fire.

I heard a roar and my mind's eye saw a white light of rage blurring everything. Did Rangers just score? Did Prso just score? Unanswered questions cutting at me like daggers as anger clouded my senses.

If these bastards have made me miss a Rangers goal I will do real damage to them was all I could think of. We all know the famous Bill Shankly, a Scotsman, quote that football is not a matter of life and death but much more important than that well I believe when you add Rangers into the mix this funny quip becomes reality.

I remember going to Dublin for the *Irish Times* Theatre Awards as my play, *In a Little World of Our Own*, had been nominated for three awards including Best New Play. When I won Best New Play I held the trophy high above my head and used my imagination to turn the Irish Catholic audience into a mix of Rangers supporters cheering me, and bitter Celtic supporters booing me, as we beat them in yet another cup final.

Earlier that evening when everybody predicted the award would go to an Irish Catholic writer who had written another play about the IRA I was reminded that Rangers once trailed by three goals to nil to Shelbourne in a preliminary round of the Champions League and I remembered the goals going in.

Travelling from Belfast to Dublin on the train even earlier would have been the first goal to Shelbourne as I met up with another nominee from Northern Ireland, a certain Owen McCafferty, who not only mocked my chances of winning but also went on to say that he had no chance of winning either and so Shelbourne took an early lead and my stomach felt sick as I relived that nightmare: 'How can Shelbourne be leading against the masters of football?' The world is upside down.

Having dinner in the beautiful auditorium I was told that people were taking bets on Best New Play and not a single person had bet on my play. I said I would take the bet and a ripple of laughter went around the spectacular hall and Shelbourne went two up. I could see my fellow players bowing their heads as we made our way back to the semi-circle to kick-off again. There was my director, nominated for Best Director for my play, and representatives of the actor, Lalor Roddy, also nominated for Best Actor for his performance as Walter in my play, and everyone agreed this night was a disaster and it was no real surprise when the third goal went in.

Half-time came and I took my customary trip to the toilet and dreamed of the second-half comeback that broke all those Shelbourne hearts as they ripped defeat fiercely from the jaws of victory.

I returned from the toilet as the second half got under way with an immediate reply from Rangers. We pulled one back, Conall Morrison won best director for directing my play and I thought this isn't over yet and Shelbourne mouths stopped singing and as panic raged through every one of them, the envelope was torn open and Lalor Roddy was revealed as the Best Actor for my play, now we're only three-two down and back in the game.

The nominations for Best New Play were read out and I was the only Protestant writer named. As each nominee was announced they were clapped but when my name was called out it was met with a ripple of silence and I knew Rangers were away from home and facing a hostile crowd. Nerves jangled and my heart pounded as the envelope was ripped open and the name of the winner appeared in large letters in the giant screen behind the stage for all to see that the winner of the inaugural *Irish Times* Theatre Award for Best New Play was . . . Gary Mitchell for *In a Little World of Our Own* and it was like I had scored a hat-trick. Rangers won the match by five goals to three.

Rangers had performed so well that even the Shelbourne supporters stood and applauded as they left the pitch in jubilant celebrations and I clutched my *Irish Times* award to my chest and was applauded off the stage by the audience of celebrities and nominees.

I, like Rangers, have had many victories on foreign soil, including my film, *As the Beast Sleeps*, finishing third in the Prix Europa Award for Best European Television film and when I was told we could have won first place if the BBC had supplied subtitles as they do for all their other films I felt gutted and was reminded of perhaps the greatest Rangers European adventure in my lifetime when they were cheated of the Champions League by Marseille, who were later punished by UEFA, but no reward or rematch was offered to us.

Another Rangers link in that particular film is that when it was first performed as a stage play in Dublin, the Abbey Theatre had no problem purchasing the Rangers kits for the actors, nor the Rangers wallpaper that plays such an important role in establishing the characters of the play and their relationships. However, when we came to the television production, problems did arise.

The director was an Englishman with as much knowledge of football as he did of the political divide in Northern Ireland. He was asked at the Edinburgh Film Festival if there was anything he didn't want to be asked about his work on *As the Beast Sleeps* – described as an important investigation into the workings of Loyalist paramilitaries during the ceasefires of the late nineteen nineties – and he said, 'Steer clear of religion and politics and I will be all right.'

Scene one was to show the audience several important points. Two Loyalist football teams were playing against one another in the Saturday morning league and as one was called Rathcoole Rangers and the other was Rathfern Rangers, they both wore Rangers kits. The home team were to be dressed in Rangers home kit and the away team in Rangers away kit.

The setting of this was very important because not only does it show the world the central characters' allegiances and identify them with the Protestant half of Glasgow but also alludes to the in-house fighting between each paramilitary cell as a football analogy of the Loyalist feud. Further, it highlighted the fact that a lot of money was spent on these football teams, revealing again just how much money was to be made from racketeering.

The BBC, however, countered that the audience would be confused and would think that the play was set in Scotland and so they refused to purchase any Rangers kits and later tried to erase Rangers from the film entirely. Television audiences are so thick you understand. Funny that during the Holy Cross film there seemed to be an abundance of Celtic tops – was it really set in Glasgow?

I digress. I don't know when it started but when I was very young I would get this tingling feeling of excitement in the pit of my stomach that no amount of food would cease. If I heard the word Rangers in a sentence the hair on the back of my neck would rise. The blood pumping to and from my heart would race and the widest smile would spread across my face. This smile could only be removed if the word Rangers was immediately followed by the word nil. Thankfully, in my lifetime that was rare and it was more frequently followed by preferred words like two Celtic nil or three Aberdeen nil. The latter sounds like it should be all one word – Aberdeenil. Until I was eight I thought Hiberniannil was a team. Rangers one Celtic nil and Rangers two Celtic nil or even Rangers five Celtic nil have a certain rhythm only bested by the very greatest of British poets or the words Celtic nil Rangers three etc.

When Rangers win it is almost impossible to upset me. Many, many people have tried and failed. Not least of all actors turning up for rehearsals wearing T-shirts with IRA slogans on or Irish writing that I don't understand. Let me tell a story about a very talented actor, Mark O'Shea, famed for turning down the role of Richard in *In a Little World of Our Own* that made way for Colin Farrell's debut performance.

Kevin Spacey loved my play and took us all out to a private club. Spacey is as generous a man as he is astounding an actor. It is his meeting and showing interest in the very young Mr Farrell that is credited with the introduction in America to Joel Schumacher and eventual roles in *Phone Booth* etc. But if we can set one very fortunate and talented Irishman to the side we can finish the story of perhaps one of the unluckiest actors; enter stage left, Mark O'Shea, and more importantly his left leg.

During rehearsals for *In a Little World of Our Own* in Dublin Mark felt so upset at having to wear a Rangers shirt every day that he went and got a Celtic tattoo on his leg. I felt sorry for him, I mean he did have to sit and listen to me ranting on and on and on about how many leagues we have won etc . . . I can still hear him chanting something about Lisburn Lions but can't remember if that was something to do with an Irish League team or what? Did Celtic beat Lisburn Distillery one year? This would upset him enormously but something good must have happened because he did deliver a powerhouse performance as Richard. I believe he was unlucky not to pick up a Best Actor Award for it, and if every actor needed a Celtic tattoo to be that good then I would gladly facilitate it.

There is something wonderful about knowing that Rangers have won a match. It makes problems seem easily solved, weights are lighter and tasks accomplished with hardly any effort. When Rangers clinch a title, regularly in my lifetime, including the awesome nine in a row, I feel elevated to a Utopia where nothing can bring me down.

5 May 2007. Early kick-off Old Firm game. Celtic visit Ibrox with the league already won but Rangers still need three points to guarantee qualification to the Champions League. As if any of the teams needed extra incentive for this match.

Unlike the average supporter I live outside the city of my favourite football team. Thinking of Manchester United perhaps it doesn't even make me exceptional to say that I don't live in the same country as my favourite team but what does make me almost unique is that I work in theatre, television and radio drama as a scriptwriter and have done for the last seventeen years. In that time I have worked in Northern Ireland, Scotland, England, the Republic of Ireland, USA, Czech Republic and Canada and although I have worked with many Celtic supporters and of course supporters of lots of other teams I have never worked with another Rangers supporter.

Then we have the same old chicken-and-egg debate. Rangers' supporters don't get involved in the arts because the arts are against them or the arts are against Rangers' supporters because they don't get involved.

Back to match day, I wish I had enough money to go and see Rangers every week. If I could afford it I would travel all over Europe and in fact the rest of the world to watch them, but in reality I can afford to go only every now and again and that's it, so I have to be choosy.

Today isn't one of those days. The game is live on Setanta Ireland and I sit down to watch it with more than a little trepidation. My dad Chuck's warning still rings in my ears, 'If Setanta Ireland are paying for the Scottish Premier League then surely everything will be set up to help Celtic win it.' My Uncle Geordie adds quickly, 'Setanta Ireland are paying the wages of the referees so who do you think will get all the decisions, kid? Use your head.'

I remember similar voices and warnings, like Wee Rab, a heavily tattooed Loyalist, 'You might as well give your money straight to the IRA as pay them Fenian bastards to watch Rangers getting cheated,' or Hatchet Higgins, 'It's fixed, there's only one Irish team in Scotland, sure they fly the tricolour and everything and if the Irish have bought and paid for the league then . . . '

Yes, I think it is safe to say that Setanta is not the channel of choice in Loyalist areas but I am a Rangers addict and I need my fix on a regular basis. Surprisingly, I didn't have to hang around in a dodgy alleyway waiting on dark characters to slide me what I need in a brown package, it was just a phone call, an easily deniable phone call should Hatchet Higgins ever ask me if I did get that Setanta subscription from close quarters, like say, hatchet length . . .

The final say goes to Chuck who believes he qualifies as a Rangers supporter through his unequivocal loathing of Manchester United and constantly reminds every person, during every conversation remotely to do with soccer, that Martin Tyler said at the start of the game between Man U and Rangers that Manchester United were the biggest Catholic football team in the world and therefore this match meant more to Rangers than beating Celtic!

Let me talk you through some typical pre-match experiences. I get up, my wife gives me a Rangers vest, a set of Rangers pyjamas and a bib with Gers printed on it . . . not for me, for Rachel, my baby daughter, three days away from being five months old and as of yet hasn't experienced defeat to the other half of the Old Firm in her entire life. My heart pounds in my chest that today might be the first. I do everything I can to make sure

I am in the house by myself, alone, in peace in front of the television screen in the living room but somehow Alison, my wife, has managed to invite most of my family to dinner, most of her family to lunch and some of Harry's friends round to play with him in case he gets bored.

'How can he be bored with an Xbox, a Playstation, a Gamecube, an arcade thing and the other twelve million toys and games I bought him?' 'Santa brought me them toys,' Harry counters and I consider bursting his bubble there and then. Alison gives me a daring look and I scan the room for something else to burst. 'Listen kid,' his older brother David offers, 'it doesn't matter what fat, bearded man got you them the point is you shouldn't be bored.' 'Don't back me up.' I respond.

The point is kids should learn as early as possible how to watch a football match quietly, they should know that this skill will help them stay up late at night, almost every night in view of Sky's football coverage, because dads everywhere put everything off until after the football unless somebody makes too much noise or becomes a nuisance in any other way and it is up to bed immediately. I fondly remember one Saturday because of an early kick-off I brought bedtime forward to 1:15 p.m. and the boy went to bed during the half-time break. This also helps avoid the nonsense that the 'experts' spout in that time.

Another bone of contention among most Rangers fans is the fact that Setanta and Sky TV before them but mainly BBC Scotland always have an anti-Rangers commentary. Chuck explains:

> How come when Celtic are live on TV the commentators are always explaining what Celtic need to do and what is so good about Celtic's play or they go on and on about a Celtic player, his hair, his socks, the way he prefers his shirt in or out of his shorts . . . whenever Rangers are playing, however, the commentators prefer to focus on what the other team need to do to beat Rangers, what the other team should be doing and what possibility there is of an upset. They relish the idea of a little team beating Rangers but when Clyde thrashed Celtic all they could do was explain how Celtic weren't interested in winning this meaningless cup any more and preferred to concentrate on Europe!

I remember listening to a dozen Rangers supporters complaining one after another about each commentator and the overall bias against Rangers in the media. A row broke out as some of the supporters vehemently bickered about the one they thought was the worst.

So this build up on this day of the Old Firm clash has no big-match build up. Did I mention that when we are in the room we turn the sound down? I remember Geordie's delight when we taught him how to put the atmosphere of the crowd on the TV without the commentary. Loved it. 'Don't have to listen to those idiots any more. Now if only they could work out a way to drown the Celtic supporters.'

I think he meant drown out the singing and the noise and the chanting.

This build up has become increasingly routine for me, now that I am married and have a growing family. If I cast my mind back I remember a very different routine. We had to get up very early in the morning and make our way to the club. Some people would have carry-outs. I use the word people loosely. We wait for the coach to arrive to take us to the ferry and then we sing many, many songs on the way to the ferry.

The last time we did this I recall two idiots drinking as much as they could en route to the ferry. It was suggested that they would be drunk soon and could risk missing the match. 'Bullshit, I can drink all fucking day and night!' Tommy declared, the burly man emptying another tin into his big mouth as his weasel-faced friend Gordon backed him up: 'We could drink for Ireland dickhead.'

Robert, a gentleman from the supporters club, noticed some small children in the middle of the coach and the uneasiness of the parents prompted him to intervene:

'Lads keep it down and mind your language, there are kids present.'
'Fuck them.'
'Hey! That's enough,' Chuck joined in. 'You're not on the ferry yet'.
'Who the fuck are you?'

Within seconds Chuck is on his feet making his way towards the two pissed idiots. I am distracted by the fact that Chuck is not John Wayne but often mistakes himself for him, but before I could think of the words to persuade him to return to his seat my legs had somehow tricked me into following him towards the danger and luckily for them we were accompanied by two other very large men who explained that they had nephews and nieces on board and wouldn't hesitate to relieve the two drunks of their seats and tickets for the game. OK, that's not the words they used but it is the sentiment.

When we got off the ferry you could cut the tension with a knife, well not actually on the ferry because they only have those plastic knives but it was getting tense. The good and decent sensible contingent made their way to the cafeteria and indulged in breakfast or various other meals, although given the 'Irish' fry that I was presented with maybe the sensible people went somewhere else.

The now-drunk Rangers fans, probably the reason the ferries are only allowed to take one group of supporters and not mix or segregate them on the same boat, are upsetting just about everybody and I can't help but think how wrong it is that the world often identifies these idiots, like the ones who attacked my house, as typical examples of Rangers supporters when in reality these are the few and True Bluenoses are usually digni-fied, sober, intelligent, fair-minded, sporting people with a great sense of pride in their team, their community, their country and perhaps their country's relationships with other countries not least of all the Union and maybe most of all with Ulster – wee Northern Ireland.

7:84, the famous Scottish theatre company, did a fantastic production of my play, *Marching On*, and I was delighted that the audiences enjoyed it so much but the experience did bring up some unsettling stories. I remember an actor telling me a story about his son being bullied in school by Rangers supporters and so he decided that he and his son would support Celtic from that day forward.

That story upset me on so many levels but I was determined it wouldn't be repeated and so I sat with our Harry after the attacks and explained to him that any idiot can buy, borrow or steal a Rangers scarf but it doesn't make them a supporter. This wasn't enough, so I told him that I thought it would be a better idea to realise the ugliness of the individual involved rather than one particular attribute. He said, 'What the hell are you talking about?' I said, 'First of all, you're not allowed to say hell and secondly I'm trying to explain that if the worst, most evil, scumbag in the world was a Rangers supporter it wouldn't be a reason to stop supporting Rangers. The man isn't evil because he supports Rangers; he's just evil because of the evil that exists in his heart or his head.'

I went on trying to reason with the boy for another ten or fifteen minutes and somehow managed to bore him to sleep but at least I didn't allow the scum to put him off his favourite football team. I asked him, at breakfast the next day, if he understood what I meant and he said, 'Yes, even if a person is really, really boring and they support Rangers it doesn't mean I should stop supporting them just because a really boring person supports them.' I like to think he didn't mean me but I'm not 100 per cent sure.

One thing I am a hundred per cent sure of is that I can't stop supporting Rangers no matter what happens in life. It is in my blood, like a virus. Sometimes I wake up in the middle of the night just worrying about how they are going to turn things around during a bad spell. I try to solve a particular tactical problem or even think of typing a letter to the manager with some suggestions. Oh and sleep is impossible in the days immediately before or after an Old Firm derby. These games are of course much more important than European Cups, World Cups, eating, sleeping or anything else for that matter.

This can be illustrated by what I call the Bert Konterman syndrome. You must remember that for a person from Northern Ireland to visit Ibrox to watch the greatest team in the world it is not a simple thing, nor an inexpensive thing. Obtaining the tickets can be hard and match day involves getting up at a hideous time of the morning, a taxi to the supporters club, a coach to the ferry, a ferry to Scotland, the coach again to the ground or near the ground and a walk, sometimes a very long walk. On the rare occasions that Rangers lose the journey home can be incredibly bad.

The name Konterman and expletives, some obvious and some not so, condemning the hapless Dutchman to hell or torture were often used after a poor performance. I remember a two-nil home defeat to Dundee that really hurt. Rangers dominated the match, peppered the Dundee goal guarded by eleven men for eighty-eight minutes, but failed to score and in two breakaways Dundee punished us and the crowd, every man, woman and child blamed Konterman for both goals.

Another remarkable thing happened that day. Thousands of unhappy Rangers supporters were making their way home, as was I, when they were suddenly taunted by three Dundee supporters who enjoyed their moment in the sun a little too much for my taste. They danced, sang and laughed as we took the long walk of shame, at one point they even danced right up to the faces of the sullen Blue Noses and mocked them from inches.

I thought to myself, if this was Belfast and three football fans of any team did this to thousands of supporters of a losing team they wouldn't make it home alive and it hit me – losing with dignity – supporting your team with honour even after a defeat or a pathetic, disappointing performance is part and parcel of being a true supporter. A representative of a team should display the qualities they love most about their team.

Many more games followed and the singing of Konterman's name always rang out in derisory tones. He seemed more hated as each game went by and I couldn't find a single person to say anything nice about the man until one day it happened – the Konterman Syndrome – the Old Firm played in the League Cup and the big Dutchman scored a wonder goal (all goals against Celtic are wonder goals) and from that day on I never heard a bad word said about him. He became a hero!

I have been working in the arts for seventeen years now and I have yet to work on a project with another 'true' Rangers supporter. I have worked with people who would claim that Rangers are their favourite team in Scotland but for 99 per cent of the people I have worked with Rangers are not even their favourite team in Glasgow.

This can lead to problems when Rangers or supporting Rangers becomes the focus of a scene. This brings me to my play *Marching On* and the problems that occurred during rehearsals for the Lyric Theatre, Belfast's production. A person representing the board came into a meeting and said that there were problems with the make up of the cast as four of the actors were Protestant and only two were Catholic.

I knew that we had been very thorough in casting the play and in trying to make sure we did everything 50–50 as is the norm in Northern Ireland now but somehow the religious make-up of the cast was unbalanced by an actor called Sean. Unlike Sean Connery this man was a Protestant even though he shared the same support for most things the famous actor did. Although, if anybody can match Connery for his ability to tackle any accent in the world, I would like to meet him. However, each tackle seems more akin to a violent assault the like of which you might expect to see from Hartson or Lennon as they foul yet another Rangers player from behind and go unpunished and Connery once more proves a master of the Scottish accent. I remember my Uncle Fra explaining that every time he eats a meat he hasn't tasted before he thinks it tastes exactly like chicken and every time he hears Sean Connery do an accent he hasn't heard before it somehow sounds like Scottish! Fra loved him anyway as most people do.

Back to my particular actor called Sean and a remarkable story that he often tells when asked why he changed his name to Sean. He explained to me, 'My dear boy, when I was a young Protestant trying to break into the world of theatre I had no success at all despite my very obvious abundance of talent. However, when I changed Jimmy to Sean and was a Protestant no more the jobs just kept coming.'

It was suggested that as Stuart Graham was directing the play and his wife was his assistant, and I had written it, the religious breakdown was now seven to two and something should be done in the interest of fair employment and equality, I was urged to understand. I suggested we go to the papers immediately and tell them of this travesty and while we were at it we should provide them and the public with a religious breakdown of every play performed in the Lyric Theatre over the last ten years and . . . the matter was dropped.

Let me conclude this particular chapter by saying that I hope I have offered a fair view of what it means to me to be a True Blue Rangers supporter and if I haven't then perhaps the final words will do the job. People who break the law or behave questionably should be shunned for those reasons and no matter what club, Celtic included, they claim to support; the club itself should not have to be punished or lose support for the actions of these people.

The Battle of Britain will not be fought with sticks and stones or guns and knives because that battle is over and remains only in our memories. Northern Ireland still hold the champions of Britain title as we were the last team to win the home internationals before the English cancelled them claiming they were too easy. Was this the same England who suggested the rest of the world play the World Cup and then the winners should come to Wembley to play England to see who the greatest team in the world is? Most Northern Ireland supporters are also Scotland supporters, it should be noted, so any victory for either over the English will do.

In terms of club football the Battle of Britain took place at Ibrox and

Elland Road when Rangers beat the Premier League champions over two legs, in both legs 2–1, to complete a satisfactory 4–2 humiliation. This I like to feel I have replicated in my work.

At home I feel I have lost a goal; since Robert Cooper, producer of *As the Beast Sleeps*, left BBC Northern Ireland I consider it a personal failure that I have not been able to persuade BBC NI to make any dramas in Northern Ireland about the Protestant community of Northern Ireland by a Protestant. 0–1. I did win Best Short Film for *Suffering*, I was writer and director of this nine-minute film, at the Belfast Film Festival, 1–1, and then most recently I won the prestigious Aisling Award for Outstanding Achievement in Culture and Arts for my play *Remnants of Fear*: 2–1 to Rangers.

Of course it was easy for Rangers to beat Leeds at Ibrox in the first leg and so as many would say of me it was easy to win awards in Belfast but the reality was very different. The English always put up a hard fight and remember the ball doesn't have to cross the line for the English to win. Or, as in Man United's case, even if the ball does cross the line by some distance, it doesn't necessarily mean you have scored against the English team.

So, the second leg brought me to England and I was appointed writer-in-residence at the National Theatre of Great Britain and Northern Ireland, 1–0 us. I failed to get my work onto Channel Four, 1–1, but then I did win the inaugural Charles Wintour Award for Most Promising Playwright (£30,000). It was for my play, *The Force of Change*, and that completed the two-one away victory and like Rangers, with the greatest respect of our opponents in mind, I must proclaim victory at the Battle of Britain!

Rangers and the Ulster Scots

Chris Williamson

As the title would suggest, the aim of this chapter is to establish whether a credible link exists between Ulster-Scots identity and the Rangers Football Club. It is necessary to ascertain exactly who the Ulster-Scots are, and what their unique contribution to history has been, and the first section is therefore devoted to that task. More importantly, in the wider context of this book, the latter part of the chapter will seek to answer why some Rangers fans are so keen to promote the Ulster-Scots culture, while seeking to determine whether official promotion of the Ulster-Scots by the club would be worthwhile.

Over the past fifteen years or so there has been a marked resurgence in Northern Ireland of the Ulster-Scots language and culture. The motivations of the great majority of people in this movement have been non-sectarian and non-political; yet, perhaps inevitably, the Ulster-Scots have become identified with the Unionist and Protestant side of the political divide. Indeed, the Ulster-Scots culture has provided a cultural confidence boost to a community that is often told by Republicans and enthusiasts for the Irish language and culture that they have no culture. In the Belfast Agreement of 1998 the Ulster-Scots language was given recognition, and there have been many educational projects around it, and media attention paid to it, since then. (The terms Ulster-Scots, Scots-Irish, and Scotch-Irish are interchangeable throughout this chapter. As Billy Kennedy notes the latter term, 'now causes offence to many of the Scots-Irish tradition in Britain and America where "Scotch" is looked upon as an alcoholic spirit,' but adds that the name, 'has an historical reality and utility.'[1] Quotations below using this phrase remain unchanged.)

According to Ron Chepesiuk, 'the Scotch-Irish story is not well known.'[2]

Mark Thompson, chairman of the Ulster-Scots Agency, maintains that, 'for too long we have forgotten our own story; we should be proud to learn it – and to share it with others.'[3] The Ulster-Scots played a substantial role in the development of the United States of America, but that achievement is 'not as widely known in modern-day society as it should be.'[4] The context of the Ulster-Scots needs to be determined and the historical factors that shaped them examined.

An Ulster-Scot is someone whose lineage can be traced to the Scottish settlers who arrived in the north of Ireland in the seventeenth century. With passing years some returned home, others remained in Ulster, while yet more emigrated to North America, Australia, New Zealand and Argentina. They were mostly, though not exclusively, Presbyterians, characterised by their unyielding faith, determination and pioneering tendencies. Maude Glasgow describes them as, 'self-denying and industrious,'[5] claiming that they had a spirit of 'self-respect and self-reliance and devotion to what was right rather than what was expedient'.[6] Their contributions to Ulster and North America are immeasurable.

At the beginning of the seventeenth century, Ireland was subject to the English Crown, but establishing authority over the northern province was troublesome, with the indigenous population in an almost perpetual state of rebellion. James I (V1 of Scotland), who succeeded Elizabeth in 1603, intended planting Ulster with loyal and reliable Protestant settlers from England, to reduce the likelihood of further uprisings. Following the Flight of the Earls in 1607, the Crown confiscated all land in counties Donegal, Coleraine (later to be renamed Londonderry), Tyrone, Fermanagh, Armagh and Cavan. This redistribution of land among English settlers would establish new towns and garrisons. The new landowners were banned from selling land to the Irish or taking them as tenants. Implementation proved difficult as insufficient numbers of settlers arrived from England. The reasons for the low numbers of English settlers in Ulster were twofold. Recruiting settlers and investors for Ireland was unattractive. Rory Fitzpatrick suggests that 'it was not easy to persuade English landowners to invest in Ireland, a place with a reputation for fighting, rain and the unreliability of its inhabitants.'[7] The Plantation of Virginia at Jamestown, taking place at around the same time, deprived Ulster of thousands of potential English settlers and proved a more attractive

The visit of Moscow Dynamo to Ibrox in November 1945 proved an enthralling prospect for a nation recovering from six years of all-out war. A crowd of 95,000 turned out and witnessed a 2–2 draw. In this photograph the Soviet side's legendary goalkeeper, Alexei 'Tiger' Khomich, foils a Rangers attack.

(courtesy PA Photos)

Davie Meiklejohn (*right*) was one of Rangers' greatest-ever captains.
He won an impressive twelve league titles and five Scottish Cups during his
Ibrox career, but is perhaps best remembered for scoring the opening goal,
a penalty, in the 1928 Scottish Cup final against Celtic. Rangers went on
to win 4–0, ending the so-called 'Hampden Hoodoo' that had seen
the club fail to win the Cup for twenty-five years.

(courtesy PA Photos)

Reverend James Currie (*with arms aloft*), who was minister of St James's church in Pollok. Although he never had an official position at Ibrox he became 'the public face of the Rangers support' in the 1970s and 1980s. His closeness to the club brought him into conflict with ministers in other quarters of the Church of Scotland, who 'at this time viewed Rangers with suspicion and even outright hostility'.

(courtesy Newsquest Media Group)

The iconic grandstand at Ibrox stadium, designed by the renowned Scottish architect, Archibald Leitch. The stand, which opened in 1929, was '. . . a powerful statement: an aspiration to greatness and world renown, which the club has largely fufilled'. It is pictured here in 1965, when Rangers' pre-eminence in the Scottish game was unquestionable.

(courtesy SNSpix)

Old Firm games are always keenly contested, but most players report
that there was always great respect shown in the heat of battle.
In an encounter from 1981 two of this book's contributors,
John MacDonald (*left*) of Rangers and Davie Provan of Celtic
(a boyhood Rangers supporter), tussle for the ball.

(courtesy SNS pix)

The Orange Order marching in Glasgow city centre in 2005.
For many years the Order conducted its Annual Divine Service
at Ibrox stadium and although the service is now held elsewhere
most of its members '. . . must be, if not Rangers supporters,
then Rangers sympathisers'.

(courtesy Newsquest Media Group)

The transfer of Maurice Johnston (*second right*) to Rangers in July 1989 was the most important in the history of Scottish football. At a stroke, chairman David Murray (*seated*) and manager Graeme Souness (*far right*) swept away the club's Protestant-only policy. (courtesy Eric McCowat)

When Dick Advocaat was manager Rangers underwent a process of 'Dutch-isation', according to one of the contributors to this book. The process reached its apotheosis in the Scottish Cup final of 2000, the so-called 'day of orange'. (courtesy Eric McCowat)

investment. Initially the Scots, given the invitation to participate in the plantation in 1609, were also slow to journey to Ulster. However, following the introduction of a new system of land tenure to Scotland in 1610 – which saw many Scottish farmers being dispossessed of their land and forced into working as hired labourers – movement increased. 'Thus, the thought of moving to Ireland and getting a new lease on life appealed to many'. [8] Within a relatively short space of time, Scots settlers established themselves as the majority community in the province. These dispossessed were not the first. They found that Scottish settlers had arrived in East Ulster as the result of private ventures headed by two enterprising Ayrshire lairds. In 1605 Hugh Montgomery and James Hamilton had managed to acquire land belonging to the Irish chieftain Con O'Neill, in exchange for breaking him out of jail and obtaining his pardon. Montgomery and Hamilton returned to the Scottish lowlands to recruit settlers; they were very successful, and before long there was a steady movement of people from the south-west of Scotland to counties Antrim and Down. Once established, these settlers then persuaded friends and relatives to come; within ten years of the first settlement, an estimated eight-thousand settlers were resident in the two counties. They became the beachhead on which thousands of Scottish settlers made their way to the north of Ireland during the seventeenth century.[9] Ulster was fertile and under used. It had woods where there was abundant game, plentiful fish in both rivers and sea, serving the settlers for food until their first harvest. Importantly, for the settler, with Ulster and Scotland fifteen miles apart at the shortest crossing point, 'the move would not mean a complete break with his past, since contact with families and their hometowns could be easily maintained'.[10]

By mid seventeenth century, there were an estimated 100,000 Scottish settlers in Ulster, compared with 20,000 English, [11] with many more to come later in the century. Fitzpatrick states that 'the Scots dominated the settlement from the beginning. Their numbers were greater and they were better suited by temperament to the task. In the hard early years the whole enterprise would have collapsed if the hard-working Scots had not provided the food supplies.'[12] Their success was partly attributed to Presbyterianism: it instilled in them fundamental values such as 'a total reverence for the Almighty, deep devotion to their families, sincere love of country and a passionate belief in their liberty'. [13] It was considered a duty to work hard and be successful.

In Ulster they were also free to practise their religion.[14] However, such freedom did not last, and their prospects looked bleak when Charles I succeeded James in 1625. Charles forced the *Book of Common Prayer* onto Scotland in 1637 and, 'declared opposition to the new liturgy as treason'. [15] The Presbyterian Scots' devotion to their beliefs meant that they would not accept the new prayer book. In response to this, and to the earlier introduction of the *Book of Canons*, the National Covenant was drawn up in February 1638 and within months had been signed by 300,000 Scots. The Covenant affirmed, 'loyalty to the monarch, [but] it nevertheless firmly restated the direct relationship between the people and God, with no interference from the king'. [16] Presbyterians in Ulster showed solidarity with their Scottish brethren with many adding their signatures to the Covenant. This angered Charles, who ordered an army to Ireland 'to enforce a counter-pledge . . . on all males over sixteen swearing them to "renounce and abjure all Covenants, oaths and bonds whatsoever". Many fled back to Scotland rather than take the oath.' [17] The penalties for refusing to swear this 'Black Oath' were severe. [18]

Resentment, in Ulster and elsewhere, eventually boiled over with the British Isles being thrown into the Wars of the Three Kingdoms. Charles's attempts to overcome Scottish resistance were thwarted by the English Parliament's refusal to grant him funds to raise an army. Charles threatened to raise an Irish Catholic army to put down the Scots. The Covenanters retaliated by intimating that they would pre-emptively deal with such a threat by invading Ireland, which in turn led to the native Irish launching a rebellion in 1641. The threat of an Irish uprising was a constant in the settlers' thoughts, and the Ulster-Scots had to live with the daily scourge of the Irish who, 'reverted to guerrilla tactics of plundering the countryside and conducting sneak attacks on the settlements'. [19] The 1641 rebellion, planned more as a coup d'etat, was foiled in Dublin when an informant alerted the authorities, who arrested two leaders. Phelim O'Neill went ahead with his planned rebellion in the north but lost control of the rank and file, who went on to butcher the settlers. Initially, they attacked the English, but soon they turned their attentions to the Scots. An estimated 12,000 lost their lives while huge numbers fled back to Scotland. Charles I was executed at the conclusion of the English Civil War in 1649. The Lord Protector, Oliver Cromwell, unleashed his New Model Army on Ireland and put an end to the Wars of the Confederates in 1652.

The wars had, according to Chepesiuk, 'led to further strengthening of the bond between the Ulster community and Scotland.' [20] A ten-thousand-strong Covenanter army came to Ulster in the aftermath of the rebellion, offering protection to their Ulster brethren. The Covenanters brought with them a number of Presbyterian ministers, and they established the first Presbyterian church in Ireland, at Carrickfergus, in 1642. Some of these ministers remained in Ulster after the war, actively encouraged to do so by Henry Cromwell, who offered Presbyterian ministers stipends of £100, with the result that, by 1660, the number of Presbyterian ministers had increased in seven years from sixty-four to seventy in the province, with over eighty parishes and 100,000 adherents.[21]

Following Cromwell's death and the restoration of the monarchy, the Ulster-Scots again faced persecution. Charles II had sworn to uphold the Solemn League and Covenant in 1650, but reneged on this oath upon taking the throne. In 1661, he imposed the Act of Uniformity under which all worshippers 'were to use the *Book of Common Prayer* under pain of deprivation.'[22] Ministers who had not been ordained according to Episcopalian rituals were subject to fines of £500 if they were found administering the sacrament and, 'anyone who by word or deed defended the Covenant should be deemed an enemy to his sacred majesty, the public peace and the church'. [23] In Ulster only seven obeyed the decree. Charles eventually softened his stance towards the Ulster Presbyterians as the 1660s wore on. In 1672 he introduced the Regium Donum, a state grant gifted to Presbyterian ministers. Presbyterians in Scotland were less fortunate. They were subject to the 'Black Act' of 1670, whereby field preaching was punishable by death. They were harassed while in the act of worship and many were hanged, tortured or imprisoned. [24] Worse followed in 1681 when the Test Act was passed: it instructed Covenanters to renounce their Presbyterianism and to accept that the king was the supreme authority in all church and civil matters. Not surprisingly, 'this was too much for the Covenanters. The religious situation in Ireland seemed good compared with their treatment and so thousands of Scots migrated in the early 1680s.' [25]

Charles II died in 1685 and James II, his brother, came to the throne. James had converted to Roman Catholicism sixteen years earlier. He faced an early threat to the throne from the Duke of Monmouth, which, though quickly and ruthlessly suppressed, resulted in James fearing future rebellions and making unpopular decisions in order to protect his interests. In Ireland James placed the anti-Protestant Earl of Tyrconnell at the head of the army. Within a short period of time the Irish forces had been purged of between two and three hundred Protestant officers and an estimated seven thousand from the rank and file. When promoted to Lord Deputy of Ireland, Tyrconnell further alarmed Protestants by removing them from positions of control and replacing them with Roman Catholics. Meanwhile, in England, James expanded his standing army and put Catholic officers in charge of several regiments. This was a highly un-popular move and brought James into direct conflict with Parliament. His response to this protest was to prorogue Parliament and rule without it. James continued to alienate his subjects, 'by dismissing judges and Lord Lieutenants who refused to support the withdrawal of laws penalizing religious dissidents, [and by] appointing Catholics to important academic posts, and to senior military and political positions'.[26] Therefore, when Queen Mary gave birth to a male heir in the middle of 1688, fears of a Roman Catholic dynasty were at fever pitch. At the end of June 1688, The Immortal Seven, a group of Protestant nobles, requested that William, Prince of Orange depose James as monarch. William landed in Torbay in November that year and quickly received the support of the English army and navy. James fled to France whereupon a Convention of Parliament ruled that he had abdicated. William and his wife, Mary (James's daughter), were proclaimed King and Queen in early 1689. Louis XIV of France supported James's attempts to regain the English throne and provided him with the troops and finances to take on William. Ireland was to be the battlefield, and it was there that the Ulster-Scots proved their mettle once again.

By November 1688 the Irish army was under Tyrconnell's command, its ranks swelled by Catholics. Tyrconnel came to the walled city of Londonderry thinking he would enter unhindered because the Bishop of Lonndonderry, Ezekiel Hopkins, maintained that James was the lawful king. Tyrconnell ordered the Earl of Antrim to replace the Protestant garrison there with men loyal to James. When his Redshanks, 1,200-strong, were almost upon the city, thirteen apprentice boys shut the gates in the faces of the Jacobite army. James, landing at Kinsale on 12 March 1689 with 6,000 French soldiers, marched north, arriving at Derry on 18 April. James from outside the walls demanded that the gates be opened. Cries of 'no surrender' were accompanied by a volley of shots, which killed two of James's soldiers and left him in no doubt as to the determination of those inside.[27] The Siege of Derry had begun and it lasted 105 days, during which time the citizens came under a barrage of mortars from the Jacobite forces whilst also having to deal with food shortages and the spread of disease. A boom was constructed across the river Foyle to prevent ships relieving the city. By the time this was broken by Mountjoy on 28 July 1689, an estimated 4,000 people had lost their lives to starvation, injury or disease. The Ulster-Scot Presbyterians claimed to have outnumbered the Anglican defenders at the Siege of Derry by a ratio of fifteen to one.[28] Among those in the forefront was Colonel Adam Murray. Murray's family originated from Selkirkshire before settling in Ling, nine miles from Londonderry, in 1648. His involvement during the Siege of Derry has gone down in legend:

> Colonel Murray raised a troop of horsemen among his neigh-
> bours and mobilised them to defend Londonderry when the
> siege began . . . Murray was welcomed by the citizens as they
> saw in him a strong character who . . . would not compro-
> mise. He immediately set about strengthening the resolve of
> the citizens to resist and he is credited with fostering the 'no
> surrender' spirit.[29]

Murray, who was shot through both thighs while venturing outside the city's walls to engage the enemy, is revered as the model Ulster-Scot: determined, brave, prepared to do what he believes is right even if it is not the easy option.

After the triumph of the Williamite forces was complete James fled the island, an act of cowardice that saw him dubbed 'James the excrement' by the native Irish. During the fighting in Ulster, the Presbyterians were to the fore. 'King William recognized the Scotch-Irish contribution and, in gratitude, he gave them more religious freedom than they had known in years.'[30] Many Scots who had left in the wake of Tyrconnell's anti-Protestant policies returned with a new generation of Scottish settlers. 'Between 1690 and 1697, an estimated fifty thousand Scots emigrated across the North Channel, settling mainly in Ulster.'[31] This period of relative calm for the Ulster-Scots was short-lived and ended after William's death in 1702. Queen Anne took the throne insisting on religious conformity under the control of the High Church. The Test Act of 1704 required, 'every person holding an office under the crown to take communion in the established church within three months of his appointment, failure to comply being regarded as the vacating of office'[32] Of course, the Presbyterians in Ulster did not submit to this and as a result the entire city government in Belfast was thrown out of office whilst in Londonderry the Act, 'drove out of the corporation . . . several of the very men who had fought through the siege of 1689'.[33] Presbyterian ministers now found themselves operating outside the law. Marriages they presided over were declared null and void, and husbands and wives were prosecuted as fornicators and their children declared illegitimate.

It was not only in religious affairs that the Ulster-Scots experienced hardship. The tens of thousands of immigrants who had arrived from Scotland in the 1690s did so with the incentive of cheap land and long leases. When these leases began to expire in the 1710s, however, landowners raised their rents by upwards of 100 per cent. This practice, of 'rack-renting', was sheer greed on the part of the landlords, who cared little for the welfare of their tenants who, as James G. Leyburn records, had toiled to transform the land.[34] Tenants who refused to pay were summarily evicted and 'the mood of the Protestant Ulstermen had changed from optimism to gloom.'[35] These unfavourable religious and economic conditions persuaded the Ulster-Scots to pursue a better life elsewhere and from 1717 they began to move in large numbers from Ulster to the New World.

There were five distinct waves of Ulster-Scots emigration during the eighteenth century.[36] Behind each wave were a combination of factors which made the decision to leave all the easier. Drought, smallpox and famine all spurred mass emigration. It is difficult to say to for certain how many Ulster-Scots actually made their way across the Atlantic during the eighteenth century, but it probably numbered between two- and three-hundred thousand.[37]

To pay for their passage, many emigrants went to America as indent-ured servants, enduring a period of contracted service once they reached American shores. For the Ulster-Scots, this was not a demeaning state of affairs; 'they saw it as a temporary loss of freedom,'[38] and while 'judged by modern standards, the bartering of a transatlantic passage for years of servitude is reprehensible, such servitude was the foundation on which many who endured it built a more successful life than would have been possible in Ireland.'[39] They were now in a place where 'a man could practice his religion without any restrictions'[40], and this made the undoubted hardships easier to bear.

The Ulster-Scots' contribution to the development of North America in the eighteenth century was immense. These frontiersmen were indis-pensable to the British in wars against the French but they later turned on the mother country in the American Revolution. In the War of Independence they were acknowledged as the most effective element in George Washington's patriot army.[41] The Ulster-Scots were to furnish no fewer than seventeen American presidents,[42] and provide a crucial impetus for educational progress. Among the numerous institutions they founded was Princeton University. Jackson argues that 'many of the characteristics with which Americans have been identified through the years, pragmatism, love of success, reform impulses, they acquired in part from these pioneering Scotch-Irish immigrants'.[43]

It is clear that the Ulster-Scots were a proud and determined people who faced persecution, refused to be cowed by it and went on to shape what would become the world's most powerful nation. But what exactly does all of the aforementioned have to do with a Glaswegian sporting institution formed towards the end of the nineteenth century? Rangers have undeniable ties to post-Plantation Ulster, ties that go back to the founding of the club. Rangers were formed in 1872 by four teenagers: Moses and Peter McNeil, Peter Campbell and William McBeath. The McNeil brothers were Ulster-Scots. Their mother, Jean Bain, hailed from County Down but moved to Scotland where she married John McNeil (from Comrie, Perthshire) and gave birth to Peter and Moses in 1854 and 1855 respectively. As Billy Kennedy attests: 'The Northern Ireland connection with The Rangers in Glasgow is far-reaching and the tens of thousands of Gers supporters in the Province will take a very special pride in the knowledge that [among the] founders of the Club were the sons of an Ulster woman.' [44]

Rangers have a large fan base in Northern Ireland and, at a conservative estimate, approximately two thousand make the trip across the North Channel every other Saturday to take in a game at Ibrox. Even back in the 1950s and 1960s, the Ulster football journalist Malcolm Brodie (a Glaswegian by birth) contributed regular articles about the club's popularity 'ower the sheuch' to the Rangers Supporters' Association annuals. It is surprising then that so few Northern Irish players have represented the club professionally and it is nigh-on impossible to determine the reasons. Was it simply poor, or non-existent, scouting that led to the likes of George Best, Danny Blanchflower, Bertie Peacock, Sammy McIlroy, Norman Whiteside and, more recently, David Healy, Aaron Hughes, Johnny Evans and Steve Davis, slipping through the net? Perhaps the lure of English football was too strong. Whatever the reasons, Rangers – now hampered by the pittance received in television rights in comparison to clubs in England, Italy and Spain – could certainly now do worse than expand scouting and youth coaching in Ulster as they look to build a home-grown squad that can dominate the Scottish game and make an impression in Europe.

Those from Ulster who have pulled on the royal blue jersey are: Bertie Manderson, Billy McCandless, Billy Simpson, Bob McDonald, John McClelland, Bob Hamilton, Jimmy Nicholl, Sam English, Albert Lyness, John Morrow, Paul McKnight, Stephen Carson, Darren Fitzgerald and Lee Feeney. (In addition, Alex Stevenson, Alex Caig, Jimmy McAuley, all of whom were born in what is now the Republic of Ireland, also spent time with the Govan club.) Rangers currently have one Northern Irish youngster on their books, eighteen-year-old Andy Little, a striker who hails from County Fermanagh and who joined the club in the summer of 2006. Of the aforementioned, Manderson, McCandless, English and Simpson were heroes to the Rangers fans. Manderson signed for Rangers in 1915 and went on to play 452 times for the Ibrox club before transferring to Bradford Park Avenue in 1927. He was regularly partnered in the Rangers defence by McCandless, previously of Linfield. Their former teammate, Tommy Muirhead, described them as, 'a fine pair of full-backs, both Ulstermen but of contrasting styles, Manderson was very fast, while

McCandless was more studied, always in control'. [45] Billy Simpson, like Manderson, has been inaugurated into the Rangers Hall of Fame and is fondly remembered by Rangers fans of a certain vintage. Simpson transferred to Rangers from Linfield on 19 October 1950 for a then record fee of £11,500. He scored 163 goals in 239 games in a Rangers career that spanned eleven years. Sam English holds the record for most league goals scored by a Rangers player in one season, forty-four in 1930/31. [46]

It is of course unfortunate that Sam English will always be remembered for an incident during an Old Firm game in September 1931, which resulted in the Celtic goalkeeper, John Thomson, losing his life. English was on the attack for Rangers when Thomson dived bravely at his feet, his head colliding with English's knee. The seriousness of the incident was immediately apparent to the players on the field. Thomson was stretchered from the pitch but never regained consciousness. 'The tragedy had a profound long-term effect on the career of Rangers player Sam English,' wrote Ferrier and McElroy. In truth the cumulative effect of the events of 5 September 1931, and of the unnecessary and wholly irresponsible comment of Celtic manager Willie Maley at the subsequent hearing – 'I hope it was an accident' – haunted English for the rest of his life, even though he was fully exonerated of any blame, both by the enquiry and by those flickering black-and-white images of the incident, which clearly illustrate that it was the unfortunate Thomson's own forward momentum which caused his head to strike the knee of the Rangers forward. [47] A wall mural featuring Sam English and dedicated to the exploits of the Ulstermen who have played for Rangers down the years stands proudly in the Ravenhill Road area of east Belfast.

But are these ties enough to say that Rangers are an Ulster-Scots club? On one level the answer would be 'no'. According to Jeff Randall, editor-at-large of the *Daily Telegraph*, Rangers are the 'quintessential British club', as he explains:

> Quintessential means the very essence, something in its purest form. And the thing about Rangers, it is based in Scotland, but first and foremost it is a British club. A lot of fans come over from Northern Ireland to support Rangers, and a lot of English fans too. Like Barcelona, it is *mas que un*

> *club* [more than a club]: it stands for something in society. It embraces the whole concept of the Union of the United Kingdom, and if you go to Ibrox you'll see the Union Flag is the one flying highest above the stadium.' (telegraph.co.uk, 'The Best of British', viewed 12 March 2007).

In general Rangers fans are comfortable with displays of support for the Union, but there are a number who would argue that the club is, in fact, quintessentially Scottish within a British context. Historically, the Ulster-Scots were more than willing to stand up to the Crown when they felt it necessary. So the question of how Rangers fans can proudly wave the Union flag while attempting to celebrate the cause of men who battled against the Crown must be addressed. As we have seen, the Covenanters were always ready to affirm their loyalty to the Crown provided that the monarch did not attempt to interfere in matters of religion. Clearly, the Covenanting Ulster-Scots were not proponents of blind loyalty; for them the relationship with authority figures was one of give and take. If the monarch was willing to trust his subjects, and allow them the freedoms that today we take for granted, then his subjects would repay him with their loyalty. What they would not stand for was an infringement of their God-given rights, and when these were threatened they vented their anger. Such principles are clearly deemed worthy of praise by many Rangers fans, who see no contradiction in their being pro-monarchy and supporters of the Union while promoting the achievements of the Ulster-Scots, and honouring the epic history of the Covenanters.

The waters of Rangers' identity as a purely Scottish club have been muddied further by the rise of Scottish Nationalism and the alienation certain Rangers fans feel from the Scottish Football Association and the national team. While for many years, at least up to the 1970s, the Rangers fans formed the backbone of the Scotland support, it is now the case that many feel uncomfortable with recent trends. The SFA has done little to endear itself to Rangers in recent years, be it through their continued refusal to offer Ibrox up as a potential venue for a European club final, or the appointment of Neil Simpson as a community coach (the argument being that a player best known for an infamous tackle on a fellow professional should not be promoted as a role model for children).

Furthermore, some members of the Tartan Army are not slow to voice their hatred of Rangers (note how Brian Laudrup was jeered when representing Denmark against Scotland at Ibrox in 1998), and their dislike of anything English, while claiming the St Andrew's Cross as their own and flying it as a symbol of Scottish Nationalism. Understandably, a growing number of Rangers fans are now more inclined to channel their energies into following club rather than country.

Unfortunately, a minority of Rangers supporters have overcompensated. The recent fad of Scottish-born Rangers fans wearing England shirts is one example of this. Though confined to a handful of supporters, it is on the same level as the 'plastic Paddies' at Parkhead, who insist on wearing Republic of Ireland jerseys. On the other hand, the Blue Order fan group and the club have recently organised successful displays of both the Union and Saltire flags and some Rangers fans have always been happy to wave the Saltire. The majority of Scottish Rangers fans apparently welcome the display of symbols relating to the close links between the people of Scotland and Ulster. That long-standing relationship was undoubtedly the inspiration behind the production of a magnificent Ulster-Scots banner that made its debut at Ibrox during the 2006/07 season. The flag is highly symbolic: it features a St Andrew's Cross, with a smaller Ulster banner in the centre and a pair of intertwined thistles and orange lilies in two of the quadrants. Unsurprisingly, the display of the flag caused a minor controversy. The Scottish media have been quick to label as bigoted any connection between Rangers and their fan base in Ulster, to such an extent that the club often appears embarrassed by its supporters from over the water. Admittedly, the demonisation of Protestants in Northern Ireland goes wider than football, with a female politician[48] and a priest [49] comparing Ulster Protestants to Nazis and a serially offended university lecturer attempting to portray an Ulster-born children's television presenter as a bigot for daring to incorporate the Red Hand into a broadcast [50] (with said lecturer embarrassingly forgetting that he had previously stated that the Red Hand was a symbol used by both sides of the community in Northern Ireland)[51].

While Celtic can play the Irish card, with few dissenting voices amongst the Scottish media, Rangers are condemned as bigots when they attempt to promote links with their supporters in Ulster. Compare the reactions to Rangers playing a pre-season friendly against Linfield in Belfast and Celtic playing host to the Republic of Ireland national team for a testimonial match – the former is denounced as a bigot-fest while the thought process behind the staging of the latter is deemed barely worthy of discussion. The mere inclusion of the orange lily on the Ulster-Scots banner will be enough to draw criticism from some people who will associate it with what they believe to be the extremism of the Orange Order. Additionally, it is perceived that the Red Hand symbol has been hijacked for the exclusive use of Loyalist paramilitaries (which quite clearly it has not been), but does that mean that those who are legitimately proud of it have to abandon it altogether? Ignoring that rhetorical question, ultimately it is the refusal of many to educate themselves about the Ulster-Scots, the constant portrayal of their heritage as somehow bigoted, and the simple denial of its validity that sticks in the craw of many Rangers fans.

Rangers fans from Ulster do not need to justify the reasons for their support for the Ibrox club, least of all to a gutter press that deals in sensationalist rubbish. Rangers should be doing what they can to remove the constant association with 'bigotry' that such links bring without alienating their Ulster fan base. It may, in fact, be in Rangers' interests not to shy away from their links to Presbyterianism, something which, as we have seen, unites the club's supporters in Scotland and Ulster. Celtic have never denied their Irish and Roman Catholic heritage, and by refusing to do so appear to face less of an inquisition into their business practices and the behaviour of their fans.

At the commercial level, there is a belief that the club should exploit links with Ulster-Scots in North America. Interest in the Ulster-Scots among North Americans is growing rapidly and Rangers should capitalise upon this phenomenon by explaining why they are the natural team for people from such a background. There are, however, a couple of stumbling blocks. Firstly, the ambitions of the current Rangers board do not appear to extend to attempting to crack a new market. The club might defend their inaction by arguing that because the Ulster-Scots became so quickly and fully assimilated into American society, their descendants do not feel the need to identify with their ancestors as strongly as the Irish-Catholic Americans or Italian Americans who arrived in the country at a later date. Therefore, it might be argued that those of

Ulster-Scots descent would have very little interest in football, much less in Rangers, and that trying to win them over would be futile.

It may also be worthwhile mentioning that certain characteristics attributed to the Ulster-Scots have been apparent in a number of players who have represented Rangers through the years, traits that are loved by the fans. While the obvious and mesmerising skills of players such as Jim Baxter, Davie Cooper, Paul Gascoigne and Brian Laudrup are more than greatly appreciated by Rangers supporters, other highly popular players have been hard working, courageous and determined, and have demonstrated a 'no surrender' attitude to the game. Harold Davis, John Greig, Alex MacDonald, Graeme Souness, Ian Ferguson, John Brown and Richard Gough, among others, would fall into this category. And this is not simply because they are Scottish Protestants: Lorenzo Amoruso and Rino Gattuso were adored for showing the same passion and will to win. Sub-consciously perhaps, the recognition of the qualities which saw the Ulster-Scots thrive still pervades the Scottish and Ulster-born supporters of Rangers.

Rangers may not be an Ulster-Scots club, but there is no denying that, through their traditional fan base in the west of Scotland and in Northern Ireland, they have unbreakable ties to those of Ulster-Scots descent. The club should not deny this, and by celebrating the achievements of the Ulster-Scots throughout the world they would be able to disassociate themselves from any negative connotations that may be raised through links to Ulster. As some observers note there appears to be no desire amongst the current Rangers board to contextualise Rangers' place in Scottish society, a move which has led to enemies of the club continually dismissing fans' expressions of their heritage as simply anti-Catholic and bigoted. This needs to be challenged and by aggressively promoting the Ulster-Scots legacy, Rangers could perhaps educate those who are all too quick to cast slurs on the club and its fans.

Notes

1   Billy Kennedy, *The Scots-Irish in the Shenandoah Valley*, (Belfast, 1996, p. 16)

2   Ron Chepesiuk, *The Scotch-Irish: From the North of Ireland to the Making of America, McFarland and Company*, (North Carolina, 2000, p. 2)

3   Mark Thompson, 'The First Presbytery, the Covenant in Ulster and the Death of Sir James Hamilton', *The Ulster-Scot*, December 2006

4   Billy Kennedy, *Faith and Freedom: The Scots-Irish in America* (Belfast, 1999, p. 20)

5   Maude Glasgow, *The Scotch-Irish in Northern Ireland and the American Colonies*, (G. P. Putnam's Sons, 1936, p. 49)

6   ibid, p. 53

7   Rory Fitzpatrick, *God's Frontiersmen: The Scots-Irish Epic*, (London, 1989, p. 11)

8   Ron Chepesiuk, op cit, p. 41

9   Ibid, p.36

10   Ron Chepesiuk, op cit, p. 42

11   James E. Johnson, *The Scots and the Scotch-Irish in America*, (Minneapolis, 1966, p. 18)

12   Rory Fitzpatrick, op cit, p. 29

13   Billy Kennedy, *Faith and Freedom*, p. 17

14   Ron Chepesiuk, op cit, p. 53

15   Scottish Covenanter Memorials Association, 'Who Were the Covenanters?', viewed 12 February 2007, www.covenanter.org.uk

16   Rampant Scotland, 'Did You Know? – Covenanters', viewed 12 February 2003 www.rampantscotland.com

17   Rory Fitzpatrick, op cit, p. 33

18   Sir John Clotworthy cited in Mark Thompson, 'Scotland's National Covenant, the Black Oath and the 1641 Massacre', *The Ulster-Scot*, November 2006

19   Ibid, p.45

20   Ron Chepesiuk, op cit, p. 68

21   ibid

22 J. M. Barkley, *A Short History of the Presbyterian Church in Ireland*, Presbyterian Church of Ireland (Belfast, 1959, p. 15)

23 House of Lords declaration cited in Margaret Dickson Falley, *Irish and Scotch-Irish Ancestral Research*, (Baltimore, 1981, p. 389)

24 Ron Chepesiuk, op cit, p. 70

25 ibid, p. 71

26 'History of the Monarchy, James II' (r. 1685–8), viewed 26 February 2007, www.royal.gov.uk

27 *Battlefield Britain*, 'The Battle of the Boyne', BBC, London, 2004

28 ATQ Stewart, *The Narrow Ground – Aspects of Ulster, 1606–1969*, (Belfast, 1997)

29 Thames and Avon Branch of the Adam Murray Club – 'Apprentice Boys of Derry, Who was Adam Murray?', viewed 24 February 2007, www.geocities.com

30 Ron Chepesiuk, op cit, p. 93

31 ibid

32 ibid, p. 94

33 ibid

34 James G. Leyburn, *The Scotch-Irish, A Social History*, (Chapel Hill, 1962, p. 163)

35 ibid

36 ibid, p. 169–173

37 Ron Chepesiuk, op cit, p. 111

38 ibid, p. 103

39 R. J. Dickson, *Ulster Immigration to Colonial America, 1718-1775*, (Ulster Historical Foundation, 1988, pp. 91–2)

40 ibid, p. 104

41 Billy Kennedy, *The Making of America*, p. 13

42 The Ulster-Scots Agency, 'Ulster-Scots & United States Presidents: Presidents with Ulster connections who helped shape America', viewed 26 February 2007 www.ulsterscotsagency.com

43 ibid

44 Billy Kennedy, 'Rangers' founder was the son of a Co. Down woman', *The Ulster-Scot*, January 2004, p. 11

45 *Rangers News*, 1971

46 For a meticulously researched article on Sam English's record-breaking season, see www.followfollow.com

47 Bob Ferrier and Robert McElroy, *Rangers: The Complete Record* (second edition), (Derby, 2005, p. 92)

48 BBCi, 'McAleese row over Nazi comments', viewed 12 February 2007, bbc.co.uk

49 BBCi, 'Witness likens Unionists to Nazis', viewed 12 February 2007, bbc.co.uk

50 *Guardian Unlimited*, 'Red faces at Blue Peter over red hand', viewed 12 February 2007, www.guardian.co.uk

51 David Miller (Strathclyde University) homepage, 'Angus man designs Ulster "peace flag" ', viewed 12 February 2007, homepages.strath.ac.uk

The Death of Sectarianism

Reverend Stuart McQuarrie

Football is the most popular sport in the world. People support football clubs as a means of expressing an identity. Who they are, who they see themselves to be, who they aspire to be. On that basis football clubs all over the world will sell millions of jerseys at inflated prices. In Scotland football supporters who believe in the Corinthian values of the amateur will support Queen's Park, whilst those who see themselves to be Irish Catholic or wish to be politically in sympathy with Irish Catholic traditions might support Celtic. It may be a geographical community identity, such as Aberdeen or Motherwell. Or within a geographical area there might be other factors that have a religious or class-based element, such as that with the teams in Dundee or Edinburgh. For me, Rangers FC represents all that is great about being both Scottish and British. It's Rangers for me.

Someone recently said to me you can divorce your wife or your husband. You can change your house, your car, even your religion. You never change your football team.

When those young rowers pulled up their boats on Glasgow Green to watch the beginnings of organised football and formed a team they were making a statement about identity. That they chose the name of an English rugby team suggests a broad-mindedness about being British and Scottish. And from the earliest days they were able to call on the support and even the finance of people who were substantial figures in the community. Rowing, then as now, was a largely middle-class activity. Rangers emerged as a club of Scottish values and aspirations very typical of the time. Success would be achieved through hard work, application, loyalty, tolerance, commitment along with a sense of duty to support those who were less well off. Those same values had categorised the Scottish Enlightenment and made Scottish engineers, doctors, scientists, writers, soldiers welcome in every corner not only of the British Empire but also of the globe; these characteristics remain essential to the Rangers story. In the book, now almost fifty years old, *We Will Follow Rangers*, the author Hugh Taylor states '. . . on the whole Rangers' style is a fine mixture of quiet craftsmanship as essentially Scottish as that on the nearby Clyde; neat and well ordered; of intense power; of fast, sweeping, spectacular raids, fierce as a border sortie'. He goes on, 'How often it is a disaster that puts Rangers back on their feet! Resilience, endurance, determination – these are really the heart and soul of Ibrox.'

The substance of Rangers Football Club is first encountered on the approach to the stadium. The vista of the solid red-glazed brickwork formed into high and magnificent arches where large-framed windows allow the natural light to filter into the internal concourse areas emphasise this is no merely functional stadium. Even the new stands completed from the late 1970s reflect the solidity that is Rangers FC – no exposed or ugly, open steel work. And then, the entry through the front door of the stadium. The mosaic crest – guarded by the oak doors – reminds visitors they enter not merely a football-club stadium, but the very portal of a Scottish institution. The hallway with its oak panels and tasteful art deco lighting is reminiscent of when the main stand was opened. An era of Clyde-built style, elegance and form. To the left, the away dressing room. To the right the Rangers dressing room. Spacious and with oak panels, the Rangers dressing room reinforces the Rangers tradition right down to the peg on which the Rangers players were expected to place their bowler hats. Ahead is the famed marble staircase leading to the Blue Room. Next to the Blue Room is the manager's office – what tales could these walls speak! Adjacent to the manager's office is the boardroom, where until comparatively recently every Tuesday the board of directors would meet to review the previous week's matches and receive a report from the manager and the secretary. The secretary's office (now the William Wilton room) still houses a huge safe, which once held the Saturday receipts. On Fridays the players would queue up outside the secretary's office to be paid their wages in cash. Of course, the world is now a very different place, but the two photographs of the Queen which hang on the dressing-room walls remind Rangers players of the club's values, its traditions and its expectations. To me, Rangers Football Club embodies in my team all that is best in being both Scottish and British.

The first Rangers game at Ibrox I can recall seeing was when I was about nine or ten years of age. It was Rangers versus Third Lanark. Third Lanark, whose origins lay in military history, was a good team in those days and were as I recall in the top three of the old Scottish first division of eighteen clubs. Rangers won 2–0. At the end, I persuaded my father to take me to the front door of Ibrox to wait on the players coming out. Seeing them in the flesh and out of the famous blue jersey just confirmed to me that we are the people! (Psalm 100)

If someone told me the 1964 treble-winning team of Ritchie, Shearer, Caldow, Greig, McKinnon, Baxter, Henderson, McMillan, Millar, Brand and Wilson would be the last Rangers team for eleven years to win the Scottish League I would have considered this inconceivable. Of course there were some triumphs including one League Cup, two Scottish Cups and, most significantly, the European Cup Winners Cup but these were occasional stars lighting up a somewhat dark period. To lose, as we did in 1968, the title in the very last game against Aberdeen was particularly hard to bear, and I only really got over it after that magnificent victory in 1991 when we beat Aberdeen in the last game to win the league. Oh, what a joyous day that was!

As a Rangers supporter I have never hated the supporters of other clubs. I may have considered them misguided people. Celtic, our greatest rivals, were never hated. In the early 1970s I used to go to Rangers–Celtic matches with my pal Liam. It is incredible to think that in those days if you had a ticket for the Rangers end you could still get into Ibrox or Parkhead at the opposite end. Liam and I would go in and stand around the halfway line talking to each other. There was no physical demarcation, just an empty space of a couple of yards. And then at quarter to three we would each go to the opposite end and meet up in the city centre after the game. In those days Rangers was very much a Scottish and British club. Celtic was also a Scottish and British club whose proud boast was to be the first British club to win the European Cup. As a Scottish club Celtic's origins and sense of identity came from the Scottish-Irish community (largely Catholic). As a Scottish club Rangers' origins and sense of identity came from the Scottish indigenous community (largely Protestant).

As a Rangers supporter on 11 April 1970 at Hampden I cheered on Aberdeen (oh the innocence of youth!) to victory over Celtic in the Scottish Cup final. Four days later on 15 April, as a Scot, I was back at Hampden and cheered Celtic to victory over Leeds United in the European Cup semi-final. Over the years of my life as a lifelong bluenose I have always enjoyed the engagement with, and the friendship of, Celtic supporters. I believe this has been on the basis of mutual respect for origins and traditions.

In recent years, there has been a significant change as Celtic have emphasised their Irish-nationalist identity at the expense of their Scottish identity. Part of this is due to a commercial exploitation of Irishness to develop a global market. Part is also due to a hardening of social, secular and religious attitudes to being Scottish and almost a resentment to being British. For many of their fans, Celtic has become an Irish club that happens to play in Scotland. A few years ago the phrase 'he is not exactly Celtic-minded' was invented by a senior official of the Celtic Supporters Association reacting to the appointment of a new chief executive officer for Celtic FC. The sectarian inference was perfectly clear. The new CEO was brought up in Lanarkshire as a Protestant, not as a Lanarkshire Catholic. Echoes sounded of the Celtic board's refusal to appoint Jock Stein – arguably the most successful football manager in Britain and who had led Celtic to win the European Cup, and a then record nine league championships in a row, plus numerous other trophies – to the Celtic board of directors. When the time came for Stein to move on from direct football management he was offered the role of managing the club's weekly lottery. Stein was the first Protestant to manage the Celtic team, but it was a step too far, despite all the honours he had won for Celtic, for him to become the first Protestant director.

The phrase 'Celtic-minded' has since spawned at least two books and generated several websites, which frequently allow racist and sectarian comments about Britain and its people, especially Protestants. The delusion is promoted of Celtic being a 'different' club, and because of this difference its supporters are somehow superior to other human beings. It is not different. It is a football club that expresses an identity to which the supporters can relate. Just as Rangers symbolise a Scottish/British identity so historically Celtic has symbolised an Irish, largely Catholic, identity. Celtic-mindedness introduced the recognition of a sectarian element to that identity. To the Celtic-minded anyone who questions Celtic FC or its supporters is motivated by bigotry and sectarianism. When I think of the Celtic-minded and sectarianism what comes to my mind is a paraphrase of Boris Johnson's description of Liverpool, which goes along the following lines:

> They see themselves whenever possible as victims, and resent their victim status; yet at the same time they wallow in it. Part of this flawed psychological state is that they cannot accept that they might have made any contribution to their misfortunes, but seek rather to blame someone else for it, thereby deepening their sense of shared tribal grievance against the rest of society.

In recent years there has been much talk of sectarianism as 'Scotland's secret shame'. The author of this particular phrase, a noted Celtic supporter, announced it as such at a public conference that was part of the Edinburgh Festival. He then went on to describe the leaders of the Reformation in quite offensive terms, comparing them with some of the worst dictators in world history. With a reference to the murderous Pol Pot he described his own discipline of music and the time of the Reformation as Year Zero. Not only was this provocative but also it simply ignored the great artistic and literary gifts Scotland has given to the world through the music of people like George Buchanan, the poetry of Burns, the writing of Stevenson, Scott and more recently Lewis Grassic Gibbon, Neil Gunn and many others. Had this insult been made to the leaders of any other racial or religious group, including and perhaps especially Irish Catholics, then all hell would have broken loose. Instead, the Scottish media merely seized on it as a justification for their own prejudices.

Celtic-minded is a sectarian term that needs a sectarian agenda. It is only that sectarian dimension which distinguishes Celtic-mindedness. Celtic-mindedness is quite different from the Roman Catholic Church as it is today, and from Ireland as it is today. It is based on a mythology. That mythology is broadly that thousands of Irish people fled Ireland in the nineteenth century to escape the Great Famine which blighted the potato crop, the staple diet of nineteenth century Ireland. The more extreme of the Celtic-minded insist the potato blight was deliberately introduced to Ireland by the British government, and liken the famine to the Nazi Holocaust. The mythological view is that all these people came to a Scotland which hated and despised them purely on the basis of their Catholic faith. The Celtic-minded view of Ireland is a romanticised 'O'Brigadoon' type of place where people still live in small rural communities, supporting each other and going to mass every Sunday. The contrast with the reality of today's modern, economically thriving Ireland, which is more European in outlook than Britain, where the young people are sophisticated and educated, cannot be understated. Celtic-mindedness can only see sectarianism in one way, with Catholics as the victims. Sectarianism is always between two or more competing factions. Think too of the sectarianism recounted in the Gospels where the Saduccees, the Samaritans and the Pharisees, who all had separate views on the Jewish faith which Jesus followed, all hated each other. It is my assertion that sectarianism arose in Scotland from around the 1920s and lasted to the late 1970s. From then it has diminished and only finds expression in a rump of people who associate themselves with both Rangers and Celtic. Celtic-mindedness is a somewhat crude and unsophisticated attempt to put some intellectual justification on the sectarianism which is associated with elements of Celtic's support. Rangers have acknowledged that element within our own support. The club has worked ever since Willie Waddell's statement more than thirty years ago to eradicate that dimension within the support.

The Scots and the Irish have strong cultural links and the movement of people between the countries has gone on from time immemorial. The name Scotland is derived from the Scotti, an Irish tribe. In AD 563 an Irish prince, Columba, left Derry with a small band of followers and established a religious community on the small island of Iona. Columba's church community was quite different in style and structure from the developing Roman Catholic Church community. It was only following the Synod of Whitby in the seventh century that the distinctive Celtic church practices regarding worship and the Christian calendar, including the timing of Easter, were absorbed into the Roman Catholic Church. From this point on the church in Britain was part of the Roman Catholic Church, until the time of the Reformation. After the Reformation people still continued to move freely between Scotland and Ireland, looking for work, trading with each other. The first people fleeing on a large scale from famine were Scots who settled in Ulster and beyond from 1695. Despite the famine the government of William of Orange was unsympathetic to the starving Scots and offered no assistance. This was in the wake of the massacre of Glencoe. Scottish Protestants and their descendants who settled in Ireland became prominent in the developing Irish Home Rule movement in the eighteenth and nineteenth centuries. From the early nineteenth century onwards increasing numbers of Irish men and women came to Scotland to take advantage of the jobs offered by the Industrial Revolution. They often came in large family groups to work on projects such as the Forth and Clyde canal, begun in 1768. These navigators, or 'navvies', worked with pick and shovel and lived in camps. It was a hard and demanding life. They stayed on in these camps seeking work when the canal was finished. They kept apart from the indigenous population because of things like language and religious practice. Often they were accompanied by priests trained in the Irish seminaries, whose role was to keep them from what they saw as the apostasy of Protestantism. One such camp was at Croy in Stirlingshire and those who lived or had a base there were ideally placed for work as navvies when the Glasgow to Edinburgh railway line began in 1842. The vast majority of Irish immigrants to Scotland came from Donegal. So by the time people fled from disease and famine from 1846 on, Scotland was well used and well adjusted to Irish immigration. There is virtually nothing in written records to suggest sectarian or other persecution. The Irish and Scottish communities tended to keep themselves apart. The Scots Presbyterians' attitude to the Irish with their strange and superstitious Roman religion spoken in the dead language of Latin by a priest who kept his back at all times to the people was mainly indifference. The Irish attitude to the Scots was of wariness, lest they be contaminated by Protestantism. Industrialisation opened up for Scots and Irish new possibilities in work, but also the squalor of overcrowded tenement life in Scotland's cities. Glasgow's population increased fivefold during the nineteenth century. By 1878 the Catholic Church in Scotland had assumed importance and more crucially the confidence to re-establish its hierarchy for the first time since the Reformation. This would not have been possible in a political or social climate that was completely hostile. Indeed three years earlier, in 1875, Hibernian FC had been founded in Edinburgh out of St Patrick's Roman Catholic church by Canon Edward Joseph Hannan.

Nineteenth-century Scotland was characterised not by sectarianism between Scottish Protestants and Irish Catholics but by sectarianism within Scottish Protestantism. The apotheosis of this came with the Disruption of 1843, which saw ministers and elders walk out of the established Church of Scotland to form the Free Church of Scotland. Congregations and families were split as attitudes hardened. The new Free Church set up an ambitious programme of building churches, schools and manses. Thus even today in most Scots cities and towns there are places known as 'holy corner', where the Free Church built a church directly across from the established Kirk. In 1900 the vast majority of the Free Church of Scotland united with the United Presbyterian Church of Scotland, which had been formed in 1847, to form the United Free Church of Scotland. This new denomination reunited with the Church of Scotland in 1929. However, a minority of the original Free Church of Scotland remained outside the Union of 1900, claiming the title Free Church of Scotland for itself, as did a minority of the United Free Church of Scotland. Both denominations continue to this day.

Catholic and Protestant communities largely kept apart in a form of splendid isolation. Catholic priests particularly warned against intermingling, as did some Protestant clergy. Any young couple who found themselves in a Romeo and Juliet situation across the religious communities was likely to be ostracised by both. And there were other Catholic communities who took up residence in Scotland, notably those from Italy and Poland.

There were occasional outbursts of what might be termed sectarian violence, although even these were predominantly local and contained within small communities. These tended to happen following an event unconnected to religion, such as followed the Blantyre mining disaster in October 1877. The disaster claimed the lives of some 240 miners. The death of a male miner usually resulted in destitution for his family. They would also be thrown out of the tied cottage. Thus when the mine owners brought in impoverished Irish Catholics to work the mine to replace those who had died there was considerable resentment. The mine owners kept themselves apart. Situations like this occurred across Scotland's mining communities as greedy mine owners sought to maximise their profits. The Irish were seen as a very cheap (and expendable) source of labour. They spoke a different language, had different customs, and followed a faith which to the indigenous Scots was superstitious and expressed in a primitive way. It is no coincidence that the remaining bastions of Orangeism, which may be interpreted as a reaction to Irish Catholic influences, are in the former traditional mining areas of Lanarkshire, parts of Ayrshire, parts of Stirlingshire and West Lothian.

The twentieth century saw the development of mass popular culture. Football was one element with theatre and music hall, then cinemas and dance halls. This exposed the Scottish and Irish to each other in ways which had never before been possible. Public houses became male bastions of escape from the demands of dirty, industrial and commercial work. The clergy – both Protestant and Catholic – railed against these changes in society, viewing them as immoral and corrupt influences that undermined the power of the churches. The pattern of people flocking to the cities in search of work and opportunity meant that areas became associated with particular communities, and therefore religions. For example, Scottish Highlanders and Islanders settled in Partick and Maryhill. The Irish, most of whom came from Donegal, settled in the Calton and Townhead areas. Then, as the prosperous merchant classes of the Gorbals moved out of their smart south-side villas to Newlands or Kelvindale, the villas were demolished to be replaced with what could charitably be called high-density housing. The football clubs then began to assume a role of expressing the identity of the people of these communities. Rangers and Queen's Park the Scottish Presbyterians, Partick Thistle the Highlanders and Islanders, and Celtic the Irish Catholics. Celtic was the only club with formal links to a church or religious community. It had been formed in a Catholic church hall with the express purpose of providing an identity and poor relief for Catholics. Poor relief was administered through the Catholic Church, and thus was not in practice available to the other poor of Glasgow's east end. Rangers has never had any formal links with the Church of Scotland. Its directors and supporters may well have been members and even elders in the Kirk, but in the way that Presbyterians are able to separate the different areas and responsibilities of their lives the matter of which football club was supported was seen like religious faith as a 'private matter'.

The onset of the first world war placed a premium on a skilled workforce which could quickly produce the armaments and ships necessary for victory. In the regular British army there were some 20,000 Irishmen already serving, with another 30,000 in the first-line reserve. The total army strength was 247,000 with 145,000 ex-regular reservists. The British Army was a volunteer army. Other countries had conscription. Britain relied on volunteers. The Great War brought Catholics and Protestants to serve together in the trenches. Religion mattered less than having someone side by side with you upon whom you could rely. Thomas Kettle, the former Nationalist MP for East Tyrone who served and was killed as a lieutenant in the 9th Royal Dublin Fusiliers, believed that: 'Used with the wisdom which is sown in tears and blood, this tragedy of Europe may be and must be the prologue to the two reconciliations of which all statesmen have dreamed, the reconciliation of Protestant Ulster with Ireland, and the reconciliation of Ireland with Great Britain.'

Sadly, Kettle's belief was misplaced. The dual blood sacrifices of 1916 that fuelled the mythologies of both Irish Nationalism and Unionism – the Easter Rising and the Battle of the Somme – followed by the Irish War of Independence, caused anti-Irish, as opposed to anti-Catholic, feeling in Britain, and intensified sectarianism in Scotland. In December 1921, a treaty between the Irish representatives and the British government was signed, leading to the establishment of a twenty-six-county Irish Free State. The six-county unit of Northern Ireland had come into being in mid-1921, as a devolved part of the United Kingdom.

In Glasgow in 1921 an incident involving the Irish Republican Army (IRA) was to create considerable resentment and to poison Protestant–Catholic relations for much of the inter-war period. This concerned the attack on a police motor van in Cathedral Square, which led to the death of one officer and the serious wounding of another. Shortly afterwards, in 1923, the Church of Scotland General Assembly received a report entitled *The Menace of the Irish Race to our Scottish Nationality*. In many ways this report summarized the anti-Irish mood which was a feature of sections of society at the time, and proposed repatriation to Ireland for the unemployed Irish who had settled in Scotland. The temper of the times was also reflected by the growth of Protestant political parties in Glasgow and Edinburgh in the 1930s, and in the gang warfare of Glasgow. The South of Ireland's neutrality during the second world war merely reinforced pejorative opinions where they were held.

On the Catholic side, the significant number of priests educated at seminaries in Ireland and who served in Scotland saw their principal duty as keeping the flock from the apostasy of Protestantism. Anti-Protestant sermons became the norm, with parishioners left in no doubt they would go straight to the eternal damnation of hell, bypassing purgatory, if they or their families dallied with Protestants. The separate school system through which the 1918 Education (Scotland) Act brought the Catholic schools within the remit of the state system (the Catholic Church was paid for the schools) guaranteed the Catholic Church rights over the schools, including access for priests to teach the catechism and doctrines of the Catholic Church. This gave enormous power to the Catholic Church and to individual parish priests. As recently as 1989 I can recall seeing a history book used in a Catholic secondary school, which blamed the Reformation on greedy Protestant landowners who wanted the Church property. That book may well still be in circulation as a teaching aid today. The modern Catholic Church though cannot be compared with the Catholic Church prior to the Second Vatican Council of the early to mid 1960s. Vatican II, as it is often called, was ordered by Pope John XXIII and in many ways it revolutionised the Catholic Church. It meant Catholics could eat meat on Fridays and the mass could be said in the local language. The priest no longer had to have his back to the congregation when saying the mass. It also opened up the prospect, for the first time since the Reformation, of ecumenical dialogue with other Christian churches. This stopped short of recognising the validity and basis of other Christian churches, but it was a start. At the time of writing it has been announced that the Latin mass has been restored by Pope Benedict XVI. Within the same week it has emerged that the Pope has also authorised a document which claims that the Orthodox churches are defective and that the other Christian denominations are not true churches.

Historically, Rangers and Celtic, whilst being rivals for football honours, have been very close. The first game Celtic played was against Rangers. The name 'Old Firm', as the historian Bill Murray's excellent researches have shown, was coined in the early part of the last century to describe that relationship as Rangers and Celtic worked together to dominate the world of Scottish football.

Celtic FC was founded to provide charitable support to the poor of Glasgow's East End. The club's founder, Brother Walfrid, a Marist priest, had been greatly impressed by what Hibernian FC had achieved in terms of support and identity for Catholics in Edinburgh. The first Celtic players were actually 'poached' from Hibernian. From the outset Celtic was an outlet for, and supporter of, Irish Nationalism. Rangers, by contrast, became a symbol of Scottish Britishness. The two clubs understood each other perfectly well. They attracted the biggest crowds. They acted together.

Rangers acquired a significant following of workers from Ulster when, in 1908, Harland and Wolff brought over many of them from their Belfast shipyard to the Clyde. These Ulster Protestants were, overwhelmingly, opposed to Irish Home Rule. Rangers with their red-white-and-blue strips were a natural team for the Ulstermen to support.

Rangers and Celtic mirrored many developments in Scotland (and Ireland's) life. Their supporters were part of these societies. Celtic continued as an expression of Irish Nationalism, Rangers of Scottish/British Unionism. In the early 1950s the Scottish Football Association passed a resolution which demanded that Celtic stop flying the flag of Eire over Celtic Park. Celtic refused and were supported in their refusal by Rangers. As post-war austerity gave way to the Swinging Sixties Rangers and Celtic players were often seen together in some of Glasgow's more sophisticated night spots. Jim Baxter in particular was friendly with a number of Celtic players. In 1967, a week after Celtic became the first British club to win the European Cup, Rangers lost the European Cup Winners Cup Final in extra time by 1–0 to Bayern Munich. The match was played only fifty miles from Munich. In 1972 Glasgow hosted an amazing night as Rangers played at Ibrox in the second leg European Cup Winners Cup semi-final and Celtic played at Celtic Park in the European Cup semi-final. Rangers won their game and went on to lift the cup in Barcelona. Celtic lost out after extra time and penalties. The Old Firm were contesting for the top trophies in Europe. Just around this time the Troubles in Northern Ireland were being seen as more than just a temporary problem. What started out as a human-rights campaign became a terrorist campaign to create a united Ireland by force. Thirty-five years on and it is only now the violence has genuinely ceased.

Again, the sectarianism of this conflict was mirrored by Rangers and Celtic fans. Celtic fans openly chanted in support of the IRA and IRA scarves/regalia/publications were openly on sale outside Celtic Park on match days. An IRA-supporting rock band was given permission to film a video at Celtic Park. Rangers fans similarly could buy UDA/UFF scarves/regalia/publications outside Ibrox on match days. But there were changes in society that were having another effect. The emergence in the early 1970s of a sizeable, educated Catholic working class with middle-class aspirations began to challenge not only the stereotypes of the previous generations, but also began entering the professions. The reforms of Vatican II took longer to filter into the Catholic Church in Scotland, but these began to have an effect. Clergy began to invite each other to their respective churches at Christmas and Easter. Joint services took place. In 1982 the largest public gathering held in Scotland saw 200,000 Catholics (with a few others!) crowd into Bellahouston Park, just half a mile away from Glasgow, as Pope John Paul II celebrated mass. The Pope publicly called on *all* of Scotland's Christians to walk together hand in hand into the future. Days earlier, the Pope had been welcomed to Scotland by the Moderator of the General Assembly of the Church of Scotland on the steps of the General Assembly, under the extended arm of a statue of John Knox.

Rangers' relationship with the Church of Scotland is often misconceived. In general, ministers of the Kirk have preferred to be associated with more middle-class sporting pursuits, although there have been particular ones who have been notable supporters down the years. The best example is probably the Reverend James Currie, minister of St. James's church in Pollok, who was ever alert to the dangers of the Kirk losing touch with its working-class flock. A charismatic man, who had a deep concern for anyone who needed his help, Currie was a popular and ken-speckle figure, never seen without his clerical collar. He became known to everyone at Ibrox from the doorman to the chairman and was adopted by the Rangers Supporters Association as their chaplain. In the hours and days following the Ibrox disaster in 1971 Currie made himself available to assist the bereaved families and supporters. He was also there to help the Rangers players and directors through what was a very public trauma. Although he never had a formal position with Rangers FC he became a very public face of the Rangers support and was never slow to defend the club in the controversies over sectarianism that dogged it during the 1970s and 1980s. This brought him into conflict with ministers from other quarters of the church, which at this time viewed Rangers with suspicion and even outright hostility. On Boxing Day 1976 Rangers were due to play Motherwell at Ibrox. Willie Waddell, then general manager and a great friend of Currie, thought this would be an opportunity to stage a carol service. Currie was enthusiastic and agreed to conduct it, believing that this would be the only 'service' many of the fans would attend during the year. However, his fellow ministers objected, the issue became controversial, and Waddell dropped the idea to prevent further embarrassment.

Rangers, it should be noted, offered clergy (Protestant and Catholic) a complimentary season ticket as a courtesy to their position if their parish was close to Ibrox. I was possibly the last beneficiary of this in 1984 when assistant minister of Govan Old Parish Church. Celtic had a similar arrangement, which was taken up enthusiastically by Catholic priests to such an extent that when Fergus McCann saved Celtic from bankruptcy in 1994 he discovered a complimentary list in excess of five hundred!

By the late twentieth century much in the social order had radically changed. More and more Catholics and Protestants were beginning to form relationships and marry each other. Rather than cause problems for either party, many of them either just set up home together or got married in a civil-marriage ceremony. Now some 35 per cent of Catholics are either married or in a relationship they consider permanent with someone who is not Catholic. The fans of Rangers and Celtic once again began to mirror the changes and challenged the accepted wisdom of the two previous generations. For me, it began in 1975, following the Rangers versus Celtic match at Ibrox which Rangers won 3–0. As I got ready to go out in a celebratory mood with my Catholic girlfriend the whole inconsistency and stupidity of it began to challenge me. How could I sing songs about Protestant victories, celebrating battles of long, long ago and think about settling down with a Catholic girl who regularly attended mass, whose parents themselves were of a 'mixed marriage'? Although that relationship ended the questioning did not. I then found myself involved with a church group which was bringing Catholics and Protestants together. Then came the influence of the Iona Community, ending up with me becoming a minister. And as a minister I have built up trust between Protestants and Catholics wherever I have served. I have been invited to speak to confirmation classes in a Catholic primary school on three occasions and have also participated in the confirmation mass. Pilgrimages to Iona have been organised and, when I was married, a Catholic priest took part in the ceremony. In the University of Glasgow I regularly attend events and mass in the Catholic chaplaincy. None of this makes me any less a Rangers supporter. Indeed all who know me quickly learn of my passion for Rangers. In any case, the world has moved on. It is no longer about Catholics and Protestants. It is about Buddhists, Christians, Hindus, Jews, Muslims and Sikhs working with Humanists and others to respect people as human beings.

Any suggestion that Rangers were a sectarian club was blown out of the water, once and for all, when in July 1989 Rangers signed Maurice Johnston. Three weeks previously he had been paraded as a new signing at Celtic Park in what was subsequently realised to be a stunt to appease the increasingly restive Celtic support. Some Rangers fans did not take kindly to the signing, and some, in a media-arranged event, were seen to be burning their Rangers season tickets and scarves. Celtic fans demonstrated outside Celtic Park and called for the board to be sacked. Maurice was called a traitor, a Judas. It was a brave signing by Rangers. Maurice was given special security by Rangers, and lived for a while in Graeme Souness's villa in Edinburgh. I rejoiced. Not only had Rangers signed themselves a very good player – and indeed a much better player than when he had left Glasgow – but also they had once and for all demolished the mythology surrounding the club. Those same Celtic supporters who then and still now consider Johnston a traitor are guilty of the very bigotry they condemn. Surely, if they are as against bigotry as they claim, they too would have rejoiced. In many ways the views people have of Maurice Johnston is an accurate indicator of their real views, as opposed to their mouthings and writings, on bigotry.

From the late 1980s Rangers FC strenuously worked a consistent and effective campaign against sectarianism. The rebuilt Ibrox stadium made it easier to identify supporters who were causing embarrassment to the club. Fans who did not wish to sit next to some foul-mouthed individual during the match realised that complaints to stewards would be addressed. Stern warnings were followed by the removal of season tickets and the banning of those who were caught making discriminatory comments and chants. Rangers did this quietly and discreetly, in a similar manner to which Rangers has conducted its business throughout its history. Emphasis was put on an appeal to the traditions of Rangers FC which were about resilience, endurance, determination – Pride over Prejudice! In early 1997 Celtic launched Bhoys Against Bigotry in a blaze of publicity. This was a sincere attempt by the then Celtic chairman (and the man who had single-handedly saved Celtic FC when it was within eight minutes of bankruptcy) to deal with the sectarian element in the Celtic support. This writer publicly backed that campaign.

When in 2006 UEFA charged Rangers fans with singing discriminatory chants, and did not initially find the club guilty, it actually reached the right verdict in describing the matter as a 'Scottish issue'. The subsequent appeal by the UEFA 'prosecutor' was upheld. Sectarianism cannot be dealt with by punishing one of the parties and praising the others. That only inflates the sense of injustice felt on all sides. Where else but in Scotland would you get a player trying to antagonise fans with a symbol of religious faith? I recall watching in amazement as a Partick Thistle player, having just been cautioned by the referee, lost the plot and ran to the stand where the Rangers fans were and started making the sign of the cross several times – most fans laughed and jeered at him. Or when a goalkeeper starts winding up the fans behind him, giving them the come-and-get-me and other hand signals, and then starts to make the sign of the cross. When this player was cautioned about his conduct the spin was put out that he was simply expressing his faith. Using symbols or actions of faith to antagonise people says more about these individuals and what their faith really means. From the 1990s onwards Rangers fans were well used to some of their players blessing themselves with the sign of the cross as they entered the field of play. Similarly, it is not sectarianism when a player elects not to play for the country of his birth, but for another country. However, can you imagine what a Rangers player would be subjected to if, given the choice of playing for Scotland on account of his birth or for England on account of his grandparents, he chose the latter?

Sectarianism on the political agenda has been a convenient diversion for politicians. Sectarianism, where it did exist, was a significant feature of life for only two generations in Scotland. It has not, as some claim, always been there. Nor has it just been one-sided. It has though for some time been in its death throes. Changes in demographic and social characteristics have seen to that. There are far fewer people who hold values that could be described as sectarian. That minority of sectarian-minded Old Firm fans who remain have an intensity about their beliefs which I guess has its roots in influences from the Northern Ireland conflict. One of the successes of Glasgow's post-war housing policy was the demolition and scattering of old communities which had developed along Catholic–Protestant lines. Catholics and Protestants now live and work side by side. Their churches now work together for the benefit of the whole community. People go to events and services in each other's churches with increasing frequency. At Rangers and Celtic matches there are often supporters of both teams in the hospitality boxes – businessmen and women who enjoy their football. Similarly, in virtually all of the weddings I conduct at Ibrox stadium there are Celtic supporters as guests or even as members of the bridal party. This often leads to good-natured banter. On one occasion the bride and groom insisted that all the male guests wore kilts in the Rangers tartan. Celtic supporters who were guests complied but maintained their purity by wearing Celtic shorts underneath!

I have no doubt there will be those who challenge some of the assertions in this chapter. They will quote individual instances to back their claims. There will inevitably be the 'what abouts?', and some example of alleged discrimination will be dredged up to support a view and justify a cause. I look forward to the debate and to quote William Struth, a Rangers great, 'I welcome the chase'. We either move on together and support our teams for all that is good in our history and heritage, or we remain locked in the mists of conflicts long ago. Rangers and Celtic fans working together would be an unstoppable force for good in our society. For Celtic, that is being a Scottish team with Irish ancestry. For Rangers it is being a Scottish team that is quintessentially British.

It's Rangers for me!

Rangers and the Orange Order

Ian Wilson

There are Orange Lodges scattered throughout Scotland, as most people know, but given that the highest proportion of the membership lives in Glasgow and the west of Scotland, then most of the members must be, if not Rangers supporters, then Rangers sympathisers. I don't think that the associations Rangers and the Orange Order have with each other has necessarily been a bad thing. I don't have an issue with it but what I would have an issue with is people who say, 'I'm a Rangers supporter so I must join the Lodge.'

There are many types of Orangemen and if you stood any ten of them against a wall and asked them independently what the Lodge means to them, and why they are an Orangeman, you could get ten totally different answers and every one of those ten answers will be the correct answer for that individual. But the one saying that they joined the Lodge because they are a Rangers fan is the one with whom I would be the least happy. Is that really what brought you into Orangeism, because you support Rangers?

But that's maybe easy for me to say because I'm not from Glasgow and I'm not a Rangers fan. The joke they make about me is: 'Ian doesn't really know much about football – he's a Hearts supporter.' And one of my Grand Lodge executive colleagues is a Hibs supporter. Everyone smiles at the very thought of that, although maybe from a Glasgow perspective it is the worst thing imaginable. I have to work hard to appreciate that part of the west of Scotland Protestant culture is bound up with Rangers and the Lodge. It is not easy for me to understand but it is a reality nevertheless. It won't be all Rangers fans following the marches, but certainly, if you go to a Glasgow parade, then by and large the flags you see will say 'Rangers'.

However, the thoughts of the Lodge in general, and me in particular, is that the most important thing is that people who attend the parades

163

behave themselves. It bothers me that we get teenage lads out of their face on drink shouting and bawling. I, too, have experienced being bumped off the pavement by the 'Buckfast brigade' as I have watched a parade. Even in mid-morning they seem to be six sheets to the wind on a cheap wine that is, oddly enough, brewed in a Roman Catholic monastery. It also bothers me that those 'air punchers' discourage family groups coming along to see the parades. It doesn't do the Lodge any favours having that image.

The Old Firm come from two different traditions, which at one time would have characterised Hibs and Hearts and Dundee United and Dundee if you go back far enough, but all of that has largely gone; it's really only in the west of Scotland that this has persisted. It would be best if the religious aspect didn't come into football; it hasn't the slightest relevance but it is there, it's part of the traditions of Glasgow and I'm not the guy to solve it. But the religious issue has dwindled. We lived through the signing of Mo Johnston and the sky didn't fall in.

I disagree with the suggestion that Rangers are trying to distance themselves from Orangeism. I think they are trying to distance themselves from bigotry and that's no bad thing. One Sunday newspaper alluded to the myth that the Lodge was chucked out of Ibrox because of behaviour problems. That is utter nonsense and we received an apology. Let's set the record straight. The Grand Lodge organises the Annual Divine Service and for years it took place at St Andrew's Halls in Glasgow until that got burned down. We had problems finding another place big enough and that's when we brokered a deal with Rangers, where we went for years. But about ten years ago we broke with that tradition. Football had changed out of recognition and the close season, as such, no longer existed. There were issues of the pitch being re-seeded and it became increasingly difficult to guarantee that we could get the use of the stadium. It got to the stage where it wasn't fair to Rangers and it wasn't fair to us so we decided to make the break, but it was amicable. A well-known director came to the last service and we presented him with an item of crystal, which I think is on display in the trophy room – along with the relatively few other things that Rangers have there at the moment! So the truth is we weren't snubbed by the club but no doubt those Orangemen who have an attachment to Rangers regret that we no longer use Ibrox.

I'm not the stereotypical Orangemen for many reasons, not only because I don't support Rangers. The Sash My Father Wore doesn't apply to me; my father wasn't an Orangemen and neither was my mother. My granny was so there is a family connection but she had no influence on me as far as the Lodge was concerned. The influence came from my best pal who, incidentally, became quite a high-ranking policeman. He was a member of the Juvenile Lodge and the colour, the parades and the bands were very attractive to a twelve-year-old so I joined. My parents believed that education was more important than the Lodge so I took a break and came back into the organisation at twenty-two. There was a group of church elders forming a new Lodge so that was what took me into the adult Lodge in my home town of Whitburn.

When I became Grand Master twelve years ago, the Orange Order faced a number of issues, one of which was that it was in gentle decline. The Lodge has been in Scotland since 1798 so you had an organisation in its third century and the membership, which peaked in the 1950s, was slowly dwindling. Another challenge was the way the Lodge saw itself; in some places the members' confidence was low. In addition to that, we had a terrible public image. To some extent it was our own fault because we didn't have an open-door policy, we were bad at selling the good things about the Orange Order, like its family aspects and charity work. And yet another challenge was the images that were coming from the Orange Lodge in Northern Ireland and the effect that was having on the Scottish organisation. These were things that have had to be dealt with over that period and I am still working on it.

The Orange Order in Scotland has a smattering of professionals but in the main it is a working-class organisation. That's not a reason to look down on an organisation but for some people it is and some see us as rather vulgar. But despite being a working-class organisation we have consciously backed away from politics in Scotland. I don't think that will change and I don't think that it should change. Again, if you asked any ten Orangemen what their politics were you would get ten different answers, including support for the SNP. That's the reality so the Lodge would not be seen to throw its weight behind any political party. We don't have this Unionist/Lodge tie-up that you have in Northern Ireland. That situation is driven by the political situation over there and it's quite different in Scotland.

There was a time in Scotland when the Lodge would have been thought of as the Tory party in Sashes, no doubt about it, and there were Unionist halls in every corner of Glasgow. But again, a lot of that was driven by the Irish politics of the time. But times have changed. For the Grand Master to seek to influence the way the membership votes would not be popular. We held a big parade in Edinburgh this year before the 2007 elections to celebrate three hundred years of the Union and I had to tell the members from the platform that, from a Unionist perspective, voting SNP would be dangerous for people like us but that was as far as I could safely go.

If people have an opinion of the Orange Order that is other than sympathetic, then at best it will be that it is an old-fashioned, stuffy, Masonic, secretive organisation that likes to dress up and bung up the roads with parades. At worst, there are people who view the Lodge as a sectarian organisation and I can see why they take that view. It worries me and we have to work harder at correcting the image, although it's not an entirely fair one.

There is no point in beating about the bush. The Orange Lodge comes from the Reformed tradition, it is an exclusively Protestant organisation; there is no question about that. But I'm fond of arguing about it being sectarian, that is a word that has been misused. I don't see us as being anti-Catholic. If you are in the Scottish National Party then you are against the Union. It's not quite the same as saying you hate the Unionists but you will take a stand against them. So, by the same token, it's not quite fair to say that the Orange Lodge is rabidly anti-Catholic. That's not to say that there aren't bigots in our organisation; I have met a few but I have encountered bigotry in every walk in life. And for anyone to suggest that the Orange Order is the single biggest sectarian problem in Scottish society is nuts. Indeed, I don't think Scotland has a big sectarian problem. If you want to see real sectarianism in action you should go to the former Yugoslavia or certain parts of North Africa.

And Scotland is not Northern Ireland. You have a totally different situation across the water, where you have a polarised society. Protestants and Catholics live in separate housing estates as a consequence of the Troubles. It's an awful situation but we don't have that in Scotland. We live cheek by jowl with Roman Catholics, Sikhs, Muslims and by and large we get on pretty well. I'm not saying that there are no sectarian issues; I just don't think it was worth all the heat that has been generated by the politicians recently. When Jack McConnell went down the road of hosting 'Sectarian Summits' – which I thought, to some extent, were stunts – he was in danger of talking up the problem and making it worse.

Nevertheless, I accept that our image is a problem, which is why two years ago we took on a firm of public-relations consultants for the first time. However, you can have the best public relations in the world but you cannot sell the unacceptable and that was one of the hard discussions we had with the company at the beginning. We have learned a lot. They have been driving us, telling us where there are problems and we have addressed them so it's been positive. But it's like turning around a tanker, it takes a while. Is the message getting through to the ordinary punter in the Lodge? Largely it is, but it is not getting through to everybody.

It annoys me that the Lodge often lets itself down but I have to say that the vast majority of members do not disgrace the colours. There are sanctions for those who do. We have our own disciplinary procedures, that we have just upgraded, and members know that if they step out of line they will be dealt with in no uncertain terms. And one of the problems we are addressing is the links between the Lodge and Northern Ireland paramilitaries. The Ulster–Scottish connection has become stronger in recent years. But there is a perception that the Lodge is linked to the para-militaries in Ulster and to some extent it has been true. As the IRA campaign continued, and the Crown forces and various governments seemed to go soft on the issue, we witnessed the rise of various paramil-itary groups like the UDA, the UVF and other splinter groups. A lot of daft people on this side of the channel, although to a lesser degree than they did in Northern Ireland, felt it was right to support groups, some of which subsequently became illegal.

However, it was never my line and never the line of the Lodge. Any studies of Scottish Orangeism, even by those not sympathetic, have always noted that we have taken a hard line against paramilitaries. It has been tough because it's been an issue of hearts and minds. A lot of our people have been caught up in the emotion of all this and they are not thinking logically. But we have a clear rule that if anybody has even tacit support for any paramilitary group then their membership is on the line and we have a long record of expelling people. I believe it's a matter of convincing members not to go down that road. There is no place for an Orangeman setting himself against the Crown forces. We are supposed to be the people of law and order, the Queen's greatest supporters, so it should not be happening.

The problem also exists within the band world. The Orange Lodge and the bands are semi-detached although it is true that that there are lots of Orangemen who play in bands and it is also true that there probably would not be flute bands in Scotland if it wasn't for the Lodge. But you don't have to be an Orangeman to play in the band, they are separate entities. The bands appear with us under stringent rules, and, over the years, and certainly during the times of the worst excesses of Northern Ireland, those rules became tighter and tighter. Bands tend to be made up of fired-up young guys, who are the most easily attracted to the paraphernalia of Loyalism and the 'standing up for the kith-and-kin' arguments. They can easily get sucked in to paramilitarism. At one stage some bands thought it was clever to parade with emblems that displayed sympathy for the UDA or UVF. We outlawed that totally, long before the Terrorism Act of 2000 made it illegal.

But if you stopped the Orange Order parading, you would not destroy the Lodge; it would not disappear. In some ways you would create a dangerous organisation by driving it underground. We are waiting to see how the new laws that impinge on parades pan out. The devil is in the detail so we will see how local authorities apply them. But at the end of the day the Lodge won't back away, and I certainly can't back away, from saying that parading is part of our tradition. It is a democratic right but you will always get me to add that it has to be done responsibly. You have to remember that other people have an equal right to get about their business. It's a question of balance.

It is highly desirable that Catholics could and would come and watch our parades. The mark of a settled and democratic society is that we have the ability to tolerate even the things that we don't accept. There are aspects of the Sikh religion that I find very odd but I would not feel offended to relate to their culture. There should not be anything offensive about an Orange parade. If people do find it offensive then they have a bigger problem than I have.

However, it is very sad – and again, I think it is driven by events in Northern Ireland – that some sections of the Protestant and Roman Catholic population in Scotland look daggers at each another and we need to overcome that. But I believe there are lots of Roman Catholics who don't have a big issue with the Order and if a parade is passing then they would stand and take it in. I met Archbishop Mario Conti at one of Jack McConnell's summits and I was chatting to him afterwards. He said to me: 'Perhaps the time will come when I can stand in George Square and review the Orange Parade.' And I replied, 'Perhaps it will.'

And I do hope that it will.

The Sash My Granny Wore

Karen Gillon MSP

Yes, I have sung 'The Sash'. I would be a liar to deny it and I'm not a liar. And I knew the words long before I went to Ibrox. I'm not particularly proud that some people take offence at the song but it's not worth lying about. My grandmother on my mother's side, Maggie Wright, came from Northern Ireland and she was a huge influence on me as I was growing up in Jedburgh. She sang the song to me and there was a sash in the house because it was part of her Orange background. You shouldn't deny where you come from and I wouldn't deny my granny for a minute. I am very proud of her and what she has achieved in her life. And I'm not going to deny that I'm a Rangers supporter either.

My home town had a large number of second-generation Irish immigrants when I was growing up. Around 1915, after a silk mill in Northern Ireland closed, the British Linen Company set up a factory in Jedburgh, which is why my granny and her compadres came over to Scotland. Irish Catholics came to work on farms in the Borders, so you had two distinct communities from the north and south of Ireland in the area. As a child, my mother was taken over to Northern Ireland for the Orange Walk and she would go to Ibrox with her twin brother so there was a natural family link and I wasn't discouraged from supporting Rangers. However, my mother, who brought me up herself, was far more at ease with religious differences between people than my granny.

I had a church upbringing and I still attend, my faith is very important to me as a Christian. Ultimately, we worship the same God although we express that faith differently. But the differences between the two faiths are far less than the similarities. My husband Jim is a Catholic and my two sons are being brought up Catholic but I suppose forty years ago it would have been a different proposition for my mother to marry a Catholic.

And it would have been challenging for my granny, if she had been alive, for me to marry a Catholic. One of her nephews married a Catholic and his mother, my gran's sister, disowned him. She never spoke to him again because it just wasn't done. And forty years ago there would probably have been resistance to Jim marrying a Protestant, but times have moved on.

I actually started to follow Rangers in the Seventies when I was at Glasgow University and at a time when they were probably the most successful domestic Gers team in a generation. Derek Johnstone was my hero and Davie Cooper was a great player but for some reason I have an everlasting memory of big Peter McCloy swinging on the bar at Hampden in the 1978 Scottish Cup final against Aberdeen after we had lost a goal.

There have been instances in the past where people have tried to make the fact that I'm a Rangers supporter something of which I should be ashamed. I suppose it's because the old structure at Ibrox discriminated against Catholics. You cannot deny that and the fact that people thought it was acceptable. But it was stupid that we lost players because of what school they attended. It's always been about football to me. I have no truck with bigotry. I don't like people who are anti-Catholic, anti-Muslim or anti any religion, I'm not in that game. I was amazed when I came to live in Glasgow and then Lanarkshire, because those places were far more divided than Jedburgh. We all went to the same school in Jedburgh. My friend was a Rangers supporter but she was a Catholic. I don't think that would have happened in the west of Scotland.

My faith and my political views are very closely related in terms of tackling injustice and making society more equal. I was brought up with the Labour Party and my mum says I was putting leaflets through doors as a child. My first recollection of an election campaign was John Home Robertson's by-election in Berwick and East Lothian in 1978, where my mother, who had been a shop steward and an activist all her life, campaigned. My granny was a Labour voter in Scotland but Ian Paisley would have been her MP if she was back in Ireland and we would talk about that. And as I got older I would ask her how those two things could go together, but she didn't have to reconcile herself with that, she was what she was and that's how she was brought up.

It is very important to me that the Labour Party is not associated with any religion and that everyone should be able to play a part in it but I accept that in some places in Scotland the Labour Party is associated with Catholicism. I can see where people are coming from with regards Glasgow but it's about who gets involved, why they get involved and the extent of their commitment. I am also a Unionist, and a monarchist. Independence is a possibility not a probability at the moment. I think we do well out of the Union but if the people of Scotland decide they want to go another way then we will have to adapt and get on with it. And I just think there is something safe about a constitutional monarch.

And contrary to what people may think, there are a fair few Rangers fans in the Labour Party, people like Andy Kerr, Alan Wilson, Alasdair Morrison and Cathie Craigie. But in saying that there was a group of school kids getting shown round the Scottish Parliament last year and someone brought one of the students over to me and said, 'Karen's a Rangers supporter'. The pupil didn't think there were any Rangers supporters in the Labour Party!

Celtic cultivate politicians who are Celtic supporters – you see them at games at Parkhead – while Rangers aren't particularly good at doing the politics bit although I have been to Ibrox in my official capacity as an MSP. I was at an anti-sectarianism event and I have also been there as a guest of the Bank of Scotland. I was like a big wean going up the marble staircase. People were saying to me, 'Karen, you shouldn't get excited, you are a politician' but I have been going to Ibrox for years and I wasn't going to pretend that I wasn't thrilled.

I think religion is an issue for some people at a lower level in the Labour Party but not for one minute do I think it's an issue for the hierarchy. I certainly wasn't going to pretend that I wasn't a Rangers supporter to get on in the party. But no way would people stop you becoming an MSP, an MP or a councillor because you were a Protestant but there's certainly a perception there and we have to tackle that because I still have the scars of the Monklands East by-election.[1] I was just a Labour Party activist at the time, before I worked with Helen Liddell, and I suppose that's when I really saw the underbelly – in terms of the split between Catholics and Protestants – that's still in Lanarkshire. It got very nasty and very vicious at different points.

What was happening in Monklands District Council was wrong and the council should have been challenged long before it actually was. Ironically, the four councillors who spoke out against the council were all Catholics so it wasn't about Protestant versus Catholic. The vast majority of the Labour Party councillors in Monklands were Catholics, but it was about an area not being properly funded. People were frustrated and it manifested itself as a religious issue and, unfortunately, to a greater or lesser extent, all the parties tried to capitalise on that aspect one way or the other. But, in my view, we nearly lost the by-election because of it.

In terms of demographics, and the share of the vote that Labour get, some of those who go to a Rangers game on a Saturday must vote Labour. It's not possible for it not to be the case, but that by-election became about religion. Politically, that was absolutely foreign to me and where I came from; it wasn't the way I was brought up. The boys on our supporters bus were wearing SNP stickers on their Rangers shirts. I would say to them, 'Come on guys, you can't be a Scottish nationalist and a Unionist, they are diametrically opposed to each other.' I could understand how, if what was important to you was Unionism, or Northern Ireland, or protecting your Protestant heritage – although these were boys who were probably never in church – that they could vote for a Tory. However, I couldn't understand why they would support a Scottish Nationalist with republican sympathies. But my analysis was purely political, theirs wasn't. They had a very simple and straightforward view: 'Karen, she's a Catholic; I'm not voting for her.' It was about which school Helen had gone to and what her maiden name was.

After everyone from the outside went away, as a youth worker in the area, I had to try and put it back together again. Protestants and Catholics had been living beside each other for years without any problems but it had brought something out that had been under the surface.

I think there are still strong forces of sectarianism inside Scotland and it has the potential to become a danger. However, tackling sectarianism is not about denying who you are or where you come from, it's about accepting that other people have different cultures and religions. I should not have to deny my background and my culture but I can celebrate it without degrading others.

I don't think the blame is only at the door of Rangers, it's there at

Celtic as well. But we don't need to be singing 'We are up to our knees in Fenian blood' at Ibrox. Rangers have not been good at getting their message across, they have not been as public as Celtic in showing that they are trying to tackle sectarianism. We are moving in the right direction, belatedly, but it's a long-term project. You have to take people with you and you can only do that by changing attitudes. The fans have to understand that they can sing other songs. We have a proud history and we don't need to denigrate others to be a great club.

We are a great club.

Note

[1] The Monklands East by-election was held on 30 June 1994, following the death of John Smith, the local MP, and leader of the Labour Party, on 12 May. For the by-election, Labour selected Helen Liddell. She was a high-profile candidate, who had been the first female general secretary of the Labour Party at only twenty-six. The Scottish National Party (SNP) selected Kay Ullrich, who had previously contested Cunninghame South and Motherwell South. Monklandsgate, as the scandal that dominated the election became known, centred on allegations of spending discrepancies between Protestant Airdrie and Catholic Coatbridge, fuelled by the fact that all seventeen of the ruling Labour group were Roman Catholics. The accusations included: £21 million spent on capital projects in Coatbridge while only £2 million was spent in Airdrie; councillors handing out green job-application forms while the Jobcentre handed out white ones; and also accusations of nepotism as dozens of council workers were related to Labour councillors. The accusations were of increased interest to the media as the Monklands West MP was Tom Clarke, the former provost of Monklands District Council and one-time shadow secretary of state for Scotland, while the Monklands East MP was the Labour leader, John Smith. Despite the allegations Helen Liddell retained the seat.

Sectarianism –
Scotland's Secret Shame?

Murdo Fraser MSP

If you are to believe some Scottish politicians, you would think that sectarianism was a problem that ran throughout all parts of Scotland and all sections of Scottish society. As Scotland's First Minister, Jack McConnell made it something of a personal crusade to tackle what he saw as 'Scotland's secret shame'. Mr McConnell certainly led the way in attempting to tackle the issue, with the publication of an eighteen-point plan in January 2006 [1], which listed local and national initiatives including a review of the legislation around marches and parades and performances of an anti-sectarian play to school pupils.

The First Minister was not alone in seeing this as a problem of national significance. At a members' debate in the Scottish Parliament on 24 May 2006, the Glasgow Anniesland Labour MSP, Bill Butler, proposed a motion welcoming the launch of the Scottish Executive's eighteen-point plan and commending those involved in highlighting the problems of bigotry and sectarianism, and also, perhaps more controversially, recognising that sectarianism was a problem throughout Scotland. That debate was well attended by members of the Scottish Parliament and in the gallery to observe it were eminent churchmen, including Cardinal Keith O'Brien, the senior Roman Catholic clergyman in Scotland, and the Moderator of the General Assembly of the Church of Scotland, the Reverend Alan Macdonald.

It was clear to those taking part in that Parliamentary debate that there was a link between sectarianism and football, and specifically the Old Firm. In his opening remarks, Bill Butler stated: 'Sectarianism is of course not merely a football problem, but it is undeniable that a sectarian element has attached to football clubs, particularly, but not exclusively, to Rangers and Celtic.' [2]

Others went even further. The SNP MSP for Glasgow, Sandra White, said: 'We cannot shy away from the fact that, for years and years, Scotland – Glasgow in particular – has suffered sectarianism, violence and abuse, all because of two football teams.' [3] She went on to accuse the Old Firm clubs of profiting in financial terms from sectarianism. Such views are often reflected in the Scottish media, when an assumption can be made that the very existence of Rangers and Celtic football clubs helps to perpetuate sectarian divisions and to stoke-up hatred between different communities.

There is no doubt that both clubs have taken great strides in recent years to try and address the problem. I have been attending matches at Ibrox on and off for the last twenty years, and in my younger days was a season-ticket holder. In that period, I have certainly seen a change in attitudes amongst both the fans and the club authorities.

Whilst the singing of what would be widely viewed as sectarian songs, and sectarian chanting, can still be heard at Ibrox, my own impression is that it has toned down somewhat in recent years. The club itself has made a great effort to encourage the singing of traditional club songs with the original words rather than more modern, and more sectarian, interpretations. That said, an Old Firm match at Ibrox or for that matter Parkhead is no place for the faint-hearted or easily offended.

That sectarianism has had its tragic consequences is not something that can be denied. The horrific murder of Glasgow youngster Mark Scott in an unprovoked attack in 1995 motivated, it appears, purely by sectarian hatred, led directly to the establishment of the charity Nil by Mouth, which campaigns against sectarianism. In 2001 the trade union UNISON carried out a study into the impact of Old Firm games on the health service, which showed that attendances as a result of assaults on the day of an Old Firm fixture increased substantially in many accident-and-emergency units across Scotland. The worst-affected unit was at Monklands General Hospital, where attendances were a staggering nine times the norm.[4]

Undoubtedly we have a problem with sectarianism in Scottish society. But I have to wonder just how widespread it is. I have to say that it has been my life experience, as a not atypical Scot, that I have had no direct personal experience of sectarianism. I was born and brought up in

Inverness, and have lived in Aberdeen, Edinburgh and now in Perthshire. I have to say that in all the communities in which I lived I have yet to encounter sectarianism or indeed meet anyone who has.

If people living in towns and cities such as Dundee, Perth, Stirling or Dumfries were asked whether they considered sectarianism to be a serious problem in their community, I doubt that many of them would feel that to be the case. Politicians who claim that sectarianism is a problem for all of Scotland are therefore somewhere off the mark and indeed such comments may provoke resentment amongst communities who feel that they should not be tarred by the same brush as others.

Many Highlanders like myself ended up as a supporters of one or other of the Old Firm teams not for any religious or sectarian reasons, but because living in an area which at the time had no senior league clubs it was natural to support one of the more popular and successful national sides. Although raised in a Presbyterian household, there was nothing automatic about my becoming a Rangers supporter. Indeed, I recall having an early affinity for Aberdeen and my allegiance to Rangers probably came about because my elder brother was a Rangers fan and in order to keep the peace in the house I changed my allegiance at a very young age to be the same as his. It was only much later that any religious or sectarian influence came to my knowledge. The fact that some of my cousins were Celtic fans rather gives the lie to the notion that support for the Old Firm clubs divides across the whole of Scotland purely on religious lines. There will certainly be areas of Scotland where the reality is different, predominantly in west-central Scotland but also in areas such as West Lothian and parts of Fife. However, it is a false assumption to make that the fan base of the Old Firm is entirely dependent upon any alleged sectarian basis for these clubs.

None of this detracts from the reality of a distinct cultural identity for both Celtic and Rangers. It seems to be quite fashionable and socially acceptable for Celtic supporters to talk proudly of their club's history and traditions and links with the Irish immigrant community in Scotland. It has been perhaps harder for supporters of Rangers to talk about their club's identity with the Scottish Protestant working class. But just as football clubs in all parts of the world will have a distinct identity and traditional links with different sections of the community, so neither Rangers nor

Celtic should be in any way ashamed of their roots. On occasion this can be taken too far as in the supposed policy of Rangers in previous generations of not signing Roman Catholic players, a policy thankfully long consigned to history. But to accuse Rangers of sectarianism for flying the Union flag, or for that matter Celtic for flying the Irish tricolour, as a reflection of their historic roots, is a ludicrous charge to make.

These issues are addressed by the Hamilton North & Bellshill Labour MSP Michael McMahon in a perceptive and thoughtful contribution to the book *Celtic Minded*[5] where he defends the right of Celtic Football Club and its supporters to celebrate their Irish ancestry. He argues that legitimate political and religious opinion is quite distinct from manifestations of religious hatred, and that some of those who pursue an 'anti-sectarian' agenda cannot differentiate between the two. McMahon also takes to task those Celtic fans who bastardise traditional songs into negative anti-Protestant chants.

What is true at Parkhead is equally true at Ibrox. Traditional Rangers songs, or for that matter historic Ulster ballads, have had their words twisted to include anti-Catholic obscenities. A song like 'The Billy Boys' – which has the line 'We're up to our knees in Fenian blood' – is deeply offensive to many, not just Catholics, and the authorities at Ibrox are to be congratulated for their attempts to stamp out the singing of such filth.

But even of those at Ibrox who sing offensive versions of club songs only a tiny minority will be genuine religious bigots or in any way a threat to their Catholic neighbours. A number of years ago a leading Nationalist politician coined the phrase 'ninety-minute nationalists' to describe those Scots who would happily sing about the glories of Scottish independence during a Scotland football match, but once they had left the ground no longer seemed interested in either voting for independence or taking any action to help bring it about. There is a parallel here with the Old Firm, in that of those who do participate in sectarian singing and chanting, the great majority will be 'ninety-minute bigots'. Once the match is over and they are safely back at home, the notion of hating or wanting to harm their work colleague, neighbour or even spouse simply because he or she were a Roman Catholic seems an utterly ludicrous one. That is in no way an attempt to excuse such behaviour or such attitudes, even if they are confined to a football ground. We would all want to see an elimination of abusive songs and chants, and the clubs supported in the efforts that they are making in this regard.

I feel that the sectarianism associated with the Old Firm clubs is tribalism, pure and simple. As I argued in my contribution to Bill Butler's members' debate in the Scottish Parliament, sectarianism has nothing whatsoever to do with religion. I know good Christian people of all denominations, whether Protestant or Roman Catholic, and I have yet to meet anyone with a strong religious faith who could be accused of being guilty of sectarianism or indeed bigotry in any form. The vast majority of those who indulge in sectarian abuse or behaviour or sing offensive songs will rarely, if ever, have seen the inside of a church or chapel. Those who are truly religious, have true faith and believe in Christ's instruction to us to love one another would have no truck with such behaviour.

How much, I wonder, of the 'sectarian' violence identified in the UNISON survey and elsewhere really has its roots in sectarian or religious division? Are the differences not mainly tribal? If someone is attacked in the street because he is wearing a Celtic shirt by a Rangers fan, is he being attacked because he is (supposedly) a Roman Catholic, or is he being attacked because he supports the wrong football team? If it is (as I would suspect in most cases) for the latter reason, is this really a 'sectarian' incident, or simply a deplorable consequence of football rivalry, which is something else altogether? When football fans in other countries engage in massed battles, as they often do, we do not pin the blame on sectarian divisions.

Even if it were possible to stamp out sectarianism based on the religious divide in Scotland, would that be an end of the matter? I seriously doubt that it would. I recall not so long ago seeing at an Old Firm match Rangers fans waving the Israeli flag in response to the display of Palestinian symbols from those in the Celtic colours. It seems that if we are not allowed to have a sectarian divide based upon our own religious differences then we will simply import a conflict from another part of the world and adopt it as our own.

I can quite understand why politicians feel the need to take sectarianism in Scottish society seriously. However, we do have to retain a sense of proportion. For millions of Scots, and particularly for those living in the north, east and south of the country, the idea of a nation riven by sectarian division seems an absurd one, and is entirely outwith their personal experience.

Politicians have a duty to tackle the serious problems in our society. But we should be wary of setting up straw men to attack. Nor should we have as our goal the eradication of the quite legitimate, distinct, historical and cultural traditions of both Rangers and Celtic football clubs.

I look forward to watching football at Ibrox in the future without hearing the obscenities and vile and abusive chants against the Pope and Roman Catholics. I look forward to watching games at Parkhead where Irish terrorist groups are not celebrated. I believe that both football clubs are taking great strides in the right direction. They should be encouraged in their efforts, but let us all keep a grip on reality when in the future we address the problem of sectarianism.

Notes

1   *Action Plan on Tackling Sectarianism in Scotland*; (Scottish Executive publication, June 2006)
2   *Scottish Parliament Official Report* 24 May 2006 col 25955
3   *Scottish Parliament Official Report* 24 May 2006 col 25959
4   UNISON press release 14 October 2002
5   *Celtic Minded*, (Argyll Publishing, 2006)

Left-Winger Leckie

Carolyn Leckie

My mum, as well as raising four children, was a machinist and my dad worked in Weirs in Cathcart, where he was a shop steward. Both were involved in the Orange Order. My dad was a Worthy Master of District 49 in the Gorbals and was president of the Hutchesontown Rangers Supporters Club. That is my background and typical of many Glaswegians born in the 1960s.

Orangeism played an important part in my upbringing. New Year's Day was an important occasion, as was Christmas Day, and then it was the 'big walk' in July, although of course there were other Orange parades. It was an exciting day, no doubt about it. I remember the early mornings, my mum making rolls for a house full of people over from Belfast, the bands playing, it was just great. I would be one of those girls at the front of the children's parade with the Bible open and wearing the crown. At other times, I would be swinging the long cord that hung from the big banners as the music played. I loved it. There was always a lot of alcohol involved but my mum and dad were really quite strict concerning behaviour. They would complain about some of the bands and they would get really upset by the behaviour of the people on the pavements. To them, that wasn't what it was supposed to be about.

I certainly think that there was a feeling of belonging in the Lodge because there was a lot of poverty. There was a great sense of occasion when there was a parade because it was all we had to make us feel a wee bit special. A lot of people don't understand their religion, or the history that is involved, but that's how they were brought up and the Lodge is what they belong to – it's their tribe. And often it's too difficult for people to break out of that mould and say, 'I'm moving away from this; this is not going to be me any more.' It almost always means seeking new friends and breaking from your past and that's not an easy thing to do. As it turned out, the Irish people who used to come over and stay with us provided a good teething ground for my politics. As I got older and more involved with politics, I would get into arguments with my family and our visitors and my mum would say, 'Oh no, she's got her soapbox out again.' She was incredibly strong, stoical and went through hell many times. She looked after my girls while I found my way in the world. She didn't always agree with me but she put up with my 'soapboxing' and supported me through everything. She died earlier this year and I miss her.

The ironic thing about my dad running the Rangers bus was that I never got on it because there were no women allowed. But whenever he took me to the football, as he did occasionally, we would always go to the main stand. He wouldn't wear a scarf, he wore a shirt and tie and it was the only place that I would hear him swear. There weren't many girls at football in those days and, because I used to wear an anorak when I was very young, I used to get mistaken for a boy. I didn't appreciate it at the time but that meant I got peace from the men. As I got older the men were horrible and when I look back I'm horrified at what happened because I had to deal with sexual harassment every time I went to a game.

My dad died when I was eleven and funnily enough I got more into the football after that. Rangers were really good at the time and I can still name the team with players in it like Davie Cooper and Bobby Russell, who were brilliant. And when we moved to Castlemilk I continued to follow Rangers. But our new house was further away from Ibrox and there was a lack of money. Often I had to walk there and back and so it tailed off. I also became more and more uncomfortable with the sectarianism, the verbal aggression and all the political associations. I had changed. I couldn't reconcile all of that stuff with my politics. There are a lot of people who can retain a loyalty to their team although there are a lot of things they disagree with surrounding the club – but I couldn't do it. Initially, the sense of loyalty to my dad and all that sort of thing was definitely an issue for me. It was tied up with my grieving process but once I came to terms with his death, I was able to leave it all behind me.

I argued with my brother about sectarianism from a very early age. I just thought that it wasn't right. He was one of those who boycotted the club when they signed Maurice Johnston. He didn't go to see Rangers for ages and I disagreed with that stance. I thought he was off his head, although he ended up going back. I considered returning to Ibrox because they *did* sign him, just to be contrary, but by that time I had lost interest. In fact, for a long time the pendulum had swung completely in the opposite direction and I wanted Rangers to lose whenever they played. It was a reaction against everything that they represented. Apart from despising the sectarian aspects of the club, I particularly despised the whole attachment with Unionism. If it had been just about football then it would be fine but it wasn't just about football.

Getting involved in politics led me to being less embarrassed about my upbringing and I suppose there is an irony in that. You would think that being a socialist, and operating in a left-wing environment, you would become more embarrassed about my kind of background but I am a lot more comfortable in my skin these days. I will get into debates with people and challenge their preconceptions about Orangeism. You hear people equating the Orange Order with the British National Party and fascism and that's nonsense. I will challenge that because I can speak from experience. The people in my childhood – my mum and dad and their pals – were certainly not fascists by any stretch of the imagination; they were involved in trade unions and had very collective attitudes towards society. Those attitudes probably trace back to the origins of Protestantism, which was a progressive movement of its time. But it's not progressive any more; it is stuck in the past. That happens to a lot of movements; they don't move on and it takes other movements or organisations to come along and take society forward.

There is a perception that the Scottish Socialist Party is a political party mainly for Catholics but it's not something that I have experienced and I would be really shocked if the percentage that we get at the polls isn't proportionate to the religious demographics. I don't know exactly how many in our party are from a background like mine but, again, like in the trade-union movement, there must be quite a few.

I do know that there are active Rangers supporters in the SSP. Although they don't hide themselves they wouldn't be as up front as Celtic supporters in revealing which team they support. Some people will not be happy about me saying this but in terms of public expression of your background, it is definitely the case that it is more acceptable to express an Irish-Catholic-Celtic-supporting background in a socialist party. For instance, it wouldn't be acceptable for me to start singing 'The Sash' after a few beers, whereas I have often seen others of a different persuasion getting steaming and signing Irish rebel songs so there is a little bit of a double standard there.

It doesn't bother me when I hear rebel songs being sung. It's not the politics that excludes me it's the sense of belonging I suppose. But I wouldn't feel that sense of belonging sitting in the company of people singing Orange songs either because I have moved away from that. I am in no-man's land. But perceptions can be difficult to overcome. Certainly that notion that Celtic supporters are more left-wing and enlightened than Rangers supporters is not true. We collected outside Ibrox and Celtic Park for the nursery nurses and we got more money outside Ibrox than we did outside the Celtic game.

I don't think most Rangers fans actually know what the SSP's policies are with regard to Ireland; they make assumptions. They probably think we would force a united Ireland but that's not the case, our policy is consent. What happens to Ireland should be up to the people of Ireland, north and south. You can't force people in the north into a united Ireland. I argued with Belfast Protestants about a united Ireland because I thought that it would be historical justice. Otherwise you'll never get peace, wherever it is, Palestine, Ireland or wherever.

I don't think Ireland should have been colonised by Britain and I don't think partition should ever have happened but you have to move from where people are now, not where they used to be. Sinn Fein have shifted their position drastically, they now support a united Ireland with the consent of the north. I think they now recognise that you cannot force political change on people.

There is a lot more movement between the north and south of Ireland these days. We were driving through Donegal in the summer of 2006, listening to a radio phone-in, and the amount of Protestants in the north calling for a united Ireland on the back of the Republic's growing prosperity was remarkable. You never heard attitudes like that in Belfast when I was young so there is definitely a shift taking place.

And for a political party that is supposed to appeal mainly to Catholics, the SSP have policies that certainly don't appeal to the Catholic Church.

We are absolutely pro-choice and we have been totally down the line in the same way that we have been with regards sexual health and contraception. These are issues very much tied up with religion and so we are always clashing with the Catholic Church. However, that won't stop me arguing for a woman's right to choose because that is completely tied up with my socialism and feminism. There is no way I would change my stance to get a few more votes. What are you there for? It's not just to get your bum on a seat in the Scottish Parliament. You are there to try and change society. Those policies mean we might struggle to take the Catholic vote from the Labour Party. But we are in it for the long term and there are policies that you have because you believe that they are right. You just become the same as the other parties if you water down your policies or change them just to get votes. That doesn't change society or move it forward.

People say you go back to your roots as you get older, perhaps for some sense of comfort or security, but I know for a fact that it will never happen to me. Orangeism is part of my identity and I'm quite comfortable with it but it's only a tiny part of it and it is far removed from who I am now. The truth is I feel that the Orange Order is an embarrassment. Most of the people you see at an Orange parade these days – and they won't thank me for saying this – look as if they have lived incredibly hard lives, they have that really poor look in their faces and wear really bad, shiny suits that look like they have been ironed about a hundred times. But that day when they are walking in a parade is the day that they feel important. I think it's quite poignant and it brings a tear to my eye.

As far as football is concerned, I actually can't stand either Old Firm club. If there is a smaller team playing Celtic or Rangers I always root for the underdog. I watch football on television but Scotland is the only team that I would go to see these days. But no matter what I say, there is an attitude towards you, particularly on the left, that once a Rangers supporter, always a Rangers supporter. They just don't believe me when I say I'm not a Rangers fan any more. For example, my partner is a Celtic fan and he accuses me of still being a Rangers fan. Mind you, my daughter is a Rangers fan and she accuses me of being a Celtic fan.

I can't win.

PLAYERS, FANS AND TRADITIONS

The Tradition–Modernity Interplay and the Relationship Between 'Old' and 'New' at Rangers Football Club

Jonathan Magee

Introduction

Professional football has its origins in the late nineteenth century but the pace of commercial transformation across Europe, and Britain in particular, has been appreciably rapid in the last two decades. Assessment of the current football market in the United Kingdom unearths a business where clubs are floated on the stock market and can be bought by American billionaires, Russian oligarchs and venture capitalists. Television companies have seemingly bottomless pits of money to buy rights for football coverage, stadiums are upgraded, expanded and even moved in some cases, the millionaire footballer is a universally common figure, and a handful of elite European clubs seek a stranglehold at the centre of the global game.

Closer inspection of the football business reveals tortuous power battles between key stakeholders – like governing bodies, tournament organisers and broadcasting companies – in the running of the game. A fundamental reason for this is that football is big business. The scale of this can be judged by assessing Deloitte's Football money league 2006 lists and the revenues accrued by the top clubs during season 2005/06. In this period the top twenty clubs had combined sales of £2.1 billion with Real Madrid topping the league with a turnover of £202 million. Consequently football clubs, especially at the elite level in Europe, are commercial entities that are part of an industry that has immense global popularity.

However, what is hidden, or perhaps even lost, within the professional football business is any recognition of the football supporter. After all, it is the supporter who parts with his or her hard-earned money to support a team and such expenditure is not only on match tickets and travel but also on merchandise and television subscriptions. The commercial emphasis of modern times has resulted in supporters becoming regarded more as customers of a business product or brand rather than supporters of a football club. Football would be a poor sport without supporters but the loyalty of the supporters often appears to be taken for granted.

As in almost every business, expansion into new markets is critical for maximising profit margins and football is now no different. Recent developments have seen elite clubs, like Manchester United and Real Madrid, seek to develop a global supporter base by extending to the Far East and North America. This search for new markets as part of the overall commercialisation of football has exposed conflict between club and supporter. Perhaps the clearest indication of this conflict is the recent establishment of supporter-founded clubs in England, such as AFC Wimbledon and FC United of Manchester. These 'alternative clubs' were formed by supporters who became disaffected with what they perceived as the 'selling out of their club' and so they established a 'supporters' club to retain what they believed to be the club's traditions. In the case of AFC Wimbledon the key motivation was the change of club name and location of Wimbledon FC in London to Milton Keynes Dons FC in Buckinghamshire. For FC United of Manchester, the purchase of Manchester United by the American tycoon Malcolm Glazier was the final straw in a sequence of financial decisions that were perceived to be removing the club from its roots by those who consider themselves 'true' supporters. The above examples graphically display how disenchanted some supporters have become by modernisation.

The study of football supporter culture is well established (see for example, Redhead, 1997; and, Brown 1998) but how clubs and supporters engage with each other in times of almost insatiable commercialism and profit maximisation is an interesting issue. Particularly central to this is the connection between tradition and modernity and this chapter will provide an assessment of how Rangers has developed within the commercially expanding football industry of the last two decades in relation to the tradition–modernity interplay.

British football and the modernising of tradition

In an article on Celtic FC and identity in modern Scotland Raymond Boyle (1994) focused on the modernisation of British football and the 'potential tensions that exist between the drive to modernize, and the need to retain some of the more 'traditional' aspects of football culture' (p.74). For Boyle (1994, p.82) 'by modernising, I mean the attraction of new money into the club which will allow it to progress both on and off the pitch'. Boyle focused on concepts such as 'tradition and identity' (p.78), 'tradition v modernization' (p.81) and 'tradition as commodity' (p.83) as important factors in Celtic's development in the late 1980s and 1990s.

Boyle and Haynes (1998) studied the modernising of tradition within British football in the mid-1990s and observed that 'aspects of marketing practice [are] becoming central to clubs as they attempt to modernise their business infrastructure' (p.21). Particular attention was directed at how different marketing models were introduced by football clubs, with the issues of tradition and modernisation receiving varying attention. One such case study in the research was 'The Celtic Revolution' of the early to mid-1990s and how the 'revolution' saw the club transform its business and commercial practices in ways that recognised the importance of the club's Irish history. The importance of traditional Irish links in the modernisation of Celtic was also noted by Boyle (1994) and is an example of how clubs attach to the past and marry up 'tradition with commercial acumen' (p.82).

The relationship between tradition and modernity and their resultant interplay at Rangers FC is the focus of this chapter, with the start point being the mid-1980s. In July 1986, and for the first time, Rangers appointed a manager (Graeme Souness) without any previous club association. This was a bold move by the club, which had previously only been managed by those with close associations to it and it is fair to say the club was seeking a 'modern' direction. The appointment of a 'modern' manager was followed two years later by sale of the club to David Murray, an entrepreneur who did not support the club (Walker, 1990; Fynn and Guest, 1994). In essence, this new investment was what Boyle (1994, p.82) regarded as modernising. Walker (1990, p.155) argues that this period heralded on-field and off-field practices that centred on 'the cultivation of a super-club status beyond the field of play; commercialism has become predominant and the aim of becoming a flourishing business enterprise vigorously pursued without reference to supporters'. This chapter is able to assess what has occurred at Rangers since Walker's comment but first it is necessary to establish the traditions of Rangers and then Rangers as a modern business.

Rangers FC and tradition

As is well known 'Rangers, of course, are the Protestant half of Scottish football's internationally known religious rivalry' (Walker, 1990, p.138). Writing about the Old Firm, Bairner (2001, p.55), notes that 'the fact that this rivalry is rooted in sectarian tensions between Scottish Protestants and Catholic immigrants from Ireland is undeniable'. Rangers and Celtic have thus come to represent opposite communities in a society founded upon division where football as a sport is second to none in terms of popularity and importance. Much academic literature has been dedicated to the study of the Old Firm (see for example, Murray, 2000 and 2003), Celtic (see, for example, Bradley, 2006 and Finn, 2000) and Rangers (see, for example, Moorhouse, 1991 and Walker, 1990) with attention largely centred on the themes of religion, politics, sectarianism, ethnicity, nationalism and the perceived prejudices involved. This chapter, whilst recognising the above, prefers to focus on the interplay between tradition (old) and modernity (new) at Rangers and thus it is important to establish the traditions of Rangers.

In existence since 1872, the location of Rangers in the Govan area of Glasgow is significant as this was a working-class area largely dominated by Protestant people who quickly attached to the club. According to Walker (1990), when the Harland and Wolff shipyard opened in Govan in 1912, an 'unquantified number of Ulster (Protestant) workers settled in Glasgow' (p.140) and 'the 1912–14 period is viewed as crucial in the "firming up" of Rangers' Protestant image' (p.141). Walker (1990) further argues that throughout Rangers' existence 'the club's Protestant image [has] stood for a powerful current of popular Protestantism' (p.138) and that supporting Rangers is, Walker (1990, p.146) adds, 'a celebration of Scottishness which was underpinned by a strong unionism or loyalism'.

Walker's (1990) assessment of the history of Rangers is littered with examples of the club's close association to Protestantism and he contends that Rangers became embedded within 'loyalist culture' (p.142) in the pre-first-world-war period. In the 1960s the club was criticised for their 'Protestant image' (p.147) yet it is beyond doubt that Rangers has a deeply rooted Scottish Protestant history. This history, in a society like Scotland where social, cultural, religious, ethnic and political tensions are vividly detectable, has vital significance not only to this paper but also to Rangers as a whole. Just as the Irish heritage of Celtic is critical to the club's identity in the eyes of its supporter base, so too are the Scottish Protestant roots of Rangers. When this chapter refers later to 'tradition' in relation to the tradition–modernity interplay at Rangers, it is Scottish Protestantism with its significant Ulster dimension that is being referred to.

Rangers as a modern business

Evidence of Rangers being one of Europe's leading clubs is provided by Deloitte's Football Money League 2006, which listed Rangers in eighteenth place, while Football's Most Valuable Clubs 2007, as provided by the leading business magazine *Forbes*, puts Rangers in twenty-fourth place with a market value of £75 million and a turnover for 2006 of £57.7 million. Whilst Rangers are a far cry from the likes of Real Madrid, Manchester United and Chelsea in terms of turnover, their commercial capacity at domestic level far outweighs other clubs in Scotland outside of Celtic. Indeed, the Old Firm monopoly on Scottish football and the resultant competitive imbalance are well known and as such 'the intense competition and rivalry that exist between Celtic and Rangers, have allowed both of these clubs to prosper financially' (Morrow, 2003, p.7). Whilst independent clubs, the Old Firm could be regarded as a business partnership, in which each member club is reliant on the other, since without a competitive other half the Old Firm would be a weak product.

As well as financial strength, Rangers attract an average crowd of 49,000 while over six hundred supporters clubs are registered with the official club network of supporters groups, Rangers Worldwide Alliance. In terms of football successes, the club is the only one in the world to have won fifty domestic championships. They reached the equivalent semi-final stage of the inaugural Champions League (in its former format) in 1992/93 and became the first Scottish club to qualify from the group stages of the revamped Champions League. While by no means one of Europe's elite, Rangers is nonetheless a club of significant stature and, like many other clubs in Europe, has been challenged to modernise itself in the rapidly changing European football market. How Rangers has responded is significant to this chapter.

A note on methodology

As a lifelong Rangers supporter the author is closely associated with the developments at Rangers in the period under question. Regular attendance at Ibrox in the last decade has permitted the author to engage with fellow Rangers supporters and witness key events at first hand. Material is also drawn from the author's collection of fanzines and whilst it is acknowledged that fanzines may not be representative of a total supporter group nonetheless they are, according to Haynes (1995), 'a rich resource of textual data' (p.19) that revolve 'around the need for representation to provide 'ordinary' fans with a voice' (p.58). The fanzines thus provide an indication of key debates and issues prevalent to Rangers supporters in the period under focus.

'We must leave the past behind . . .'

The historical associations of Rangers with Protestantism have left the club open to criticism of ethnic exclusivity, particularly in terms of its employment practices and team composition (Bairner, 2001). Finn provides a comprehensive critique of perceived prejudices and discriminatory practices against Scots-Irish Catholics at Rangers over the years, particularly the absence of Catholic players in the Rangers team. Finn subsequently concludes that 'Catholics were unacceptable at Ibrox; by its signing policy Rangers showed that it was an anti-Catholic club, not simply a Protestant one' (2000, p.72). For the likes of Finn, Ibrox stadium and the Rangers team were unwelcoming places for Catholics, especially those from Scotland.

In 1986, Ibrox was one of the most modern stadiums in Britain because of the necessity to revamp it following the 1971 Ibrox disaster, yet the team was experiencing a period of on-field mediocrity and sought to appoint a 'modern' manager to lift the club from its doldrums. Consequently, Graeme Souness, a Scotland internationalist with a glittering playing career in England and Italy, was appointed as player-manager in July 1986. Souness had no previous connection to the club so was a non-traditional appointment, though the fact that he was a Scottish Protestant did not go unnoticed by the supporters.

The team that Souness took over was almost exclusively Scottish Protestant but by the end of Souness's first season Rangers delivered a championship title with a team consisting of a mix of Scottish and English players. Moorhouse (1994) provides a historical account of the traditional migratory path of Scottish players to England but Souness set about reversing this trend with the acquisition of England international players such as Terry Butcher, Ray Wilkins and Gary Stevens. Internationalists from the former Soviet Union, Oleg Kuznetsov and Alexie Mikhailichenko, were also recruited as Rangers developed a cosmopolitan outlook on the field. However, the glaring exception in the Rangers team was the Scottish Catholic player, a point noted at the time by those critical of the club's policy in this area.

1988 was a significant year for Rangers in terms of off-field direction as the club received new investment following its £6 million purchase by Scottish multi-millionaire businessman David Murray. Although a supporter of Ayr United Murray was a personal friend of Souness and a successful entrepreneur with a portfolio of fifty companies. At the time of Murray's purchase Souness was quoted as saying 'Rangers are the biggest club in Britain and we have to stand alongside the European giants' (cited in Fynn and Guest, 1994, p.156) and he saw Murray as having the character and business acumen to take Rangers to 'the next level'. The next level in terms of off-field business was a restructuring of the club's commercial practices, while the next level for on-field performance was success in European football.

Fynn and Guest (1994, p.156–172) detail the success of the Murray–Souness partnership in the late 1980s and early 1990s as Rangers progressed both on and off the field. Murray set about restructuring Rangers' business practices, with corporate hospitality, sponsorship, advertising, and merchandising to the fore. However, and most critically, the vision for Murray and Souness in terms of improving future prosperity was to have an inclusive recruitment policy so that Rangers could sign the best players on the market, including those of Scottish Catholic heritage. In consequence Rangers signed former Celtic player Maurice Johnston in the middle of July 1989, a significant time in the Protestant calendar and one now firmly etched in the history of Rangers.

The acrimony caused by this signing has been well covered elsewhere (see for example, Walker, 1990; Bairner, 2001) with Walker (1990) concluding of the Johnston signing that despite initial protests, scarf-burning and general hostility among some supporters 'signing Catholic players has evidently not led to the loss of more than an insignificant minority' (p.155). The following extract is significant when one considers the traditions of Rangers and the context of the Johnston transfer:

> David Murray, the chairman who sanctioned the purchase of Johnston, showed that he was no longer concerned with parochial issues like sectarianism and wanted to take Rangers into a new era. 'We mustn't be narrow-minded,' he said. 'We have got to rise above that as something from the past and leave it behind' (cited in Fynn and Guest, 1994, p.161).

Souness and Johnston were both successful at Rangers. They left the club in 1991 and there is no doubt that their quite distinct legacies were highly significant. Souness had revolutionised Rangers and the signing of Johnston was arguably his greatest single act in turning Rangers into a 'modern' club. Johnston contributed to on-field successes and his commitment brought acceptance from Rangers supporters. Consequently, the club could now operate an inclusive recruitment policy, which was a significant factor in the early 1990s as a genuinely international transfer market was developing following the break up of the former Soviet Union. By 1991, and under Murray's stewardship, Rangers had spent £26 million on redeveloping Ibrox and £9 million net on players (Fynn and Guest, 1994, p.162). Therefore Murray had taken Rangers to 'the next level' in business terms and the Murray-Souness-Johnston triumvirate had permitted Rangers to sign non-traditional players, including Scottish Catholic players. It appeared that the club was leaving behind the narrow-mindedness David Murray had wished to dispense with.

However, and given the traditions of Rangers, Murray's desire to transform Rangers was not a straightforward process. Writing in 1990 – a time when Rangers was developing its business strategies under Murray – Walker questioned the 'type' of supporter Rangers wished to attract in the future and identified two supporter types available to Rangers at this time of modernisation: the business or professional supporter who has limited loyalty or inclination to attend Ibrox Park (tentatively suggestive of a 'modern' supporter); and, the passionate one who attends without question and 'follows' the club everywhere (tentatively suggestive of a 'traditional' supporter). Given the time that has passed since Walker's speculation it is possible in this chapter to address what has happened at Rangers with particular emphasis on the interplay between tradition and modernity.

Simply the best

Walter Smith, Souness's assistant, took over as Rangers manager in April 1991 with a handful of games remaining and Rangers under severe pressure from Aberdeen at the top of the table. As fate would have it, the title was decided in a final day head-to-head clash at Ibrox, which Rangers had to win to secure the title. An incident-packed game saw Rangers triumph 2–0 and retain the championship.

At this time many major clubs were attempting to develop a brand identity and the 1990/91 championship success resulted in Rangers presenting their brand identity of 'Simply the Best', the title of a song by Tina Turner. The first time the 'Simply the Best' label appeared on merchandising was on the front cover of a video commemorating the 1990/91 championship success. An initiative to generate pre-match atmosphere at football grounds at the time was to play a song to announce the arrival of the team and, from the beginning of the following season, 'Simply the Best' welcomed Rangers players onto the pitch. This adoption of the club's 'Simply the Best' brand identity was well received by the supporters and needs explaining.

The timing of the branding was appropriate as Rangers was experiencing a successful period. In season 1992/93 Rangers not only secured a domestic treble but also defeated English champions Leeds United home and away en route to the equivalent semi-final stage of the inaugural Champions

League. Indeed, domestic success would continue as Rangers secured nine league championships in a row between 1988/89 and 1996/97 to equal Celtic's nine-in-a-row record of the late 1960s and early 1970s. Following this success the 'Simply the Best' song was used by the club on the *Rangers – Club Anthems* CD in celebration of nine-in-a-row. It is clear then that the branding of the club as 'Simply the Best' occurred at a time when the club was very successful and supporters could hardly be faulted for attaching to the label so readily.

However, this apparently innocuous song soon became controversial when some fans supplied 'add on' lyrics about the Pope and the IRA. The sentiments were clearly sectarian and resulted in 'Simply the Best' becoming another in a long line of Ibrox anthems that did not just celebrate Rangers, but ventured crudely into the arenas of religion and politics. The practice of word insertion continued for years at Ibrox and came in for criticism even from people who contributed to Rangers fanzines. In March 2007, at the away UEFA Cup fixture against Osasuna, footage of a group of fans singing the song with the add-ons landed the club in trouble with UEFA for the second year running.

'Simply the Best', having been dropped as the song to greet the team because of the actions of some fans, has returned by popular demand although with warnings about the inserted words. Whilst critics note that the song may not be applicable when Rangers are experiencing a poor season, nonetheless supporters insist on its appropriateness given that Rangers hold the world record for the number of league titles won. Indeed, it was the 'Simply the Best' ethos that prompted the Rangers Supporters Trust, the independent Rangers supporters body, to lobby the club to alter its club badge to incorporate five stars (one star for every tenth championship) in recognition of the club's fiftieth championship success. Initially, the hierarchy at Rangers resisted but the clamour for recognition of the world record grew rapidly among supporters, so much so that Rangers introduced a new club badge in 2004 that featured five stars above the traditional club crest. The club badge now demonstrates a modernised badge that incorporates a reference to past successes and, in a sense, marries 'old' and 'new' Rangers.

The 'Dutch-isation' of Rangers

At the end of season 1997/98 Walter Smith's tenure as Rangers manager came to an unsuccessful end with Rangers denied a record-breaking tenth league championship in a row. Key to Smith's departure however was the lack of progress in Europe. At this time, David Murray was reaching a decade in charge and in this period Rangers had spent £90 million on players and £52 million on stadium development. Murray's ambitions included turning Rangers into a European force (Fynn and Guest, 1994, p.156–62) and, following the failures of first Souness and then Smith to deliver, Rangers looked beyond the Scottish Protestant community for a manager for the first time in their history.

In the summer of 1998 the club appointed Dick Advocaat, the former national team manager of Holland, as their first non-Scottish-Protestant manager. The appointment of Advocaat, a manager with an impressive pedigree, was regarded as a further illustration of the modernisation of Rangers.

Significantly in the context of the tradition–modernity interplay, the club was no longer managed by 'one of their own', that is, a Scottish Protestant, so Advocaat's recruitment had the potential to be contentious. However, he was instantly received by the Rangers support but for reasons that had as much to do with his Dutch nationality as it did his managerial prowess. The reasons for this approval are evidence of the fusion between tradition and modernity at Rangers, as one needs to look within Protestant history to account for Advocaat's instant acceptance among supporters. In essence, even though the appointment of Advocaat was central to any notion of a 'new and modern' Rangers it permitted the alignment of tradition and modernity through a 'Dutch-isation' process.

The appointment of a Dutch manager had strong approval amongst Rangers supporters because of the cultural and religious importance of the Netherlands within Protestant history and in particular the role performed by Prince William of Orange in the seventeenth century. Born in The Hague into the ruling Dutch House of Orange-Nassau in 1650, William was a Prince of Orange from birth and crusaded on behalf of Protestants against powerful Catholic rulers King James II of Britain and Louis XIV of France. In 1689, Prince William defeated King James at the Battle of the

Boyne in Ireland and subsequently became King William III. This battle has a special place in Protestant culture in relation to freedom from Roman Catholicism and is celebrated annually on the twelfth of July, particularly in Northern Ireland and Scotland.

Thus the club's first non-Scottish-Protestant manager was in fact regarded, if for the most part light-heartedly, by many supporters as 'one of their own' on cultural, historical and religious grounds. Hence Advocaat's appointment was a double-sided coin in the tradition–modernity relationship at Rangers: on the one hand his appointment was taking Rangers in a 'new' direction yet on the other a Dutch manager permitted supporters to reinforce the traditions of the club as Protestant even though it did not have a Scottish Protestant manager at the helm. This linkage was capitalised on by both club and supporter during Advocaat's spell with the club.

Advocaat instantly set about instilling a core of Dutch players whilst still maintaining a Scottish element to his Rangers team and this blend provided the opportunity for supporters to display Protestant imagery in two ways. Firstly, it is common practice for supporters to display national flags of non-indigenous players in their team and Rangers supporters did this with the Dutch national flag. As this flag is composed of red, white and blue horizontal bars, Rangers supporters were able to display a flag that related to the Dutch element in their team composition but also provided a chance to display colours central to Protestantism within the United Kingdom. This was not restricted merely to the Dutch flag as Rangers signed players in this era from Chile, United States of America and France (flags that are also red, white and blue) and while they too were displayed they did not have the same resonance with supporters as the Dutch flag. Secondly, there was the wearing of replica Holland shirts and it was the orange colour of this shirt that was significant. Orange, along with red, white and blue, is a core colour in Protestant popular culture and Rangers is familiarly associated with the red, white and blue combination in terms of team kits and supporter apparel. Consequently, wearing replica Holland shirts to honour the strong Dutch influence at the club also permitted supporters to reinforce the Protestant history of Rangers.

This integration of orange as part of the 'Dutch-isation' of Rangers was visible at the 2000 Scottish Cup final. Rangers was seeking victory to secure a league-championship-and-cup double to bring Advocaat's trophy haul to five in two seasons. In the weeks leading up to the game a campaign among supporters to display orange regalia instead of the traditional red-white-and-blue combination gathered pace and it was decided that the supporters should hold a 'day of orange'. It was certainly a novel idea to dispense with club colours, but the popularity of the 'day of orange' owed as much to symbolism as it did to the strong Dutch influence on the club's successes. Subsequently Rangers produced orange T-shirts with a picture of manager Advocaat below the slogan 'Advocaat – A Dutch of class'. However, alternative and unofficial T-shirts were available outside Hampden Park in the build-up to the game, which were orange in colour but had Advocaat's photograph associated with the following slogans:

Advocaat – The second great Dutchman to lead us to victory
Advocaat – The Prince of Orange
On the march with Advocaat's Orange Army

These slogans clearly associate Advocaat's Dutch nationality and his successes with Prince William of Orange and the Battle of the Boyne. Indeed, Advocaat was heralded as a leader of a modern-day Protestant 'army' and the celebrating crowd departing the streets around Hampden Park mirrored an Orange Order parade with its celebration of Protestantism. Advocaat offered an insightful summary of the ethos when he said of the 'day of orange' that 'you have to remember that we have our blue noses to go along with the orange shirts' (cited in Cameron, 2004, p.137). Hence, the 'day of orange' was an example of the club capitalising on the tradition–modernity interplay in ways that outwardly demonstrated 'new' Rangers but permitted supporters to reinforce 'old' Rangers and its Protestant history at the same time.

The 'Dutch-isation' process also extended to replica jerseys and the club produced two away shirts during Advocaat's reign that integrated Dutch references. Firstly, the club produced a white shirt with red and blue bars on the chest, which resembled a Dutch flag even though the logo of the club's sponsor appeared between the bars. The other shirt however was more contentious as Rangers produced an orange shirt for matches in which the home colour of blue, and away colour of white, could not be used. The use of 'third' shirts is common in modern football but in this case it was the choice of colour that was controversial. With this shirt, the club was formalising orange as part of the club's fabric and providing supporters with a legitimate opportunity to wear an orange club shirt. The shirt was widely popular and perhaps not surprisingly twice sold out in Northern Ireland. What the shirt demonstrated was the vitality of the 'Dutch-isation' process and how the club sought to fuse tradition and modernity in a way that was good for business as it appealed to the broader supporter culture. The club however received strong criticism because of the centrality of the colour orange in Protestant culture but defended the shirt under the 'Dutch-isation' banner. Despite supporter popularity the shirt was only worn twice, and replaced the next year, but it is an interesting example of how tradition and modernity can connect.

Despite significant investment in players and a domestic treble and double in Advocaat's first two seasons Rangers did not make the necessary progress in Europe and were trophy-less in season 2000/01. A disappointing start to the next campaign saw Advocaat replaced by Alex McLeish in November 2001 and Advocaat took on the position of general manager until the end of the season, when he became manager of the Holland national team. Reflecting upon Advocaat's association with Rangers it is clear the club sought a 'modern' manager and given Advocaat's nationality and his recruitment of many Dutch players, a 'Dutch-isation' process occurred. This presented Rangers supporters with a significant opportunity to reinforce the traditions of the club through this 'modern' manager. In essence, the 'Dutch-isation' era at Rangers highlighted the curious and complex alliance between tradition and modernity and the relationship between 'old' and 'new' at Rangers. It is possible to conclude that the appointment of Advocaat was made with an eye on using 'tradition as commodity' (Boyle, 1994, p. 83) as a business strategy for the club though it is also possible that the commodification of Dutchness owed more to the ironic humour of the supporters than to the business acumen of the board.

Amo! Amo! Amo!

The inclusive transfer policy that was initiated by Souness and then internationalised during his, Smith's and Advocaat's reigns advanced the cosmopolitan composition of the Rangers team and in doing so reduced the centrality of the Scottish Protestant player. The case of Maurice Johnston was important in demonstrating that Rangers supporters were willing to accept and support non-traditional players. However, the shift in emphasis toward recruiting large numbers of foreign players was evidence of a new Rangers, in which the role, number and significance of the traditional player was reduced. Supporters subsequently had to become accustomed to many non-traditional players in their team with the recruitment of players from Catholic countries like France, Italy, Spain, Argentina and Chile.

For a club with traditions like Rangers this was clearly a significant development and was potentially damaging to relations between club and supporter. However, it is significant that the case of the Argentine player Gabriel Amato, who made the sign of the cross as he went out on 11 August 1998 to play in a qualifying tie for the European Champions League, caused no adverse comment from fans (Bairner, 2001, p.55). This incident was evidence as to how Rangers supporters had adapted to the cosmopolitan nature of the team and the presence of Catholic players in it and the supporter group must be praised for this.

An interesting case regarding Catholic players at Rangers was Lorenzo Amoruso, an Italian player signed by Walter Smith for £5 million in the close season of 1997. Following a difficult initial period Amoruso became an established member of the team to the point that he became the first Catholic captain of Rangers. This was in preference to some Scottish Protestant players, but Amoruso was a successful and admired captain because of his leadership qualities and commitment to Rangers. Thus, under Advocaat, Rangers subsequently had a non-traditional manager and a Catholic captain. A new Rangers clearly existed. Nonetheless relations between Advocaat and Amoruso deteriorated to the point where Amoruso was stripped of the captaincy, which prompted him to say 'I remember the date as if it were yesterday: Monday, October 30, 2000. The day Dick Advocaat tried to rip my heart out' (cited in Cameron, 2004, p.14).

Amoruso remained at Rangers until the summer of 2003 with the captaincy passing to Barry Ferguson, a boyhood Rangers supporter and thus one regarded as a traditional player, though this brought about some interesting developments. Ferguson – despite his Scottish Protestant suitability as captain and the successes Rangers enjoyed at the time – was not overwhelmingly popular with supporters, with some considering that he lacked the leadership qualities necessary at a club of Rangers' stature. Indeed it would not have been an unpopular move if the captaincy had been returned to Amoruso by McLeish yet, somewhat ironically, both players were transferred to Blackburn Rovers in the summer of 2003 although in completely different circumstances. Rangers received an offer for Amoruso, by then into his thirties, that they felt could not turn down and transferred the player against his wishes but for Ferguson it was different. Ferguson was in his mid-twenties, the Rangers captain and a pivotal player. Despite being tied to a long-term contract, he made no secret of his desire to leave the club he professed to have so much loyalty toward and engineered, through his agent, a transfer to Blackburn. While Rangers did not sell Ferguson on the cheap the club had little option and the whole saga caused deep disgruntlement amongst the supporters. The starkly different circumstances of these transfers highlighted the supporter reverence afforded to Amoruso and the open disgruntlement directed to Ferguson.

In a way this Amoruso–Ferguson situation is another contradictory example of the interplay between tradition and modernity at Rangers as an Italian Catholic was a more popular choice for captain than a Scottish Protestant one. Critically, Ferguson was to be reunited with Rangers and played a further role in the tradition–modernity interplay at Rangers as the next section will demonstrate.

Replacing the new with the old: coming full circle and the return of Walter Smith

As mentioned above Dick Advocaat was replaced as manager by Alex McLeish, which returned Rangers to the hands of a Scottish Protestant manager. However, McLeish was not of traditional ilk as he had no prior involvement with the club. At the time of his appointment McLeish claimed boyhood support of Rangers though this appeared a little tenuous and was never fully accepted by the Rangers support. Even though McLeish remained in charge for almost five seasons and won seven trophies in that time his tenure was one characterised by financial constraints. Rangers signed a series of free transfer or low-budget players and the side was a shadow of the great teams witnessed under Advocaat. Nevertheless

McLeish gained the respect of the supporters through his professional conduct and dignified manner.

Significantly, McLeish signed Barry Ferguson from Blackburn Rovers in January 2005, a controversial move given the acrimonious circumstances of Ferguson's departure. Some supporters were openly and understandably hostile to Ferguson's return, but others welcomed Ferguson with open arms as the returning hero. Even more contentious was the reinstatement of Ferguson as captain, with many supporters regarding the player as unbefitting of the captaincy given his previous show of disloyalty to the club. There is no doubt that Ferguson is a talented player but his controversial return and reappointment as captain is something not forgotten by some supporters.

Despite initial success under McLeish Rangers struggled domestically and despite becoming the first Scottish club to qualify for the last sixteen of the Champions League his tenure ended at the end of season 2005/06. Rangers had finished without any silverware and did not even qualify for the Champions League but remarkably David Murray secured the services of one of the most sought after managers in Europe to replace McLeish. The highly successful and much respected former Lyon manager Paul Le Guen became the second non-Scottish-Protestant manager of Rangers in June 2006. Even more significant was the fact that Le Guen became the first Catholic manager of Rangers, a point forcibly made by the club's detractors who speculated that this would cause significant unrest amongst the supporter base. The appointment was evidence that Rangers was again entering another 'new' phase as Le Guen was a highly technical and forward-thinking manager.

Le Guen himself was aware of what faced him at Rangers and not long after his appointment he said that 'when you start working for a new club you have to respect the past, and the traditions, and the way the club has been built' (*Scotland on Sunday*, 26 May 2006). Understanding the club's traditions was significant to the solidification of the Rangers–Le Guen partnership and he duly received a rapturous welcome on his first match at Ibrox with his name being chanted from before kick-off. When he arrived in the dugout at kick-off the Broomloan Road stand displayed cards that replicated the French flag, an act of support that contradicted predictions in the media that Le Guen would not be accepted because of his religion.

Under Le Guen Rangers had a poor start to their domestic campaign but progressed well in the UEFA Cup. A limited transfer budget meant the manager had been unable to improve the quality of the squad and by December it was clear that Rangers were not going to challenge Celtic for the championship. Pressure on Le Guen intensified, especially within the media, and tetchy relations surfaced between the manager and captain Ferguson. Le Guen's management style was that of a disciplinarian founded upon a scientific approach to training, diet and lifestyle. He was a fitness fanatic who refrained from alcohol, expected the same level of dedication from his squad and questioned the lifestyle of Scottish players, especially in relation to alcohol. Ferguson publicly criticised the methods of the manager and also the quality of some of the foreign signings made by Le Guen and the media speculated that there was a split between Scottish and foreign players.

As Rangers lost further ground on Celtic over the Christmas period the pressure mounted on Le Guen. The opening of the January transfer window saw Le Guen strip Ferguson of the captaincy and place the player on the transfer list, reasoning that Ferguson 'tries to have too much influence. I thought of the interests of the team, the squad and Rangers. You need to have a captain who gives the right message and provides an example.' (BBC Sport website, 2 January 2007). This was a sensational move as Ferguson was arguably the best player in the team and a traditional Rangers captain who had known past success. Le Guen also acknowledged that the move could result in the termination of his contract. However, the strength of Le Guen's management style was clear: he felt he could not be undermined by any player, let alone the captain, and Ferguson was not selected for the next match.

The Le Guen–Ferguson dispute highlighted a tension between a modern manager and traditional player and the supporter base was split. On the one hand some supporters sided with the manager as it was he who had ultimate authority and put their faith in him given his impressive record at Lyon. Also, the circumstances of Ferguson's transfer to Blackburn Rovers was not lost on some supporters, who felt that he was further undeserving of the captaincy by undermining the manager and therefore should leave the club. However, Ferguson received support from those who felt that the manager had misunderstood the importance of the role of Rangers captain, especially a traditional one like Ferguson, whilst others backed the captain because they felt that in his short time in charge Le Guen did not possess the management skills required for Scottish football.

At the next game, away to Motherwell, Le Guen faced supporter protests before and after the game with many chanting the name of the absent Ferguson. Despite victory the match turned out to be the Frenchman's last because at a meeting with David Murray the next day both parties agreed that it was best Le Guen left his post. Ferguson was reinstated, as player but not captain, by the acting manager in the next game. It seemed that the methods of the 'modern' manager had not found favour with the 'traditional' captain and this clash fractured the club. The outcome of the Le Guen–Ferguson split still causes consternation among supporters despite its ultimate resolution. Indeed, Ferguson has acquired the nickname 'Captain Undermine' amongst some supporters who question his suitability as captain. What the situation demonstrates is the powerful undercurrents that exist at Rangers in relation to the tradition–modernity interplay.

At a time of turmoil David Murray reappointed Walter Smith as manager in January 2007. Smith appointed Ally McCoist, Rangers' record goal scorer, as his assistant and reinstated Ferguson as captain. Ultimately, following two 'new' and 'modern' managers in Advocaat and Le Guen Rangers returned to the past and reinstated an 'old' and traditional manager. This however was not universally popular as Smith's previous tenure had ended in repeated European failure. On the other hand, others were more welcoming as Smith's teams of the nine-in-a-row years were founded upon a Scottish backbone that was interspersed with foreign players of repute and more of the same was anticipated. To such supporters managerial control of the club had returned to a capable and traditional manager. Almost true to form, Smith began to pick more Scottish players and managed to defeat Celtic twice before the end of the season, although he suffered a disappointing exit at the last-sixteen stage in the UEFA Cup. What is clear is that managerial appointments in the last two decades are a microcosm of the tradition–modernity interplay and how the relationship between 'old' and 'new' at Rangers is highly complex.

Conclusion: The future needs the past

It is evident that much of significance has occurred at Rangers in the last two decades, providing an illuminating insight into the complex developments fashioned by modernisation. Rangers – a club founded upon Scottish Protestant roots – has sought to adapt to the changing European football market and in so doing it has been necessary for the club to recruit non-traditional players and appoint non-traditional managers. One might assume that these developments would have reduced the significance of the club's traditions but this chapter has shown this not to be the case. Clearly the traditions of 'old' rangers have retained an important position in the development of 'new' Rangers in the last two decades.

Fundamental to the retention of the club's traditions has been the important role played by Rangers supporters in retaining a 'Protestant image' (Walker, 1990, p.138) to the club. This chapter has highlighted how this was achieved, and despite the marginalisation of the traditional Scottish Protestant player and the appointment of non-traditional managers, Rangers continues to stand 'for a powerful current of popular Protestantism' (Walker, 1990, p. 138) in the eyes of many of its supporters. On the other hand, Rangers supporters have not demonstrated anti-Catholic feeling toward Catholic players or managers. Thus, overall, despite the emergence of this 'new' Rangers, the presence of 'old' Rangers is still very much in evidence wherever the team plays.

In the last two seasons Rangers has been investigated by UEFA for the alleged singing of sectarian songs at European matches. Indeed UEFA fined Rangers because some fans sang the popular Loyalist song, 'The Billy Boys', at both legs of the 2005/6 Champions League tie with Spanish club Villarreal and the governing body warned that the club would be removed from the competition if it happened again. It cannot be denied that Rangers attracts a minority of supporters who engage in sectarian behaviour but the club and supporters groups have worked hard to remove this element. However, it remains difficult to ignore the importance of Protestant historical links to Rangers. This is a hugely important issue to those Rangers supporters who feel that the rich history and traditions of the club should be celebrated in the same way that clubs like Celtic (Irish Catholic heritage), Barcelona (Catalan nationalism), Athletic Bilbao (Basque separatism) celebrate their history and traditions. UEFA, however, has appeared to adopt an inconsistent line with regard to this issue and their recent actions against Rangers have been, in the eyes of the vast majority of Rangers supporters, unfair.

It should be remembered that the club operates a Pride over Prejudice policy, which ethos is summarised in the following extract:

> Pride. It's what being a Rangers fan is all about. It's history, future, passion and success. And it's about holding our heads high as one of the leading clubs in world football. . . . It's important that every single fan protects and enhances Rangers reputation so that we can all be proud (*Wee Blue Book Season 06/07*, p. 7).

The reference to history is significant in that it recognises within the public image of 'new' Rangers that the traditions of 'old' Rangers are important. When it comes to songs, the club is keen to move supporters away from those with Loyalist sentiments and, through the Pride over Prejudice initiative, is actively encouraging them to regale Ibrox with traditional club songs that relate to Rangers' history. Therefore, at the first home match of the 2006/7 season – Paul le Guen's first at Ibrox – Rangers relaunched the *Wee Blue Book*, a traditional publication that was once given to Rangers supporters at the start of a new season. In the publication a list of traditional club songs like 'Follow Follow', 'Wolverhampton Town', 'The Blue Sea of Ibrox' and 'Loyal Men in Blue' was included. The editorial comment explains that these are:

> Songs and words agreed between the fans' representatives and the Club. All of us want the best for Rangers – both on and off the pitch. This includes showing to the world that Rangers fans are proud and not prejudiced. This is the real Rangers. This is our fans. (*Wee Blue Book Season 06/07*, p.3)

The fact that the *Wee Blue Book* was reintroduced for a new purpose, at a time when the Rangers team was managed by a French Catholic who selected Catholic players, graphically exposes the nuances of the tradition–

modernity interplay at Rangers and the relationship between 'old' and 'new'.

David Murray is in his third decade as Rangers chairman and has established 'new' Rangers but – and it is debatable if Murray likes it or not – the importance of 'old' Rangers has not been lost. Walker (1990) wondered what type of supporter 'new' Rangers would attract and from this chapter it is clear that the current supporter group is largely made up of those who 'follow follow' everywhere (p. 156). Whatever the business strategies, whoever manages the club and whoever plays for the team, it is clear that supporters will try to uphold the traditions of the institution that is Rangers. It is possible to conclude that what is currently evident at Rangers is simply a modernised version of 'old' Rangers, and it is clear that the tradition–modernity interplay will remain a significant issue in the future development of the club.

Bibliography

Bairner, A. (2001) *Sport, Nationalism and Globalization: European and North American Perspectives* State University of New York Press: Albany

Boyle, R. (1994) 'We are Celtic supporters . . .': Questions of football and identity in modern Scotland' in R. Giulianotti and J. Williams (eds.) *Games Without Frontiers: Football, Identity and Modernity* (Aldershot: Arena, p.73–102)

Boyle, R. and Haynes, R. (1998) 'Modernising Tradition? The Changing Face of British Football' in U. Merkel, G. Lines and I. McDonald (eds.) *The Production and Consumption of Sport Cultures: Leisure, Culture and Commerce* (University of Brighton: Leisure Studies Association Publication, pp.21–36)

Bradley, J. (2006) *Celtic Minded 2: Essays on Celtic, Football Culture and Identity* (Argyll: Glendaruel)

Brown, A. (1998) *Fanatics: Power, Identity and Fandom in Football* (London: Routledge)

Cameron, N. (2004) (ed) *The Little Book of Rangers: Over 150 quotes about the Gers* (London: Carlton Books)

Finn, G. (2000) 'Scottish Myopia and Global Prejudices' in G. Finn and

R. Giulianotti (eds.) *Football Culture: Local Contests, Global Visions* (London: Frank Cass, pp.54–99)

Fynn, A. and Guest, L. (1994) *Out Of Time: Why football isn't working!* (Simon & Schuster: London)

Haynes, R. (1995) *The Football Imagination: The Rise of Football Fanzine Culture* (Arena: Aldershot)

http://news.bbc.co.uk/sport1/hi/football/teams/r/rangers/6225469.stm Accessed 29 May 2007

Moorhouse, H. F. (1991) 'On the Periphery: Scotland, Scottish Football and the New Europe' in J. Williams and S. Wagg (eds.) *British Football and Social Change: Getting into Europe* (Leicester: Leicester University Press, pp.201–19)

Moorhouse, H. F. (1994) 'Blue Bonnets across the Border: Scotland and the Migration of Footballers' in J. Bale and J. Maguire (eds.) *The Global Sports Arena: Athletic Talent Migration in an Interdependent World* (London: Frank Cass, pp.78–96)

Morrow, S. (2003) *The People's Game? Football, Finance and Society* (Hampshire: Palgrave MacMillan)

Murray, W. (2000) *The Old Firm: Sectarianism, Sport and Society in Scotland* (Edinburgh: John Donald Publishers)

Murray, W. (2003) *Bhoys, Bears and Bigotry: the Old Firm in the New Age* (Edinburgh: Mainstream)

Redhead, S. (1997) *Post-fandom and the Millennial Blues: Transformation of Soccer Culture* (Routledge: London)

Scotland on Sunday, 26 May 2006

Walker, G. (1990) 'There's not a team like the Glasgow Rangers': football and religious identity in Scotland' in G. Walker and T. Gallagher (eds.) *Sermons and Battle Hymns: Protestant Popular Culture in Modern Scotland*, (Edinburgh: Edinburgh University Press, pp.137–59).

Wee Blue Book Season 06/07, (Rangers Football Club publication)

It Was Rangers for Me

Gordon Smith

The perception of my old Rangers boss Jock Wallace is that he was anti-Celtic and would lead the players in singing 'The Sash' and other Orange songs in the dressing room and on the team bus, but I don't know where it comes from. In the three years that I was at Ibrox there was never an Orange or Protestant sing-song, either on the bus or after games. Never once did big Jock say anything bigoted, sing an Orange song or say anything gratuitous against Celtic or Catholics; there was nothing like that at all. When he did team talks there was never any 'into these Papes' or 'into these Fenians' or anything like that; there was nothing like that mentioned.

Jock Wallace was very pro-Rangers but he had a lot of time for Celtic. It was made clear that we had to beat them but 'them' were our rivals, there was no religious stuff. You had to go into another gear for an Old Firm game because it would be harder and all those things, but it was just football. He once pulled me up for wearing a green shirt and one time he gave me a row for saying that we had been lucky to beat Celtic but, in my eyes, it was because I might have got stick from the Rangers supporters.

Jock was a big hard man, that was true, but I had a lot of time for him. He fashioned my career and he once said that if he had stayed at Ibrox then I would have become a Rangers legend, which meant a lot to me given the players he had at the club at that time. But he was always good with the players in terms of training and how positive he was about games and it was like a death in the family when he left the club at the end of the 1978 season. We were a treble-winning team, he had played me in the position that I wanted to play in. I found him perfect. So the perception of Jock Wallace is flawed.

The only time I came across Orange songs was when I went to supporters-club functions and they wanted you to sing one. The story I tell in my book (*And Smith Did Score*) is of me singing 'Mull of Kintyre' because I didn't know the words of 'The Sash' or anything like that. I told them that I didn't do party songs and I still say that these days when I'm invited to supporters' functions. I have never sung any of those songs because I grew up in a different environment.

In saying that I don't have anything against those Rangers fans who see these songs as part of their tradition. Celtic make a point of extolling their background and tradition. They are quite happy to say that they have a tradition of Irish Catholicism, that they are a club founded by Brother Walfrid and immigrants to this country and I'm very comfortable with that. But why is there a problem when Rangers come out with the very same things? Why is it a problem when Rangers come out and say that they were set up by people from a Church of Scotland upbringing and that they have a Unionist background?

Growing up in Ayrshire – although places like Stevenston were Protestant strongholds – the biggest factor I encountered in terms of the Catholic–Protestant divide was in schools football. I think it is one of the saddest things about our society. I have nothing against Catholic schools but there is no doubt about it: in the west of Scotland it brings in an inclination right away to think of people being different. We played against schools with names like St Mary's or St Peter's and the games were very competitive and when they are competitive with someone then you automatically think they are the enemy. That was the case with me.

I never encountered any sectarianism from Celtic players during Old Firm games. Rangers and Celtic players are almost a mirror image of each other; they went through the same things that we went through and you had respect for them. The only thing that happened to me in that regard was when we played Partick Thistle and one of their players spat in my face and called me an 'Orange bastard'. As I wiped the spit off my face, I said to him, 'that's what I would expect from you'. He apologised to me for the rest of the game and every time I played against him after that he would say sorry.

You would get the odd comment from Celtic fans but it wasn't a problem. In fact, I got more stick from Celtic fans when I was a pundit than I got as a Rangers player. We went about Glasgow a lot more than Rangers players do these days. Bobby Russell, Davie Cooper, Derek Parlane and I would go into town for lunch and there was seldom any bother. Wee Doddy got a bit more stick than me; he was the Neil Lennon-type figure in those days, although obviously a Rangers player. I wasn't a hate-figure as such and so I never really got that much hassle. Most of the time Celtic fans were complimentary. Rangers had a reputation as hammer throwers and hard tacklers but I wasn't that type of player. So some Celtic fans would say I should have been playing for them instead of Rangers. In saying that, win, lose or draw I wouldn't go out in Glasgow after an Old Firm game and it was a conscious decision. After the League Cup win over Celtic in 1978 we went to a hotel in Giffnock to celebrate and all our cars got smashed up. Celtic fans must have found out we were in there.

The issue of sectarianism is topical again but we have to be careful that we don't become over-sensitive to it all. You have to remember that rivalry exists in football all over the world and it can be simply a case of blue against red. I watched my son play in the Bristol City versus Bristol Rovers derby last season and we were kept behind after the game because of battles in the street. So what it is they hate about each other? It's not religion, it's just rivalry. It's about my team against your team and so we have to be a bit more logical when we discuss bigotry or sectarianism and the idea of people 'being offended'.

You can't simply make rules or laws because people say they are offended. If I am sitting in the Rangers end, and I am one of those super-sensitive souls, then I could say to a steward or a policeman, 'that Celtic strip over there offends me, can you have that man lifted?' Rangers fans sing 'God Save The Queen' and Celtic fans boo it: does that mean the national anthem is offensive? Both sides need to have a good look at themselves. We need to get a definitive list of what is offensive. Everyone should be offended about 'being up to our knees in Fenian blood' and hearing IRA songs. If those sorts of songs are sung then perhaps action needs to be taken, but just to say that everything is offensive is a dangerous route to go down.

There was no tradition in my family of supporting Rangers. My grandfather had been a Kilmarnock player so my family were all Killie fans. In fact, I had the impression that my dad didn't like Rangers. When you consider my background was Boys Brigade and Church of Scotland, you would think he would have been more inclined to lean towards Rangers, but no, that wasn't the case at all. In fact, I thought he was more comfortable with Celtic than he was with Rangers. Maybe it was because Rangers were seen as the establishment team in those days and we were a socialist family, with my dad a Labour councillor. Certainly my parents were very clear about the whole bigotry issue. The message that I was getting all the time when I was growing up was that there was no difference between Catholics and Protestants.

I became a Rangers fan when I saw Jim Baxter play against Killie at Rugby Park. I wanted to be like him and even decided to be a left-footed player like him. My close pal Davie Paterson, who ended up signing a schoolboy form for Rangers, knew I was a Rangers fan but I kept it very quiet. I was worried in case it got back to my dad and the rest of my family. To most strangers, when asked, I was a Kilmarnock fan.

I had a lot of affection for Killie as well of course and my dad took me to the 1964 Scottish Cup semi-final where a great Dundee team beat Kilmarnock at Ibrox. I had said that I wanted to go to the final to see Dundee but I actually wanted to see Rangers. I had never been to a Rangers game in Glasgow before so my dad was there supporting Dundee and I was supporting Rangers.

I had no problems with Celtic as I was growing up. I remember sitting with my family in 1967 and watching Celtic in the European Cup final and we were all cheering them on, me included. I was delighted that Rangers came in for me but if it had been Celtic then I would have signed, no problem at all.

It was a huge thrill for me to sign for the club I had supported as a boy. And, to be fair, my dad was also thrilled when I joined Rangers from Kilmarnock, he knew that it was an achievement for me. When other clubs were in for me when I was young, he told me to go to Kilmarnock, saying I would get my chance there first and he was proved right.

When I arrived at Ibrox I never thought anything much about the religious side of things. I didn't think, 'It's ridiculous that we haven't got Catholics', it was just the way it was and the way it had been for decades. Did I think Rangers would one day sign a Catholic again when I played for them? No, I probably didn't but, surprising as it may seem today, there was no big fuss about it then. The issues of discrimination didn't really come through until the Eighties.

I accepted that every player at Ibrox was a Protestant but it was different when I moved to Brighton and then Manchester City because religion is not an issue at all in England. The occasional player would ask: 'Are Rangers the Protestant or Catholic team?' that was as much as they knew about the Old Firm. The Irish players in the team knew Rangers were the Protestant side and a couple of them thought Celtic only had Catholic players. At Manchester City, big Mick McCarthy would ask me about the Old Firm probably not thinking for a minute he would end up playing for Celtic.

But the Old Firm permeates every club in Scotland and it was typified when I was assistant to Davie Hay at St Mirren. When there was an Old Firm game on at the same times as ours, the players would be asking the score as they came into the dressing room after our match. If, for example, Celtic had won 2–1, two or three of the boys would shout 'yes!' while two or three others would grumble 'bastards'. But there was never a problem with it and you can't deny that players have teams that they support.

However, many football fans have a big problem determining the difference between neutrality and objectivity. They think you should be neutral, which means you have never supported any team. But if you haven't supported any team, how can you have anything to offer? Referees are the same; they must have supported someone to get involved in football in the first place. Consequently, there are very few people in the media – like myself when I was involved – who will say, 'yes, I'm a Rangers fan' and that's a sad thing. It would be quite easy for me to go down the line of saying that I'm a Kilmarnock fan but I am honest about it.

I was more exposed to bigotry working in the media than I was as a player. I found that people disliked me just because of my Rangers background. Before I had even opened my mouth some people were saying, 'look at him, he hates us'. People emailed the BBC about me being biased and I was called an Orange bastard a few times but that doesn't bother me and it doesn't demean me, it demeans them. I always try to be objective and the most frustrating thing is that people can't see that, they see what they want to see.

Some of the points made didn't even make sense. If I noted that Rangers had ten shots on target and Celtic had one, then apparently that was me being biased even though I was only stating a fact. The season that Celtic got to the UEFA Cup final in Seville, someone wrote into a newspaper saying he could tell by my face that I was gutted. But I was delighted that they got through; I'm right behind Celtic and every other Scottish team in Europe. So that is what you are up against. I witnessed that on a day-to-day basis and there is nothing you can do about it.

I have also had stick from Rangers fans. During the Dick Advocaat era I was quite critical, saying that he wasn't as good as everyone thought and Rangers fans would have a go at me for that. I was at Ibrox one afternoon – the first time that my son had been there actually – and I was asked if I would go down to the pitch at half-time and draw the raffle. Even after three years as a Rangers player, being sold for a record fee and still a supporter of the club, I got roundly booed. But I was bracing myself for it because I knew there was a lot of discontent with me among the fans. I laughed because I recognised why it had happened. One journalist wrote that it was a tribute to me because it showed that I was a pundit who didn't toe the party line and said what I thought – even about the team that I support. It didn't bother me as much as many Rangers fans thought. Some people said I changed after that but I didn't; there just happened to be some issues surrounding Rangers that I backed them on.

Rangers are going through a hard time with UEFA at the moment and, to a certain degree, there is an agenda against them. Celtic have always thought that people were against them, but now Rangers are starting to feel the same. It is not a media bias, it is just that reports about chants and what have you reached UEFA and they took action. But people are trying portray Rangers as the only club that have bigots. I just think they should be even-handed about it but, unfortunately, because I'm an ex-Rangers player, a lot people don't see that balance.

I don't hide it, playing for Rangers was fantastic. Playing for the club gave me what I wanted out of my football career. It was the best set of players I ever played with, a great bunch of guys. I was playing for the team I supported, at the highest level, and winning trophies – the same as my grandfather had done for Kilmarnock. That's all I wanted from life and that's why my feelings for Rangers are still strong. It was a great achievement for me and, even to this day, I can still live off it although I was only at the club for three years.

It's funny the things you remember though. In my first season at Ibrox I was still living in a council house in Stevenston and I think I was the first person from the area to have played for the club. It couldn't have gone much better. I scored twenty-seven goals from midfield and we won the treble. The Stevenston Rangers Supporters Club's player of the year that season? Derek Johnstone.

A prophet in his own land, eh?

Whereza Bears?

Jonathan Watson

You get very few people in my line of work admitting to being a Rangers fan. It's seen to be more fashionable to be a Celtic fan and I think it's always been that way. It would be fair to say that show business has always tended to be a leftist environment so that's why the link is there with the east end of the city. A lot of people feel that if you want to show you are a socialist then you should support Celtic.

My politics veer towards the left but I don't see anything wrong with supporting Labour and supporting Rangers. I can think of some Rangers fans who don't admit it; they say that they are Partick Thistle fans. I don't want to name names because they would deny it but I suppose that says something in itself. I think the religious issue that surrounded Rangers is also a problem. Although it has changed greatly in recent time, it only began to resolve itself when Graeme Souness arrived at Ibrox.

But Rangers are my team. I don't have any problem admitting it and anybody that knows me knows that I'm not a bigot or racist although it sounds terrible having to use those words when talking about football. I have always been up front about it and I wouldn't have much time for people who prejudge you on which team you support.

There has never been an adverse reaction to me being a Rangers fan. I do most of my work with the BBC these days; there is always great banter there and, for the most part, that has always been the case. I left drama college in 1979 but I didn't start in comedy right away; I played in theatre companies all over Scotland. Then I got involved with the Comedy Unit when it was within the BBC, doing *Naked Radio*, and I was the only Rangers fan there; Philip Differ and Tony Roper were Celtic fans. But it was great because there was plenty of banter and it was always good natured.

I wasn't really brought up in a Rangers family, although my dad was from Larkhall! Rangers were his team, I suppose, but he wasn't a big football fan. He was, and is, a mild-mannered man, totally opposed to any kind of bigotry or racism. My grandfather, however, was a good footballer, he was a Scottish Junior internationalist and, in fact, around 1910, Rangers wanted him on trial. But my grandmother wouldn't allow it and he ended up working in a diamond mine in South Africa and played semi-professional football over there. I was brought up in St George's Cross in Glasgow and I got into Rangers through my pals at school. I went to Hillhead and I think there was only one Celtic fan in our class.

My parents never had a problem with me supporting Rangers. I went to the junior course of the Royal Scottish Academy of Music and Drama from about ten until seventeen and with that being on a Saturday it limited me a bit. But I got into Rangers in a big way after they won the Cup Winners Cup in 1972. I used to go to a lot of away games on the old, horrible football specials and my mum and dad were absolutely fine about it. I never got into any trouble and they trusted me. In my first Old Firm game, Rangers were beaten 3–1 by Celtic in the League Cup at Hampden. Harry Hood scored a hat-trick and Alex MacDonald got Rangers' goal. I went with a couple of school pals and I managed to get a bus all the way back to St George's Cross after the game, which was the only good thing about it all.

When I was a wee boy in the 1960s my favourite player was Davie Wilson. I was shipped out to Kilbarchan in the summer holidays where my granny Ramage used to stay and Davie also lived there in a house called the Left Wing. I remember my cousin Freddy and me walking the length of Kilbarchan with a piece of blue Basildon Bond writing paper and ringing his doorbell to ask for his autograph. He said 'sure son' and signed it 'Davie Wilson, Rangers FC'; a few days later he signed for Dundee United. I've still got the autograph to this day.

In the Seventies I enjoyed watching Derek Johnstone and big Greigy and I thought Alex MacDonald was absolutely brilliant. I was a season-ticket holder prior to Souness coming – when it was easy to get a season ticket – but I never went along with the no-Catholic policy. I didn't see the sense in it and I'm glad that it was ended – and what a way to do it with Maurice Johnston. If you were going to blow it away that was the way to do it and Maurice did a great job when he played for Rangers.

Ibrox is a fantastic stadium and I love the sense of history that surrounds the place. I don't think the atmosphere at Ibrox has changed that much over the years; there is still an excitement about the games. I still love the European nights, I still get a fantastic buzz going over to the stadium and seeing the floodlights. My wee boy is seven and he is on to me to take him but I've held back so far. The attention span at that age is about half an hour but I will take him in time.

I lived down in London for a couple of years in the late Eighties and I used to go to Highbury now and again and that was very similar to Ibrox. The Ibrox interior was designed by guys who worked on the Queen Elizabeth and Queen Mary and it's just a wonderful place. I have been fortunate enough to have been in the Blue Room and in the manager's office and I have also filmed in the trophy room. When I was starting out in my career, I was privileged to be a guest at Willie Waddell's and Willie Thornton's tables in the corporate suites. These guys are legends. After I spoke at a sponsor's event Willie Waddell came up to me and, in his easily recognisable voice, said, 'well done son'. That was great.

I used to do a few things for Rangers when Walter Smith was manager the first time. Before important games Walter would phone me and ask if I would go down to the Turnberry hotel and do twenty minutes for the players. Philip Differ would come down with me and it wasn't the easiest audience to please. You had players like Mikhailichenko just sitting there looking at you, puzzled, but guys like Ally McCoist, Ian Durrant and John Brown would help you out by laughing like drains. Walter and Graeme Souness were fine with me poking fun at them and, when I was doing after-dinner speaking at a Rangers function, I was encouraged to have a go at people at the club. I once had dinner with Souness and his wife and she asked me to impersonate him. I was reluctant but eventually I did a little bit and, to be fair to Graeme, he took it in good spirit. He even said at one point, 'It's a better Chinese meal than I first thought' so he was aware of that little catchphrase I had for him. I felt absolutely privileged to do all those things and I have great memories of those days.

Philip and I believe humour is important in the Old Firm context and we like to poke fun at both sides. We have a couple of characters that we do to represent the fans: Sean Lourdes the Third is the Celtic fan with the monobrow and the lisp; while the Rangers fan 'Woodsie', with the feather cut and a scar, is deranged. Philip and I were at a Scottish Professional

Footballers Association dinner in the Thistle hotel in Glasgow one night and one of the Dundee players asked us which of us supported Celtic and who supported Rangers. We liked that. Although I have done things on Rangers Television recently, as well as the stuff I've done for the club in the past, a lot of people don't know that I'm a Rangers fan. Indeed, the first time I went to the club deck at Ibrox a punter asked me: 'What are you doing here, are you not one of them?'

The only time I had a slight problem with Celtic fans was when I was invited by the producers of *Sportscene*, along with Chick Young, to make a League Cup draw. We did it live and it wasn't just a case of Chick and I taking it in turn to pick out a ball. He had to pick one out, I had to pick one out, then I had to pick another ball out, then it was back to him. It was something to do with seedings and the home-and-away aspect of it but it was a bit confusing for the viewers. I handed Rangers what was thought to be an easy draw while Celtic got quite a hard one. And when I picked Rangers out I made a joke saying, 'this is a cold ball here' and then Chick made some remark like 'Walter will be happy with that'. To my surprise, some people took it seriously. The BBC was inundated with phone calls with the most popular question being: 'Why are those two Orange bastards doing the draw?' It shows you the intensity that still exists in Glasgow with regards to the Old Firm.

I think the club is going in the right direction on and off the park. I'm really pleased about the current set-up because I never really wanted Walter to leave in the first place. With Walter, Ally, Ian Durrant and Kenny McDowall, the club is in safe hands although obviously there isn't the money to spend that was there a few years ago.

Rangers and Celtic are doing as much as they can to eradicate the sectarianism but you will still get some nutters who will do things that embarrass the clubs. But I do think there is a shift in mindset and there will have to be over the next couple of years otherwise the clubs will be punished; UEFA will come down hard on them. Of course, the sectarianism problem is not confined to Rangers; it's across so many areas of society, but I do think that it will be a thing of the past in the next few years.

One That Got Away

Davie Provan

Although I played most of my career for Celtic I came from a typical west of Scotland Rangers family. We lived in Gourock and my dad, David senior, my brother Roddy and I were all Rangers supporters. There was no Masonic or Orange influences but we were a churchgoing family and my brother and I regularly attended Sunday school. By the time I was seven or eight, we were being taken to Ibrox by my dad, where we watched players like Baxter and Henderson.

Of course there was also a player at Ibrox called Davie Provan, a big full back, which was strange, because, of course, he had the same name as my dad and me. I actually met him when he came to our Boys Brigade parade with Rangers goalkeeper Eric Sorenson and I got him to sign my autograph book, 'to Davie Provan from Davie Provan'. My brother and I had Rangers strips, some of the neighbours had Celtic strips and we would play 'Old Firm' games all the time. Morton were my local team and because Ibrox seemed so far away in those days before decent road links, bypasses and so forth, I would go and watch them a lot but when Rangers came to Cappielow, it was a game I wouldn't miss.

When I first heard Celtic were interested, I was surprised, not because of my background but because a club like Celtic would consider signing me. Obviously the family would have preferred that I had gone to Rangers but it was never a problem in the house and I had total support from them. Both my parents just wanted me to be what I wanted to be and my brother told me to do what I felt was right. Despite being from a Rangers family there was enormous respect for Celtic and what they had achieved under Jock Stein. Signing for Celtic was a chance to play top-class foot-ball and that's what I wanted to do.

I was a part-timer at my first club Kilmarnock and in 1978 we drew

1–1 with Celtic in the Scottish Cup at Parkhead. Jock Stein stopped me before the game and spoke to me for quite a bit of time, which I thought was unusual. I had heard that he had offered Kilmarnock money for me but apparently the two clubs couldn't agree a fee. So I suppose it was all the more reason to try and impress and I played pretty well. And in the replay I probably had my best game for Kilmarnock playing against John Dowie. It one of those nights where everything went right, and we won the game with a Derek McDicken goal.

But the trail then went cold and I heard nothing more about it. At twenty-two, I thought I had missed my chance to move to a big club. Then one Tuesday night I got a phone call – and I have never spoken about this before – after I had come home from training. On the other end of the line was John Clark, assistant to Billy McNeill who by that time had taken over from big Jock. I remember the conversation well.

John said, 'Look, we know about your background but would you come to Celtic?'

'Yes, in a minute, not a problem at all.' I replied.

He said, 'Okay, I just wanted to know that you would be in the right frame of mind to play for us.'

I played against Stirling Albion on Saturday, 16 September 1978 – I recall that date easily – and before the game Killie's manager at the time, David Sneddon, had intimated that a couple of clubs were looking at me. I played really well, scored, and we won 4–1. The next day I was having a kick-about in Gourock with some pals, and my best pal's dad came up and told me to go home right away because Kilmarnock had phoned. I called Davie Sneddon and he told me that Killie had accepted an offer from Celtic and I was to sign in the morning. It was brilliant and I will never forget going into Parkhead. Although I had played against Billy McNeill, it was the first time that I had met him properly.

At the time I was serving a commercial apprenticeship with Chivas Brothers in Paisley and studying for an HNC in business studies. They could have asked me to work a period of notice but most of my bosses were Celtic supporters so they were quite happy to let me go almost right away. I signed on the Monday and started full time the following Monday. It was over all the papers the next day and there I was, a new Celtic player, sitting behind a desk writing out Custom and Excise warrants. Celtic and

Rangers fans who worked in the same place were popping in to wish me all the best; they were really pleased for me.

The first time I actually met my new teammates was at Parkhead before we got on the bus to go and play Partick Thistle on my debut. Walking into any new dressing room is intimidating, especially at a club that size. Basically, I had been signed to replace Johnny Doyle and I was really wary of meeting him but as it turned out he became one of my best pals at the club.

But he was at the wind-up right away saying, 'there's another currant bun in the dressing room'. There were other players from a Rangers background at Celtic such as Danny McGrain and Tom McAdam while Murdo MacLeod signed about eight weeks after me but the other 'currant bun' was Alfie Conn, who, of course, had played for Rangers. But it wouldn't have bothered me what the make up in the dressing room was or who was in it.

There was always religious banter at Parkhead, most of it started by Johnny, but it was always good natured, there was never the slightest inkling of any undercurrent. I had moved to Langbank within a year of signing for Celtic and I travelled with Mike Conroy, who had signed from Port Glasgow Juniors. Mike was Celtic through and through and had wanted to play for the club all his life. He would give me stick about being a Rangers man but it was just a laugh, no more than that.

The Celtic fans took to me right away. I got a terrific reception from them at Firhill in my first game and I was always under the impression that as long as I did the business on the Saturday then they would forget that I had been a Rangers fan. It sounds ridiculous now but Celtic had paid £125,000 for me, which was a record between two Scottish clubs, so there was a fair bit of pressure on me but I started reasonably well, which was important. But it's a bit of a myth that supporters stand by you through thick and thin. If you are not doing the business then they soon let you know about it. There was no hiding place in front of the old Jungle at times but you just had to get through it. You've got to be strong mentally to play for either half of the Old Firm because there will be times when you are not playing well and you'll get heavily criticised. You won't last if you let it get to you.

In games against Rangers, I felt I had to do a bit more. I would be lying if I said otherwise and I think one or two others from the same background would tell you the same. You would never leave yourself open in an Old Firm game. If there is such a thing as another 10 per cent that was the match where you had to make sure you found it. You could have a bad game, but you didn't want anyone to think, 'Well, maybe he's not giving it his best shot.' So you always did the full shift and a bit more.

My first Old Firm game was at Hampden because Ibrox was being reconstructed at the time. I played against Alex Forsyth, who had just signed from Manchester United, and it ended in a 1–1 draw. The will to win was astonishing in those games, where you had guys like Johnny Doyle and Alex MacDonald who probably epitomised what each club was about. But although there would be a lot of verbals going on during the game I never heard any sectarian comment at all and I am being perfectly honest. We didn't hear it when we played teams other than Rangers either. That might surprise people but it is true. There is a great respect between Celtic and Rangers players because they know what each other are going through. Every player was out there trying to do their best under immense pressure and that's why there was always a warm handshake at the end of the game – win, lose or draw. You were always delighted to win the game but it was important that you didn't lose it. After a drawn game you could see the look of relief all around – you could go out the house the next day!

Part of your job in those days was to meet the fans. It wasn't written into your contract but whether it was Belfast, Aberdeen or Dumfries, you were expected to go to supporters' functions if invited. One season I won numerous of player-of-the-year awards and it seemed as if I was out every Saturday night. That's the disappointing thing these days: players wouldn't cross the street to go to a supporters-club function. In the early 1980s Frank McGarvey and I were invited to the New Lodge Celtic Supporters Club in Belfast. At that time the Hunger Strike was coming to an end and you could have cut the atmosphere in Belfast with a knife. I suppose I could have called off but although the background was a bit surreal it was still expected that you would turn up.

I had never been in Belfast before and it was intimidating. Frank and I stayed in the infamous Europa hotel which had been blown up countless times. You had to go through a metal detector to get into the place, which was unusual to say the least. I went for a walk during the day and saw young kids throwing rocks at the soldiers, who were walking down the street with their rifles. As I said: all very surreal. All the Republican pubs had closed down as a mark of respect to the hunger strikers but the Celtic Supporters Club had received permission to stay open. As we entered the hall I noticed that there were portraits of the hunger strikers all around the walls. It was a bit spooky to be honest and I was glad to get out of Belfast and back to Scotland.

When I first signed for Celtic I got a bit of stick from some people in Gourock, not friends but acquaintances who would give me the usual 'turncoat' stuff. And it became apparent very early on that hassle was part of the deal of being an Old Firm player. I was reasonably good at handling that kind of stuff but it was difficult at times. In a Glasgow pub one night, a guy called me a turncoat then spat in my face; that was quite hard to take. But most of the nasty element was verbal, usually after some punter had too much to drink and I never found myself in a scrap. I used to walk away before it got to that stage and it never stopped me going out. There were usually four or five Celtic players together any time we were in the town and I never felt unsafe. I'm sure you could speak to Rangers players who got stick from Celtic fans; that's just the way it is in Glasgow.

I don't have any problems with Rangers fans these days. Some shake my hand and say they respected me as a player and some will say they wish I had signed for Rangers. I get a bit of stick from some Celtic supporters because of the things I write or say about the club but I can live with that as long as I know my comments are honest. But most of the time the Celtic fans are very warm towards me; they will talk about the old times. I played over three hundred times in the hoops so I think most of them remember me for that rather than what I say or write these days. I have to admit that the relationship between me and the club is uneasy at times. Some people feel that as a former player I shouldn't have anything critical to say about the Celtic. It gives me no pleasure to be critical of Celtic but if it has to be said then it should be said.

It has been years since I played my last Old Firm game but the sectarian issue is still ongoing at both clubs. I applaud former First Minister Jack McConnell for having the bottle to tackle sectarianism, but he was wrong to say it is Scotland's secret shame, because it's not a secret. It shames every one of us and however long it takes this clampdown has got to continue.

There is a real purge on sectarian songs these days but when I played it was quite normal for Old Firm supporters to sing them and everyone had become accustomed to it. We don't have the overt sectarian element in the grounds simply because they are not allowed to get away with it but I'm not convinced that there has been progress made outwith the stadiums. The biggest problem, as far as I'm concerned, is the intelligent, professional, middle-class bigots and there are those on either side. You can understand the knuckleheads who don't know any better but if you have an intelligent man who can't open his mind and see the stupidity in all of this, then Scottish society is going to have a problem for a long time.

I certainly wouldn't have moved to Rangers from Celtic and Maurice Johnston was probably the only one daft enough to do what he did. At the time, people said he was brave; I just think he was daft. If you look at the hassle that it brought him; who needs that in their life? Kenny Miller and Steven Pressley moving to Celtic after being at Ibrox has helped the situation and ten out of ten for these guys for having the bottle to do it, to be strong enough to ignore the idiots who say that if you have worn a blue jersey, you should never play for Celtic and vice versa.

But I can't see the direct transfer from one Old Firm club to the other coming soon. I suppose we are getting closer to it but I don't see what player would want to put his family through it all and that's an indictment on the west of Scotland.

The Rangers thing is gone for me. There is no part of me now that wishes I had played at Ibrox. It was my upbringing and it was ingrained into me but I wouldn't swap my Celtic career for anything. The irony is, between signing for Celtic in 1978 and 1986, when I played my last game for the club, Rangers didn't win the title. I won four championship medals and Rangers were never at the races. Who knows what would have happened if I had signed for Rangers but I don't have an ounce of regret, none whatsoever.

I still have an allegiance to Celtic and my two daughters are Celtic fans. I try not to let it interfere with my work, I try to be neutral but – put it this way – I'm never unhappy to see Celtic win.

Life Before Souness

John MacDonald

Everyone thinks you are loaded because you played for Rangers – I wish. I never made any money at Ibrox. There was a rigid wage structure when I was there and it had always been that way. Everybody was on £300 per week. When I went to Barnsley they were bottom of the old English second division but they gave me £350 and I was thinking, 'How does that work?' We never had big bonuses either; it was £80 for a win, then it went up to £100, then £120. When we won the Scottish Cup in 1981 we got £1,000. Big Derek Johnstone told us it was the same as he had got in 1970 for winning the League Cup. And when we played Hibs three times in the 1979 Scottish Cup final, they got more bonus money than us because they got bonuses for draws. We only got a bonus for winning it.

John McClelland left Rangers for Watford because of money. He had been at other clubs where every time he signed a new contract he got a signing-on fee. He didn't get it at Ibrox and so he left. I got £250 when I signed on as a schoolboy and it was the only signing-on fee I got from Rangers. We had to play for the jersey – agents weren't really about at that time!

I was brought up in Maryhill until I was five and my dad used to take me to Thistle. When we moved to Drumchapel he still took me to Firhill at first but when I got to nine and ten all the boys were going to Rangers so I ended up going to see them. I went to Kingsridge secondary in Drumchapel, which produced players like Andy Gray, Danny McGrain, Alex Miller, Gregor Stevens and also Kenny McDowall – who was a couple of years younger than me – and his brother Gary, who also played professional football.

When I was fourteen I played in a semi-final for the school and we won 7–6 after extra time and I scored six goals. An Ipswich scout was up to watch the schoolboy international later that day and he asked me to go down to Portman Road. So I would go down south during every holiday with Alan Brazil and then I got to know John Wark, who is from Scotstoun. One day the Rangers chief scout came up to the school, got me into a room with the headmaster and said: 'You would love to play for Rangers, wouldn't you?' Of course, I said yes, as you do, but I was enjoying the way Ipswich were treating me. He told me he would come up to the house with the forms the next night. I told my mum and dad and they asked: 'What about Ipswich?' I told them that I still wanted to go there. When I told the scout he said, 'You told me in front of your headmaster that you wanted to play for Rangers.' He then came up to the house and talked me into it. He said he would give me a liver a week expenses, which was megabucks in 1976, so I signed an S-form.

There was no youth structure at Rangers then, I just kept on playing with my boys club and I would go into Ibrox during the school holidays. Rangers had good crop of boys, better than they have now, but a lot of them didn't make it. Boys don't want to play football nowadays; they have so many other things to do. I played with the Cubs on the Saturday morning, the Boys Brigade in the afternoon and my boys club on the Sunday. Now I'm coaching boys at under-sixteen who get cramp because they don't play enough or take enough exercise.

A lot of people were very critical of Jim Denny when he was in the first team. He said he used to warm up at the Celtic end because he got less stick there! But when I first started playing for the reserves I couldn't have had better help than I got from him. We had a great reserve team, with players like Davie Armour, Gordon Boyd, Eric Morris and Derek Strickland – and I remember beating Celtic reserves 7–0 – but a lot of them just moved on. They just didn't get a chance.

Jock Wallace had signed me as an S-form but he left after Rangers won the treble in 1978. We never knew why. John Greig became manager and I was his first signing at seventeen. Greigy didn't have managerial experience; he came from the dressing room with all his pals and he was trying to become a manager to them. He travelled with Sandy Jardine and his best mates were Alex MacDonald, Tom Forsyth and Tommy McLean and he had to change it and bring other players in. He let those players go but the players he brought in weren't as good. Sandy Jardine could have played another three or four years at sweeper, as he did when he went to Hearts.

When Greig was appointed manager Davie Cooper was a bit wary of him. He kept getting subbed and I heard him in the corridor asking, 'why do you keep subbing me?' and Greigy replying 'well, start playing better then'. I know guys like Davie Armour complained because every time things went wrong Greigy would bring in seasoned pros like Alex Miller rather than the young boys.

People say John didn't do that well but we got to five Scottish Cup finals and four League Cup finals and were one game away from a treble in 1978/79. I was in the dugout the night we lost 4–2 at Celtic Park. Greigy had put me in the squad to stop me going away with one of the Scotland youth teams and it was like a morgue in the dressing room after the game. But if we had won Greigy would have become a managerial legend! I more or less took Tommy McLean's place in the side. Coop moved to the right wing and I was on the left before moving into the middle as a striker.

Before I signed as a professional I was injured and in at Ibrox for treatment. I played heady-tennis with Coop and you couldn't get a nicer guy. He was a huffy bugger as everyone knew but he was one of the best players ever to play for Rangers. The senior players from Derek Johnstone right through were fantastic, even Tommy McLean, and they helped me settle in. They weren't going to let your confidence go, they wanted the team to succeed and it didn't matter who came in. We were all professionals; we knew that if you weren't playing well somebody else would come in.

I had watched guys like Jardine, McLean, Johnstone and Greig and then I got to play with them. I had seen Parlane and Jardine scoring against Bayern Munich in the '72 Cup Winners Cup semi-final at Ibrox and I was going into training with them. It was fantastic. Even going in as a school-boy was great. You would sit in the corner and not say anything. It's changed days now; young boys just don't respect the pros the way we used to respect them. We were scared to speak in their company, now the young boys slaughter the senior professionals.

I used to think training was hard but when I think back it wasn't. Tuesday was your only hard day but it was enjoyable. Pre-season was hard though. We would meet at Ibrox at eight in the morning and go to Gullane: that was a killer; that was really hard. We would go round the different dunes doing little runs then we would move on to 'The Hill'. We would be sick running up it and by the end you were on your knees crawling.

Most of my pals in Drumchapel supported Celtic and I didn't get any hassle there in all the time I played for Rangers. I stayed with my mum and dad until I got married in 1982. You would get hassle now though, staying in a council house in Drumchapel as a Rangers player. People knew where I lived and you used to hear them walking up the street singing, 'There's only one John MacDonald' after they had had a few beers.

Football has changed since then and there probably was a tactical naivety in those days. In European games we played the same formation home and away, mainly 4-3-3, two wingers, Derek Johnstone through the middle with Gordon Smith pushing on. We went to Valencia and drew 1–1 and we thought we had a chance to get through but Mario Kempes came to Ibrox and ripped the backside out of us and they beat us 3–1. Videos weren't common then so Joe Mason had gone over to see Valencia in Spain. He told us to keep showing Kempes onto his left peg, saying that he couldn't kick with his left foot. At Ibrox he was shown on to his left peg and he hit a twenty-five-yarder into the top corner. Aye show him on to his left peg!

And in Cologne we were 4–0 down after about seventeen minutes. It was one of these nights; every time they shot they scored. We were 2–1 up from the first leg so we maybe could have sat back for the first twenty minutes but we didn't have that mentality then; we didn't prepare that way. The season we got to the quarter-final of the European Cup we played the same formation; it was the players who just rose to the occasion. I don't think formations make much of a difference. If your players don't perform on the night then you will get beat anyway.

The highlight of my Rangers career was probably the 1981 Scottish Cup-final replay against Dundee United at Hampden when we won 4–1. Dundee United were a good team then and they had beaten us 4–1 earlier in the season. Coop and I were left out in the first game and we hadn't even played in the semi-final. Redford missed the penalty on Saturday at Hampden and did us a favour. Coop was magnificent in the replay but I scored twice and was asking, 'how did he get man of the match?' But I watched a video of the game not too long ago and I was shite. Every time I got the ball I seemed to give it away, but I scored two goals and I was happy with that.

Jock Wallace came back when Greigy decided enough was enough. Losing 3–0 at Chesterfield was probably the low point of his time as manager; that was a bad night. I came on as substitute and won a penalty but Colin McAdam even missed that. One time when Jock was ill, his assistant Alex Totten played me in three games in a row and I scored in each one. Big Jock returned and I started against Dundee in the Scottish Cup when Bomber Brown scored against us to put us out. I was substitute against Hearts the next week and then I was left out altogether. I was asking myself, 'Have I got to score every game to keep my place?'

Souness was fine with me. When he arrived in April 1986 he offered me another year. He had let about ten players go and I probably wasn't going to get a game so it was time to move on. Rangers were looking for money for me at first but I got a free transfer in September. I took it on the chin. If I knew I would have got signing-on fees then I might have moved earlier! I moved to Barnsley and struck up a friendship with three former Celtic players: Jim Dobbin, who was already there, Paul McGuigan and Owen Archdeacon. We would have fun with the English players asking who the Protestants were and who the Catholics were and they of course were completely bemused by it all.

But we never really spoke about religion in the dressing room at Ibrox. I don't think Greig or Wallace were men who wanted to change it. They were quite happy with the way it was. It was a big step by Souness but it had to be done; you couldn't just keep on signing Protestant players. There are the stories about Souness asking: 'Does anyone object to Maurice Johnston signing?' and Coop replying, 'Aye me'. I don't know if that is true but I was also fired-up when I came up against Celtic and I don't hold that against anybody. That's the way we were. We hated getting beat against them. That's the difference nowadays; it's just like another game to some of the players.

I scored four goals against Celtic as a Rangers player but it should have been five. I got a goal chalked off at Parkhead. Ian Redford cut the ball back to me and I headed it in only for referee Brian McGinlay to chalk it off. I couldn't believe it. He later told me that he thought that the linesman had his flag up for offside but it had been a steward's jacket behind the linesman that he had seen!

As far as the carry-on with UEFA recently is concerned, they are just nitpicking and it always seems to be Rangers and Celtic; they are an easy target. There are far more things going on in the world for them to be worrying about than what people are singing. I think it's ridiculous. The fans are not allowed to sing those songs at the stadium but away from the grounds, at their dances, they still sing them. The SFA are now involved talking about docking points but if they take points from Rangers and Celtic there will be outrage.

I've always had a good relationship with the Rangers fans. In the course of a season I would be invited to ten or twelve supporters' functions and I wanted to go. A supporters' function was a night out for me when I was a player. I would tell the wife, 'We've got a great night out darling – we're going to another supporters dance!' In fact, the fans still ask me to go to their functions these days because they can't get any current players to attend. I was in Dubai twice recently. It's great to meet up with guys like Willie Johnston and even the older players like Jimmy Millar. You are still treated the same these days, the younger ones don't remember who you are but some of the older ones will say, 'You were my hero.'

Players are spoiled now. Before Souness came you wore the same training kit every day and you can imagine what it was like by the Friday. He changed all that, there was new training gear every day. Souness transformed it all and brought Rangers into the twentieth century. It would have been great to have been starting out when Souness came, just for the money aspect, but I can't complain. I enjoyed my time as a Rangers player. I scored goals in cup finals and against Celtic and won trophies and nobody can take it away from me.

If We Only Had the Rangers Over Here

Stewart McDougall

I was born into a well-established Rangers family. I don't know of one member of my family that didn't support Rangers, even the in-laws and outlaws. My dad Hughie's mum and dad came from Bridgeton and Gorgie respectively and my mum Ina's side from Cambuslang, where I grew up. I was taken to my first Rangers game on my third birthday, forty-five years ago, but the first game I can truly remember was against Dundee United at Tannadice on 12 December 1964, which we won 3–1. It was my first away game (outside of Glasgow) and Jim Forrest scored a hat-trick. Funnily enough he was not to become my hero: that would be the one and only Willie Johnston.

We were not only a Rangers family but also a family entrenched in the Orange Order and Orange parade bands. At that time it was not looked down upon by Rangers as it seems to be now. My dad and his brother Sam were founder members of the Cambuslang Bluebell Accordion Band. I joined the band when I was three, playing the triangle, moving on to the cymbals when I was five. I attended Cathkin and Fernhill church, had perfect attendance for seven years, and proudly marched with the 246 Boys Brigade. Basically my life was set out for me and that upbringing made me the Rangers fanatic that I am today.

I was a well-behaved child but I knew that if I didn't behave then I would not get to see Rangers on Saturday or even Cambuslang Rangers when the 'big Rangers' were away from home. I learned to read a lot through poring over the match programmes that my dad brought home from every game and I would actually try and write a match report on each game from what I saw or heard on the radio. I knew that we had 'won everything' in season 1963/64 because of the pennants and pictures we had in the house but Rangers would not win the Scottish first division again until 1975. I attended every game that season except one: the 1–1 draw with Hibs at Easter Road on the day we won the league. I was in France on a school skiing trip at the time and I got a telegram at the hotel. It was read out to me in private as they thought something bad had happened at home. I was told 'Calling Steen, champagne we roll the papers.' My dad had called up the GPO, which the post office was known as in those days, and, in an inebriated Glasgow accent, had said. 'Colin Stein, champions. We are the people.'

The night we won the 1972 European Cup Winners Cup, against Moscow Dynamo in Barcelona, we all sat around the radio as the game was not shown on television. I had never seen my dad so happy. We were out on the street in Skye Road in Cathkin dancing and signing, with dad playing the accordion. We all got up early to get the papers, which were sadly plastered with the one-sided view of what happened after the game with Franco's mob.

A Rangers supporters club was formed in our area, called the Springhall and Cathkin RSC. This was now the way to get to every game as the club had it written into its constitution that a bus must go to all Rangers games even if it was just a minibus, which was rare. Going on the bus was the greatest thing for me. We sang all the way there and all the way back, even up to Aberdeen and down to Wembley with Scotland. My dad would get the accordion out for away games and that's how I learned all the old songs and every Rangers and Orange song. Jessie Murdoch and Nellie Brodie were always on the bus and they would feed the young guys while the dads had a few haufs. We all behaved under the threat of 'nae biscuits'.

We had guys from all walks of life on our bus, but mostly there were three common factors which united us: Rangers, the Orange Order/bands and the Masons. At that time, due to what was going on in Ulster, other songs were sung too. But no matter what, we were all in it together. The first trophy I saw Rangers win was the 1973 Scottish Cup final and, when Tam Forsyth's goal went in, I experienced the greatest high I had ever known.

As I said, Willie Johnston had become my hero. I was involved in a bike crash and was rushed by my uncle Jim to Hairmyres hospital in East

Kilbride. As an undertaker, he somehow got me in to see the doctor without going through the usual paperwork. When my mum and dad came up to see me they could not find a Stewart McDougall; the only person who had been admitted was a 'Willie Johnston'. I wore a Willie Johnston medallion round my neck and they thought that was my name!

Life was good. I followed Rangers everywhere. My work was very accommodating to the extent that I would get to work late to make up for time off. I was a junior officer in the Masons, a member of the Orange Order and band sergeant of the Cambuslang Young Conquerors flute band. Then, when I was planning to get married, I got a phone call to go to West Germany on a three-month contract. I had always wanted to go there and had even tried to learn German. My last game before I left Scotland was the game against Celtic at Parkhead, when Alex Miller scored the winner. When you see television pictures of the Rangers end after that goal, that's me on my friend Sandy Knox's back. Everyone has blue on except Sandy, who was wearing a bright-red jumper.

I'd call my mum from Germany for the report on the Rangers game and by Wednesday I'd have read all the papers that had been mailed to me. Unbeknown to me I was never to permanently live in Scotland again but that didn't stop me from following the Rangers and staying strong in my beliefs. In 1984 I learnt that Rangers were to tour Switzerland and Germany. I finally tracked down the agent organising the tour and he reluctantly told me that they were playing the first game in Einsiedeln, a non-English-speaking village. We were there a day before the team and, being able to speak German, I was helping some of the Rangers lads get hotels; I even found a room for a couple on their honeymoon. The next day about forty of us, seven of whom were from Cambuslang, were all sitting on the grass at the end of the stadium drinking beer and sunbathing before the game when two guys marched right across the park towards us. Someone shouted: 'It's Big Jock.' He marched up and asked if we were enjoying ourselves, then told us to behave or we'd answer to him! Then he shouted, 'Who's the gentleman that speaks German?' All fingers pointed to me and Jock said, 'Right come with me, you're my translator.' The agent had bailed out and there I was, translating for a Rangers legend. I was so proud I called my mum.

Scotland qualified for the 1986 World Cup in Mexico and I wanted to go so I got a job in California and left Munich with two suitcases, my Bible, my Rangers gear and my flute, thinking that I was going back. I never returned again to Germany until this year. My dad's last letter to me was written in March 1988 and the last line in the PS was, 'Get ready son for signing a Catholic.' He could not have imagined who it was and the drastic change it made to Rangers.

In America, a group of us started the Anaheim Loyal RSC. My mum, who was the honorary president of our club, would hold the phone to a radio and we all sat round and listened to the games from Scotland. It cost us $200, a massive amount of money then, but we didn't care. Eventually we grew in numbers and, in 1991 – as we realised fans were coming in from further afield than Anaheim – we became the Orange County Rangers Supporters Club. There were four founder members: Bruce Craig, Tam White, Iain Porter and me. The club went on to greater things and still stands strong. However, with the internet and games live on television, our crowds are not as big. There is not the same immigration to North America from Scotland and Ireland as there used to be, so we rely on our own kids and the occasional new member to bolster the numbers. But we are still loyal and true blues, still getting up sometimes at 3:30 a.m. to go and watch a match an hour later.

Since LA Galaxy were founded, we have been getting some of their fans coming along and, when the Rangers fulfilled my dream this summer by playing on my own doorstep, the Galaxy fans became Rangers fans. I had got a text from a friend, Gordon Mathers, in April 2007, saying that Rangers were coming to play the LA Galaxy in southern California. That was it; we decided that we were going to make it the greatest day for all Rangers fans in our club and for all the travelling fans. It was just a three-day trip for the team, and it was a midweek game, but we had to make sure word got out. By the morning after the game, which was on 24 May, everyone would know who the Rangers were.

We began by taking out newspaper adverts and setting up a website to buy tickets. Through the support of the North American Rangers Supporters Association and the Orange County Rangers SC, Gordon Mathers and I sold over 1,500 tickets, a lot of them on trust. People turned up at my sister Barbara's house in Cathkin with cash and cashiers cheques. Some were mailing cheques with the names of their wives or girlfriends on them, and we had no idea who the tickets were for! I met the Rangers team late Monday night and returned at noon on the Tuesday to take Super Ally, Walter and Nacho Novo to the press conference (Nacho was for the Mexican televisions stations). I had asked Ally if there was any chance of a 'meet and greet' with the team and that we would arrange a hotel somewhere near the airport. He said he would speak to the gaffer. After the press conference as we were driving down the 405 freeway, I asked Walter where he was watching the Champions League final, which was on the day of the game. It was a noon kick-off here and the players had to nap from 3 p.m. until 5 p.m. He asked for directions to a sports bar and I told him that our club was only a mile away. He replied: 'That's it then, we'll bring the whole team to your club!' I was dying to call Gordon Mathers and tell him but, as we were having a nice chat, I did not want to show how ecstatic I was.

The next day, at 11:30 a.m., I arrived at the hotel and the bus was there with the Rangers team on it ready to go. Ally shouted, 'Hey Stewarty, yer late!' Imagine Ally McCoist pulling anyone up for being late! I got the bus to 'follow follow' me down Carson Boulevard towards the Orange County RSC and to the Rangers fans who, of course, did not have a clue who was coming to visit them. I had tears in my eyes as I sat at the traffic lights. All I could think of was my dad, wee Hughie, who had started me out on this fantastic Rangers journey and my mum, wee Ina, who sat by the phone all those years while we listened to the games and I started to sing, 'If we only had the Rangers over here.'

I pulled into the car park, walked into the pub and announced: 'Ladies and gentlemen, the world-famous Rangers Football Club.' To a man, the players and staff were great; after they left, we were still shell shocked. Gordon Mathers had booked a bus for the twenty-minute journey from the pub to the LA Galaxy stadium but that quickly turned into a five-bus convoy full of happy Rangers fans. The game went by too quickly but I had all my friends and family there, and I sang my heart out with my four-year-old daughter Maggie on my shoulders. To this day she'll ask me: 'Daddy, sing the "all together now" song . . .'

I have just returned from my first visit to Germany in twenty years. I was also in Glasgow on the seventh of July to walk with my mother Lodge in Cambuslang; then on the twelfth I walked in Belfast with

Ballyhackamore 1053 in front of the Cambuslang Britannia (formerly the Young Conquerors). I am currently Worthy Master of LOL 1690, Ulster Scots, in Los Angeles and president of the Orange County Rangers SC. I am still a Masonic man, I still attend church and will 'follow follow' the Rangers proudly till the day I die.

THE CONTRIBUTORS

Professor Graham Walker

Born and raised in Glasgow, Walker is professor of politics at the Queen's University of Belfast. He has authored and edited several books on Irish, Scottish and British history and politics. These books include *Intimate Strangers: Political and Cultural Interaction Between Scotland and Ulster* (1995), *A Biographical Dictionary of British Prime Ministers* (co-edited with B. Eccleshall, 1998) and *A History of the Ulster Unionist Party* (2004). He has also published many articles on football and the politics of sport in journals and newspapers, and co-edited the book *Scottish Sport in the Making of the Nation*. He has written the most authoritative account to date of the Ibrox disaster of 1971, a match he attended. His forty-five years of supporting Rangers involved enduring one nine-in-a-row and revelling in another.

Ronnie Esplin

Esplin is a graduate of Strathclyde University where he gained a BA honours degree in history. He was managing editor of Guildford-based Arena Leisure's football website in the Nineties before returning north of the border to become a freelance sports writer. His work has appeared in a wide range of titles, such as *Scotland on Sunday*, *Sunday Times*, *Sunday Mirror*, *The Times*, *Scottish Mirror*, *When Saturday Comes* and *FourFourTwo* as well as on several sport websites. Esplin is now a reporter for PA Sport (Press Association) in Glasgow. He is the author of *Down the Copland Road* (Argyll, 2000) and co-writer of both, *Barcelona Here We Come: The Story of Rangers' European Cup Winners Cup Win 1972* (Argyll, 2002) and *The Advocaat Years* (Argyll, 2004). He also edited *Ten Days That Shook Rangers* (Fort Publishing, 2005). He is currently working on the autobiography of Frank McGarvey.

Tommy Malcolm

There are few people in Scotland who know more about the history of Rangers than Tommy Malcolm. Many football fans will have encountered him in his role in the Scottish Football Museum at Hampden Park as historian/researcher/tour guide, a role that is ideal for someone who is 'football crazy'. Malcolm played in the Juniors, but the highlight of his playing career was at senior level when he captained Glasgow Transport into the second round of the Scottish Cup in 1971. Malcolm was born in St Vincent Street, Glasgow in 1944 and as a boy knew only two teams: Rangers and Celtic. However, his first match was around 1949 at Firhill when Partick Thistle entertained Hibernian and he was at a loss as to why 'Rangers didn't wear blue!' His first Rangers match was against Aberdeen at Ibrox in 1954, when the home side won 3–1, and he has been Rangers daft ever since. The greatest player Malcolm ever had the pleasure of seeing was the late, great Jim Baxter and he doubts we will ever see his like again.

Archie Mackenzie

Archie Mackenzie was born in Glasgow on 22 October 1915 and is therefore now in his nineties. He grew up in Ibrox, went to Bellahouston Academy and then Glasgow University where he studied philosophy. Subsequently, he was awarded scholarships to the universities of Oxford, Chicago and Harvard. During the second world war he was co-opted onto the British Embassy staff in Washington and later became a professional diplomat, serving in France, Thailand, Burma, Cyprus, Yugoslavia and the USA. In 1945, in San Francisco, he helped to draft the United Nations charter and was British ambassador to Tunisia from 1970–3 and Economic Minister to the United Nations from 1973–5. After retiring Mackenzie was appointed special assistant to Prime Minister Edward Heath on the influential Brandt Commission, dealing with world-poverty issues, and helped to draft the final report. He has been a Rangers supporter all his life and now lives with his wife on the eastern shore of Loch Lomond.

George Hewitt

George Hewitt is a Rangers supporter of sixty years' standing, though nowadays it mainly involves sitting, courtesy of Setanta Television. A distinguished historian, he is the author of *Scotland under Morton* (the regent, not the football club), and, with Ian Donnachie, *Historic New Lanark*, as well as various dictionaries of, and companions to, Scottish history. He is a tutor at the University of Dundee, specialising in Scottish history, and plays trombone with the New Orleans Joymakers.

Graham Spiers

Spiers, a divinity graduate of St Andrews University, works for *The Times* and is one of Scotland's most-renowned sportswriters. He has played and followed football since he was four years old, after attending his first senior match between East Fife and Aberdeen at the old Bayview Park, sometime in the late 1960s. After moving to Glasgow, Spiers became a Rangers fan and was present at most of the club's memorable moments of the 1970s and 1980s. In his career he has written for the *Sunday Times*, *The Guardian* and *Scotland on Sunday*, and was chief sports writer on *The Herald* from 2001 to 2007. He has been honoured seven times at the Scottish Press Awards, including being voted Sportswriter of the Year on four occasions. Spiers also broadcasts on the BBC and STV.

Dolan Cummings

Cummings is editorial and research director at the influential Institute of Ideas in London, an organisation with a mission to 'expand the boundaries of public debate' through a 'new academy of ideas'. He is the co-convener of the annual Battle of Ideas festival and also edits the IOI's reviews website Culture Wars, for which he writes on theatre, film and books. He has edited two collections of essays, *The Changing Role of the Public Intellectual* (2005), and *Debating Humanism* (2006). He is a co-founder of the radical humanist Manifesto Club. He gets to Ibrox whenever he can, but can more often be found watching Rangers games in dingy London pubs. He has more Celtic-minded friends than he cares to admit.

Gary Mitchell

Born in Belfast, Mitchell is from a working-class, Protestant background. He is now one of Britain's most-eminent playwrights, and his works have been produced by the Donmar Theatre, London, the Royal Court Theatre, London, the Abbey Theatre, Dublin, the Lyric Theatre, Belfast and by the BBC. He won the *Irish Times* Theatre Award for *In a Little World of Our Own*, a gripping, unflinching account of Loyalist culture. His play *Drumcree* was short-listed for the Sony Award. His other awards include the BBC Young Playwrights Award, the Stewart Parker Award for Independent Voice, the George Devine Award and the *Evening Standard* Charles Wintour Award for Most Promising Playwright. He has also been writer-in-residence at the Royal National Theatre, London.

Chris Williamson

A native of east Belfast, Chris Williamson has supported Rangers for as long as he can remember. He graduated from the University of Stirling in 2003, and plies his trade as a freelance sports writer and reporter. He is a regular features contributor to *Total Football* magazine in his homeland and has covered numerous international youth tournaments, including the 2005 FIFA world youth championships.

Reverend Stuart McQuarrie

Stuart McQuarrie was born in Glasgow, and is a lifelong Rangers supporter. After leaving Cranhill secondary school he worked for several years in sales and purchasing. He was called to the ministry and studied at Edinburgh University, graduating in divinity (1982) and politics (1983). He became assistant minister in Govan Old parish church, and was ordained as parish minister of Toryglen parish church in 1984. He has also been locum minister in Dennistoun Blackfriars parish church. He was an elected Labour councillor on Glasgow City Council (1988–96) and on South Lanarkshire Council (1995–9). In his personal and professional life he has worked to eradicate prejudice and bigotry. In 1993 he was one of the key organisers of the much-lauded visit to Glasgow by Nelson Mandela. He graduated MBA in 2002, the subject of his dissertation being ethical leadership. He has been chaplain to the University of Glasgow since 2001 and is active in interfaith and equality issues. Reverend McQuarrie has, on occasions, acted as unofficial chaplain to Rangers and in 2001 he spoke at the funeral service in Glasgow Cathedral for the late, great Jim Baxter, a man he got to know well in the last weeks of his life.

Worthy Grand Master Ian Wilson

Ian Wilson is Worthy Grand Master of the Grand Orange Lodge of Scotland. He was born in 1948 in Harthill, Lanarkshire. The family moved to nearby Whitburn while he was still a toddler. Schooling was at the local primary followed by Bathgate Academy. He went on to complete a B.Sc. degree at

Edinburgh University and this was followed by a career in the pharmaceutical industry. For the past twenty years he has run his own business in speciality automotive chemicals. Married with two daughters he is an elder in his local church, in which he is also organist and choirmaster. In his twelve years as Grand Master he has steered the Order through a difficult period in its two-hundred-year history. Widely regarded within and without the Order as radical and innovative, he has sought to modernise its workings and establish a better public image. Wilson is also a 'long-suffering Hearts fan'.

Karen Gillon MSP

Karen Gillon was born in Edinburgh in 1967 and attended Jedburgh Grammar School. She studied at Birmingham University where she obtained a certificate in youth and community work in 1991. Gillon is married to Jim and has two sons, James and Matthew. During the 1990s she was an active member of Unison and served on the Scottish Trade Union Congress general council and on the Labour Party's Scottish Executive. At this time she also worked as a youth worker in Blantyre, North Lanarkshire and later as a community education worker with North Lanarkshire Council. In 1997 she took up the post of personal assistant to Rt. Hon Helen Liddell MP and, in 1999, became the first woman to be elected to the Scottish Parliament, as MSP for Clydesdale.

Murdo Fraser MSP

Born in 1965 and educated at Inverness Royal Academy, Murdo Fraser graduated LLB from Aberdeen University in 1986, and went on to pass the postgraduate diploma in legal studies. He has since worked as a solicitor in Aberdeen and Edinburgh and prior to his election to the Scottish Parliament was an associate with Ketchen and Stevens WS in Edinburgh, specialising in commercial law. Fraser first became active in politics at Aberdeen University. He held office as chairman of the Scottish Young Conservatives from 1989 to 1992, and thereafter became the first Scot to be elected chairman of the National Young Conservatives, a position he held for one year from 1991. He was an active member and then deputy chairman of Edinburgh Central Conservative Association. In the 1997 general election, he stood as the Conservative candidate for East Lothian, finishing in second place. He fought the North Tayside constituency for the Tories in the 1999 Scottish Parliament elections and again at the 2001 general election. He became a member of the Scottish Parliament in August 2001 following the resignation of the previous list member for Mid-Scotland and Fife, and was re-elected in 2003 and in 2007. Fraser became deputy leader of the Scottish Conservatives in November 2005 and was appointed spokesman on education and lifelong learning in 2007. His publications include the pamphlets: *Defending our British Heritage* (1993); *Full Fiscal Freedom* (1998) and *Scotland and the Euro* (1999).

Carolyn Leckie

Carolyn Leckie, along with her sister and two brothers, grew up in the Gorbals. She attended Blackfriars primary and Adelphi secondary before moving to Castlemilk at the age of fourteen. She worked in the tax assessor's office in Glasgow, where she became a NALGO shop steward. She started midwifery education in 1992 and qualified in 1995, after which she worked in Rutherglen maternity hospital and became a UNISON shop steward in the wake of the hospital's controversial closure. She moved to Rottenrow and became branch secretary of UNISON at North Glasgow Hospitals in 2000. Leckie joined the Scottish Socialist Party in 1998 and was a candidate for that party in the 1999 elections for the Scottish Parliament. She was an SSP list MSP for Central Scotland between 2003 and 2007. She now works for Women's Aid.

Dr Jonathan Magee

Magee is based in the Division of Sport and Leisure at the University of Central Lancashire, following spells at Edge Hill University and University of Wales Institute Cardiff. He has published from his doctorate on the football labour market, as well as on football and the Protestant community in Northern Ireland, rugby-union labour migration and coursing history in Ireland. Magee represented Northern Ireland at football at all levels up to under-21 and played for Northern Ireland, Ireland, and Great Britain in international student tournaments. In a successful Irish League career, he played for Linfield, Bangor and Portadown among others.

Gordon Smith

The current chief executive of the Scottish Football Association started his career in professional football with Kilmarnock and was sold to Rangers in 1977 for £65,000, helping the Ibrox club win the treble in his first season. Smith was sold to Brighton and Hove Albion in 1980 for a then-record transfer fee of £440,000. On leaving Brighton in March 1984, Smith joined Manchester City, moving on to Admira Wacker in Austria and FC Basel in Switzerland before retiring as a player in 1988 after a short spell with Stirling Albion. He had a spell as assistant manager of St Mirren between 1990 and 1993 before taking up a career in the media and as an agent. Smith also found time to set up a successful business in financial services. In 1999, he was voted into the one hundred greatest Rangers players of all time. Smith became chief executive of the SFA in June 2007; it was an imaginative appointment that most informed observers believe broke the mould of football administration in this country.

Jonathan Watson

Jonathan Watson is one of Scotland's leading comedians and impressionists, best known for the perennially popular sketch show *Only an Excuse?*, which parodies people and events from the world of Scottish football. His impersonations of Sir Alex Ferguson, Graeme Souness and Frank McAvennie are particularly memorable. Watson has recently turned his hand to political satire with his highly popular *Watson's Wind Up*, which is recorded every Friday at the Glasgow Film Theatre and broadcast on BBC Radio Scotland. He also does occasional work as an actor and was a cast member of all five *Naked Video* series and also appeared in the BBC Scotland sitcom *City Lights*. Other credits include 'Jonathan' in the film *Local Hero*, an episode of BBC Television's *Casualty* in 2001 as 'Billy Shears' and also an episode of ITV's *The Bill* in 2005 as 'Rev Lewis'.

Davie Provan

Provan played for Kilmarnock and Celtic (despite his upbringing in a 'traditional' Rangers family), primarily on the right wing. He earned ten caps for Scotland and was a member of the Scotland World Cup squad in 1982. Since his retirement from playing he has worked in the media and is recognised as one of our most knowledgeable and objective pundits. He is a football commentator for Sky Sports and writes a weekly column on the game for the *News of the World*. He is also a regular contributor to *Super Scoreboard* on the Glasgow station, Radio Clyde.

John MacDonald

An Ibrox hero, Glasgow-born MacDonald was generally reckoned to be one of the finest Scottish strikers of his generation and was chased by a host of clubs before he even left school. He played for Rangers between 1978 and 1986, at which time he moved to Barnsley. He made 230 appearances for Rangers, scoring 77 goals, and won the 1981 Scottish Cup. He also picked up League Cup winners' medals in 1982 and 1984.

Stewart McDougall

Stewart McDougall is a lifelong Rangers fan. He attended his first Rangers game at the age of three, forty-five years ago, and continued in his support after emigrating from Scotland, first to Germany and then to the United States. McDougall was a member of the Springhall and Cathkin RSC while he lived in Glasgow. In 1991, he was one of four founder members of the Orange County (California) RSC, of which he is currently president. His all-time Ibrox hero is Willie Johnston.